For Joy

" . . . and her deeds shall
praise her in the gates"
(Proverbs 31:31)

TABLE OF CONTENTS

APPROACHES TO JUDAISM IN MEDIEVAL TIMES
Volume II

Number 57

APPROACHES TO JUDAISM IN MEDIEVAL TIMES
Volume II

Edited by
David R. Blumenthal

APPROACHES TO JUDAISM IN MEDIEVAL TIMES
Volume II

Edited by
David R. Blumenthal

Scholars Press
Chico, California

APPROACHES TO JUDAISM IN MEDIEVAL TIMES
Volume II

Edited by
David R. Blumenthal

Library of Congress Cataloging in Publication Data

(Revised for volume 2)
Main entry under title:

Approaches to Judaism in medieval times.

(Brown Judaic studies ; no. 54,)
Includes bibliographical references and indexes.
1. Judaism—History—Medieval and early modern period, 425-1789—Addresses, essays, lectures. 2. Judaism—Controversial literature—History and criticism—Addresses, essays, lectures. 3. Christianity and antisemitism—Addresses, essays, lectures.
I. Blumenthal, David R. II. Series; Brown Judaic studies ; no. 54, etc.
BM180.A66 1984 296'.09'02 83-18886
ISBN 0-89130-659-5 (pbk. : v. 1)
ISBN 0-89130-848-2 (v. 2)
ISBN 0-89130-849-0 (pbk : v. 2)

Printed in the United States of America
on acid-free paper

PREFACE

One of the rewards of scholarship is the opportunity of reading essays which shed new light on hitherto unknown or misunderstood aspects of the intellectual and spiritual life. As editor of these volumes, I am particularly exposed to this, and grateful to Professor Jacob Neusner for the opportunity. The following essays each shed some of this special light on different aspects of medieval Judaism.

In "Attitudes Toward Childhood and Children in Medieval Jewish Society," Ephraim Kanarfogel takes up a topic that has become central in scholarly discussions of medieval society in the last few years. He sets the scholarly stage by surveying the main approaches to the field, reports the general Jewish attitudes on the subject (using especially **Sefer Ḥasidim**), presents the legal, educational, and marital status of children, and draws important conclusions indicating that the Jewish attitude toward childhood and children differed from that of the Christian environment. Kanarfogel also includes an appendix on nursing practices.

In "The Modern Study of Responsa," Peter Haas traces and critiques three approaches to the study of the responsa which have been in use for the past 150 years. The first approach sees the responsa as incidental sources for historical facts (e.g., names, prices, customs, social structures). This method is limited because it does not control for the intellectual bias of the sources. The second approach sees the responsa as historical sources for Jewish law or as a system motivated by values. This method is inadequate because it yields self-contained studies which lack social context. The third approach sees the responsa as literature within a periodized catalogue of Jewish literature. This is the most promising approach but it lacks wholistic analysis.

In "Yiddish and the Settlement History of Ashkenazic Jews," Alice Faber and Robert King point to the usual account of the origin of Polish Jewry in the Rhineland. But, through a detailed linguistic analysis of the source dialect of Yiddish and of the influence of Yiddish on liturgical Hebrew, they reach the conclusion that favors an origin from southeastern Germany. Faber and King, then, study the demographic data and reject the accepted hypotheses of a Rhineland or Turkish origin for Polish Jewry, thus supporting the conclusion of a southeastern German provenance based on the linguistic evidence. This article appeared in **The Mankind Quarterly,** 24:4 (Summer 1984) 393-425; it is reprinted with permission of the Institute for the Study of Man.

In "New Light on the Life and Writings of Leon Modena," Howard Adelman shows how a scholar sympathetic to the early Reform molded Modena's image, how a more traditional scholar then destroyed it, and how the former distorted it even more, embroiling nineteenth century intellectuals (including Geiger and Graetz) in a scholarly-religious polemic. Adelman then reconstructs the historical Leon Modena as a literate expounder and defender of Rabbinic Judaism and a musician.

In "Maimonides on Mind and Metaphoric Language," I translate and explicate the key paragraph from Maimonides' "Hilkhot Yesode ha-Torah" in which he outlines what one can believe and then say about God. There, Maimonides deals, in an authoritative halakhic text, with the problem of metaphoric language within an intellectualist theology.

In "Royal Power and Rabbinic Authority in Fourteenth Century France," Roger Kohn recapitulates the conflict between Johanan ben Mattathias Trêves and Isaiah ben Abba-Meir. He summarizes the three main theories of interpretation (Güdemann, Hershman-Breuer, Zunz-Zeitlin) and then proposes a theory of his own based on a fresh reading of the documents in their historical context.

In "'The Eastern Dawn of Wisdom': The Problem of the Relationship Between Islamic and Jewish Mysticism," David Ariel traces the early influence of the Isra^{c}iliyat on Islam and publishes a tradition on the transmission of Jewish mysticism from Bagdad to the West. He also presents a text on mystical calligraphy and light mysticism as evidence of Islamic influence on the early Kabbala.

And in "The **Haqdamah** of Immanuel of Rome to the Book of Ruth," Murray Rosenthal sets forth the background to this work, describes the manuscripts, and gives the text and translation of the **Haqdamah.** He notes with interest that Immanuel of Rome avoided the socio-political tensions of his setting as well as the intellectual tensions which derive from the contrast between the philosophic-kabbalisitic and the literal exegesis of the Biblical text.

There are also troubles in editing books, one of which is the confusion which occasionally results from lack of adequate communication. In Volume I of this series, I was privileged to publish as the lead article an essay by our distinguished colleague, Gavin Langmuir, entitled "Historiographic Crucifixion." This essay was intended for the **Mélanges offerts à Bernhard Blumenkranz** edited by M. Gilbert Dahan. Through no one's fault other than my own, I inadvertently published it in Volume I of this series and I take this opportunity to publicly apologize to Professor Langmuir and to M. Dahan.

One of the real joys of scholarship is getting to know people whose lives are motivated by a deep love of Jewish culture and a desire to further that effort. I have known Joy Ungerleider-Mayerson for twenty years and, in that time, I have been deeply impressed by her love for all aspects of Jewish civilization. She has, among many other activities, been Director of the Jewish Museum and has worked on various archaeological expeditions; she is now publishing a book on Jewish folk art. And Joy has done all this with an infectious excitement and enthusiasm. I have also been deeply impressed by the hard work Joy has put forward in support of education in Jewish culture. Her gracious gifts to various institutions are always generous. They are also carefully conceived so as to provide the maximum educational opportunity for students of Jewish life and civilization. Indeed, her own work and her support for the work of others--her deeds--"shall praise her in the gates." To her this book is dedicated in warm friendship.

Parashat Noah, 5745
Atlanta, Ga.

ATTITUDES TOWARD CHILDHOOD AND CHILDREN IN MEDIEVAL JEWISH SOCIETY

Ephraim Kanarfogel

In European Society: The Controversy

In 1960, Phillipe Ariès published a controversial book entitled **L'enfant et la vie familiale sous l'ancien régime.**[1] The book was translated into English in 1962 and entitled **Centuries of Childhood: A Social History of Family Life.**[2] Ariès maintains that in western Europe until the sixteenth century, no one paid much attention to children during the **enfances** stage of childhood (birth to age seven). This does not mean that all children in the Middle Ages were necessarily despised or neglected. Rather, the awareness of what distinguished a child from an adult was lacking and, as a result, there was no appreciation of childhood for its own sake.[3] Citing evidence from iconography which depicted the "ages of children," the history of games and children's dress, and a vast array of medieval texts, Ariès argues that in medieval society, there was a complete lack of attribution of any special character to childhood.[4] Parents did not accept children on their own terms, enjoy them or coddle them.[5] There was also no attempt made by parents to inculcate self-control or supervise the young child's moral development.[6] The new-born baby who had not yet acquired certain physical and intellectual skills was treated with indifference.[7] The death of a small child was not a cause for great sorrow.[8] Indeed, Prof. Lynn White, who accepts Ariès thesis, sees the relative indifference of adults toward children as directly related to the high infant and child mortality rate. It did not pay to invest great emotional capital in a child whose chance of survival was less than fifty percent.[9]

Ariès further claimed that once the child reached the post-**enfances** stage and did not need to be cared for as much as before, he immediately became part of the adult world. Thus medieval education was not geared to children but to "little adults." There was no structured primary education at all. When children did begin their schooling, there was no attempt made to separate students of different ages and abilities.[10] The educational process was such that in most cases, the child was removed from his family and was taken by the teacher or tutor to live in a different household or location. This further loosened the bonds between parents and children and encouraged these students, because of a lack of discipline, to become rowdy.[11] The loosely knit family prevailed throughout the Middle Ages and it was not until the modern period that the concept of a nuclear family, centering around children and their parents, became firmly established.[12]

Ariès' book evoked varied responses but most certainly revitalized interest in children and childhood. Some scholars, while generally accepting Ariès' thesis, attempted to blunt the force of some of his conclusions by finding sources which ran counter to the thesis. Thus, U. T. Holmes in a 1968 review of Ariès' work, gathered some anecdotal texts which show an appreciation of childhood on the part of the central figures in those texts.[13] For example, in **The Life of William Marshall**, little William's cute childish talk and mannerisms while at play gave pleasure to King Stephen and indeed saved William's life while he was being held hostage.[14] Chrêtian de Troyes writes of a father who embraces his young daughter and protects her from being teased by her older sister.[15] Holmes claims that children did have their own toys and did amuse themselves with a variety of games. The fact that adults would amuse themselves with some of these games, which led Ariès to conclude that children did not have their own "childish" games, is considered by Holmes to be inconsequential. Evidence from art, which shows that children were not well-depicted or were drawn as little adults, may have been due to the poor drawing techniques employed before 1400. As for education, Holmes shows that in the upper strata of society, a child was often given a **maistre** or **garde.** The **maistre,** who was often not much older, supervised the child's studies and served **in loco parentis.** Holmes concludes however, that in the majority of cases, children between the ages of seven and fourteen were sent away from the home to be educated or received training without any form of parental control. L. Stone claims that as a result of this practice, even if the parents selected their child's marriage partner, the couple normally set up house independently, often at some distance from the parents.[16]

In the 1970's, new interest in the history of childhood fostered directly and indirectly by Ariès' work, brought forth additional material. Most of the research centered around the first part of Ariès' thesis, that childhood as a distinct entity and parental appreciation of childhood were not to be found in medieval society. David Hunt, writing in 1970, questioned the plausibility of some of Ariès' conclusions in light of the basic tenets of human psychology. If the indifference of the parents to their younger offspring was as deep and pervasive as Ariès suggests, the very lives of these children would be threatened.[17] In the mid-seventies, several papers presented additional sources and materials which showed among other things, that medieval art did portray children's faces and bodies as distinct from those of adults.[18] The most significant and heavily documented article produced at this time was an article by Mary McLaughlin entitled "Survivors and Surrogates: Children and Parents from the Ninth to the Thirteenth Centuries," published in a volume entitled **History of Childhood.**[19] Using a wide range of sources, McLaughlin shows that from the twelfth century on, tenderness toward children, interest in the stages of childhood development and responsiveness to the beauty of children can be documented in poems, tales, philosophical and scientific works and hagiography.[20] Greater interest in developing the morality of children can also be found especially in the thirteenth century encyclopedia of Bartholomew of England and the work of his contemporary Vincent of Beauvais on the education of noble children entitled **De Eruditione filiorum nobilum.**[21] It is striking however, that, as McLaughlin herself notes, few of these sources represent the views of actual parents. They may reflect an ideal rather than a practice, although the idea itself is significant. Indeed, in entitling her paper "Survivors and Surrogates," McLaughlin claims to sum up the actual position of children in medieval society. There is ample evidence for children who were neglected, beaten and even murdered. The enactment of corrective legislation, ecclesiastic and secular, indicates that such occurrences were not rare.[22]

It is not the purpose of this study to confirm or deny Ariès' conclusions per se. This study will demonstrate that if the questions which Ariès raised are asked about Jewish society in western Europe in the Middle Ages, the answers will not always be the same as those of Ariès.[23]

In Jewish Society: General Attitudes

Let us begin with a most revealing description found in the commentary on **Ethics of the Fathers** heretofore attributed to R. Yedeyah ha-Penini of Beziers.[24] Prof. Marc Saperstein has shown that this commentary is in reality not the work of R. Yedayah but of a certain R. Isaac b. Yedayah.[25] R. Isaac flourished in Provence in the middle of the thirteenth century. A mishnah in the third chapter of **Avot** reads in part: "Sleep of the morning and wine in the afternoon and the conversation of children remove one from the world."[26] In explaining why children's conversation causes this result, R. Isaac writes that the nature of man is to love the small child more than the older one. The child teaches or causes the father to speak of idle matters, perhaps to talk baby talk and whatever the child says is pleasing to the father.[27] R. Isaac further asserts that it is the nature of man that the father expends more effort with the younger child than with the older one who knows the difference between right and wrong and who is weaned and can take care of himself.[28] The small child who cannot tell the difference between right and wrong will die an abrupt death if his father does not help him. The purpose of this mishnah in R. Isaac's view, is to teach that devoting excessive unstructured attention to the child will harm both father and son. When the father is supposed to be developing his own intellect, the child burdens him with his idle talk and his playing. The time that the father should spend teaching the son will likewise be occupied with childish inanities.

The child being discussed in this comment is one who has not yet been weaned. It is precisely this child who according to Ariès did not count. Ariès finds no evidence for parents enjoying the childish behavior of their offspring. R. Isaac assumes that quite to the contrary, there is a natural yearning on the part of a parent to play with this child as a child; to talk baby talk with the child and to almost resist the notion that the child will grow up. The purpose of the mishnaic statement is indeed to prevent this sentiment from becoming overpowering, so that when the child can talk and can begin to appreciate more serious subjects, the father is prepared to begin his training. While R. Isaac's comment is the teaching of a moralist, it would make no sense to preach these principles in such a lengthy and well-developed formulation, if the parents he was addressing did not do what he claims they did. He is certainly not preaching against parental love. It is the manifestation of this love which causes the parents to become addicted to the sweetness and child-like behavior of their offspring which R. Isaac seeks to control. The existence of such feelings in the parents is beyond question.[29]

A different approach to children's speech is found in the **Ẓedah la-Derekh** of R. Menaḥem b. Aaron Ibn Zeraḥ.[30] R. Menaḥem offers practical advice on the washing and anointing of a newborn child and on nursing as well.[31] When a wet nurse is used, she must make sure that the child sleeps well. When the child is awake, R. Menaḥem recommends that his sensory organs be developed and most important that he be taught to speak: "**vi-yelammedo ledabber ki hem meḥakkim ha-medabber ʿimmahem.**" Children imitate those who speak to them. Appreciation of this aspect of the child's development is significant as is R. Menaḥem's interest in the earliest efforts of the child to walk.[32] R. Menaḥem outlines a proper diet for the child and concludes that "from the beginning, the attempt should be made to develop good character traits, that the child shouldn't get angry or be afraid or be stubborn or worry." This (development of equanimity) will contribute to the child's health. This is what King Solomon meant when he said: "Educate the child according to his way . . . " (Proverbs 22:6). R. Menaḥem then discusses the beginning of the child's formal education at school which occurs when the child reaches age five or six. Thus, the development of the character of a child advocated by R. Menaḥem should be undertaken when the child is very young, perhaps three or four. The ability of the child to imitate those who speak to him is appreciated and can be used to inculcate values and morality and develop the child's future proclivities at a very young age.

The verse in Proverbs cited by R. Menaḥem is interpreted by R. Menaḥem ha-Meiri as referring to the development of **mussar** and **middot** in children as young as age five.[33] Similarly, Shem Ṭov Ibn Falqera (Spain, 1225-95) in his **Iggeret ha-Mussar** discusses the development of acceptable social behavior in young children.[34]

Ariès had noted that in the Middle Ages, owing largely to the fact that there was no nuclear family and that a whole host of characters lived in the house with the family, children were exposed both physically and verbally to sexual abuse, immodesty and misconduct.[35] Intuitively, medieval Jewish historians would argue that the observance of normative Jewish law by a significant portion of the Jewish population would preclude these abuses.[36] A text in the polemical tract **Sefer ha-Berit** by R. Joseph Kimḥi argues precisely that: "The **ma^ɔamin** said: Oppression and theft are not as widespread among Jews as among Christians . . . . Those Jews and Jewesses, who are modest in all their deeds, raise their children, from the youngest to the oldest, in the study of Torah. If they hear a vile word from the mouth [of a child], they beat him and chastise him so that he would no longer swear with his lips. They also train him to pray every day . . . Their daughters, because of modesty, are not to be seen about nor found in a wanton manner like the daughters of the Gentiles."[37] The basic statement of the Jew about Jewish morality and educational practices is not contested by the Christian. Even if the debate in **Sefer ha-Berit** is an imaginary one,[38] we possess several revealing statements by Christians in their scholarly literature which acknowledge that on the whole Jews are more interested in educating their children than Christians and that Jewish morality is generally on a higher level.[39] Another aspect of childhood development raised by this source is the role of the synagogue. As we will see shortly, the Jewish communities welcomed children into the synagogues, not as little adults but as children, and encouraged their attendance.

The Evidence from **Sefer Ḥasidim**

A most important source for our study of medieval Jewish attitudes toward childhood is the **Sefer Ḥasidim**. Ascribed to R. Yehudah he-Ḥasid, who died in Regensburg in 1217, this work is the handbook of the **Ḥasidei Ashkenaz**, the German Pietists, who lived alongside the Tosafists in twelfth century Ashkenaz.[40] While many sections of the book are devoted to the proper beliefs and practices of the Pietist community, the book as a whole often has the flavor of a work designed to promote self-improvement of the individual in a wide range of areas. The eminent Jewish historian Fritz Baer, in a pioneering article written almost fifty years ago but still considered a most important study of **Sefer Ḥasidim**, points to the similarities between this work and the **exempla** produced in Christian monastic circles at this time.[41] The actions of a particular rabbi or scholar in **Sefer Ḥasidim** cannot very often be taken as historical fact. They may be acting or reacting, in effect, to help make the point of the author. But attitudes or practices which **Sefer Ḥasidim** seeks to correct or embellish, or which form the silent backdrop for the Hasid's discussions can be considered as actual attitudes of the period. Thus, a recent article uses **Sefer Ḥasidim** as an important source for shedding light on medical practices among Jews in medieval Germany.[42] Bearing this methodological **caveat** in mind, we find several sections in **Sefer Ḥasidim** which indicate that parents truly enjoyed playing with or being with their small children and normally took time to do so, that they were concerned with and attuned to the emotional well-being of their small children, and that the death of a small child was a cause for great sorrow.[43]

A most instructive example is this section: "Towards evening, a man should not take a child onto his lap, lest the child dirty his [father's] clothes. If you were to suggest that he can wash his clothes, [this is not satisfactory because] they will not be as clean as before. Also while the father looks for water, the time for praying the Minhah service may pass . . . and he will arrive late, after the congregation has begun to pray. In addition, it is possible that when the father tries to put the child down, the child will cry. The father will be most concerned with the child and not with giving honor to his Creator (**yaḥus ʿal ha-yeled ve-lo ʿal kevod qono**)."[44] Moreover, talking or playing with a small child was a source of pleasure for the parent. The author of **Sefer Ḥasidim** welcomes these activities at the appropriate time as helpful diversions, while cautioning that they should not cause the father to be remiss in his religious duties such as prayer and study. Thus, the following suggestion: "A person who is troubled and his mind cannot comprehend because of the pain should remove the pain by taking a walk and then return to the study of Torah. Also, a person of troubled mind on the Sabbath should speak with a youth in order to remove the melancholy from his heart. But he should not stroll [idly] with the child or kiss him in the synagogue."[45]

It is interesting that in both these sections (in the case of the first, just prior to the material cited), the author of **Sefer Ḥasidim** seeks to restrict the father's kissing of the child in the synagogue, in order that the father show love and devotion only for his Creator. In other sections, **Sefer Ḥasidim** wishes to minimize this practice because it would show insensitivity to those who did not have or who had lost children.[46]

It would seem that the synagogue was a place where children were normally brought and treated in a way that would encourage their attendance. While they were in attendance, the father would pay great attention to them and display his love for the child.[47] There is a passage found in several volumes of the **sifrut devei Rashi** which asserts that a Rhineland scholar, perhaps R. Eliezer ha-Gadol, the great teacher of Mainz in the first half of the eleventh century, would pray with a small child (**tinnoq**) in his lap (or perhaps on his shoulders). He would remove the child only when it came time to recite the **Shemaᶜ**.[48] Moreover, a passage in **Sefer Or Zaruᶜa** encourages parents to bring little children, both male and female, to the synagogue. Thus, R. Isaac Or Zaruᶜa heartily endorses the prevalent custom of allowing the children to kiss the Torah while it is being rolled up. This will heighten the sensitivity of the children to the performance of religious precepts. Their attendance generally will inculcate **yirʾat shamayim.**[49] Other synagogue customs of this period, such as the reading of certain verses of the Book of Esther in a loud voice and the drowning out of Haman's name, are explained by medieval halakhists as customs initiated to make the young children happy and thereby retain their interest.[50] Several customs at the Passover Seder also developed for this reason.[51]

The material cited thus far from **Sefer Ḥasidim** is significant because it shows the practices and attitudes of Jewish parents in this period. Other sections in **Sefer Ḥasidim** indicate that the author of **Sefer Ḥasidim** himself had a noteworthy appreciation of childhood which he wanted to share with his readers. In counseling that tutors for young children be hired not only on the basis of their grasp of the material to be taught but on their ability to use the material to teach religious values, he describes the nature of a young child's intellect in this way: "A child's intellect (**libbo**) is like the intellect of an adult who is dreaming; dreamers assume that all [they dream] is true. So too children; they assume that all your words are true, until he is indoctrinated by bad friends."[52] Several sections in **Sefer Ḥasidim** show awareness of the great curiosity of children and advise that precautions be taken in light of this curiosity. An example: "'Place not blood in your house' (Deut. 22:8) . . . if a person falls, even though he does not die, Scripture accuses him [the homeowner] of spilling blood. A person should not place a pitcher of water in his home because it is the nature of children to look at their images in water. Maybe the child will bend over and will fall into the water . . ."[53]

Arbitrarily halting our investigation at this point, we can conclude that there is evidence for scholarly and lay appreciation of children within Jewish society in western Europe. A passage in **Tosafot ha-Rosh** proclaims this appreciation most clearly. The Amora R. Judah, on the basis of a verse in Isaiah, claims that Jacob spared Abraham from the travails of raising children (**ẓaʿar giddul banim**). Rashi interprets that Jacob fathered the twelve tribes in place of Abraham. **Tosafot ha-Rosh** states: "**Ein ha-banim ẓaʿar la-ʾadam ʾela simḥah.**" Having children and raising them is on balance a positive, happy occurrence. Jacob spared Abraham from the specific problems generated by Joseph, Dinah and Simeon. But having children in and of itself is a cause for joy, not an automatic dose of pain.[54] Parents did enjoy their children and some were clearly cognizant of the distinct nature of childhood.[55] Undoubtedly related to this conclusion is the very strong impression that Jewish children were on the whole simply treated in a manner far superior to their Christian counterparts.

In Jewish Society: Legal Status, Education, and Marriage

There are several responsa which deal with child custody in cases of divorce and death and with the responsibilities of a father who abandons his wife and children.[56] There was an ordinance promulgated by R. Tam that a father who is away from his home for an extended period of time to collect his debts or to conduct his business or to study (all of which required court permission to begin with) had to continue to support his family and provide for the children's education in six-month installments.[57] All these sources leave one with the impression that the children in question were provided for, and the sources do not have either a threatening or hopeless tone. This impression is very different from the one which McLaughlin emerges with at the end of her study.[58] Indicative of the Jewish literature is a responsum of R. Joseph Ibn Megash concerning the parental custody of a four year old girl whose parents were divorced.[59] The father left town after the divorce and the child remained in the mother's custody. When the father returned two years later, he wished to gain custody of the child. The mother resisted saying that she had supported the child for the past two years and that the child at this point felt closer to her mother. The child herself broke into tears when the matter was broached. The father claimed that he was obligated to support the child and that he would do so. On the basis of Geonic precedent, R. Megash ruled that the child should remain with her mother, adding that the mother is generally more concerned with the child's welfare than the father and is better equipped to instruct the girl in living her life. The response of R. Megash is interesting, as is the position of the father. Apparently, the father was significantly attached to his child to wish to return to his role, although R. Joseph writes in his response that he does not believe that the father can be trusted to remain with the child in light of his initial departure.

As for Ariès' findings concerning the educational process and its contribution to the weakening of family bonds in the Middle Ages, my own extensive research into the educational structures of Ashkenazic Jewry in the twelfth and thirteenth centuries has yielded the following conclusions: there was no system of primary education in the modern sense of the term in Ashkenazic communities. However, there is evidence for children being given a reading familiarity with the Biblical text, through tutoring, beginning before the child was seven years old.[60] The more than forty Ashkenazic responsa dealing with elementary education show clearly that this level of education always took place under parental control either in the student's home or in the tutor's home or in rented rooms in the same town.[61] In one responsum of R. Gershom, the father hires a tutor (older student) who will take his son and acclimate him to life in a yeshiva out of town.[62] This seems similar to the **maistre** described by Holmes, but the process is still under the father's control. Other sources show that the decision to leave town to study in a higher academy was made around the time of bar-miẓvah.[63] As such, the educational process in Jewish society was very much connected to the child's home and cannot be seen as disruptive to family life.

In addition, we do find in **Sefer Ḥasidim** and in **Sefer Ḥuggei ha-Torah**[64] attempts to separate students with differing abilities and to direct students with different proclivities into different disciplines. Both **Sefer Ḥasidim** and **Sefer Ḥuggei ha-Torah** direct the struggling Talmud student into midrash or codes. Both works attempt to monitor the elementary level student to see if he is making progress. If the student is not, these sources call for changing either the teacher or the subject matter. This is done to help both the weaker and the stronger student who might be held back as a result of the weaker one.[65] While these works should be viewed as attempts at reform and do not reflect normative practice, their existence in light of Ariès' conclusions is significant.

In medieval Jewish society, even the marriage of the child did not automatically lead to a dissolution of the family. There is ample evidence that married children lived near at least one set of parents, usually the groom's. This development can be found in Ashkenaz as early as the eleventh century. Two questions in the **Sefer Ha-Dinim** of R. Yehudah ha-Kohen refer to this practice as their point of departure.[66] In a responsum addressed to R. Meir ha-Levi Abulafia, the scenario presented is of a suitor who comes to a city, marries a girl from that city and brings the girl back to his home town to live in his mother's home.[67] In light of the clearly documented practice in medieval Jewish society of children marrying at a young age,[68] this development concerning where the young couple lived is hardly surprising. To be sure, not every young couple lived with their parents during the early years of their married life. R. Solomon Ibn Adret (Rashba) held however, that " . . . a woman must live with her father-in-law and mother-in-law, for her husband is obliged to honor and fear them, and may not depart from them."[69]

That the son and daughter-in-law actually lived in the home of his parents is seen from another responsum of Rashba. The questioner asked Rashba if a woman, who does not wish to continue to live together with her mother-in-law because the mother-in-law causes quarrels between husband and wife, may force her husband to move. Rashba responds that the wife can demand this of her husband but that he only need move out of his parents' house but not to another neighborhood in honoring his wife's request.[70]

A section in **Sefer Ḥasidim** mandates that the son live near his parents so that the son can continue to fulfill his filial obligations: "Parents who command their son not to marry so that he might serve them make an inadmissable request; let him marry and live near them. But if he cannot find a wife in the town in which his parents live, let him not leave town . . . But if the son is wealthy and can have someone else serve his parents, he may then go to another town to take a wife."[71] The following section shows that in thirteenth century Ashkenazic society, it was still in vogue for the young couple to live in close proximity to their parents: "If one's parents constantly argue with one's wife and if he would tell his wife to keep silent she would become quarrelsome with him . . . let him keep silent himself . . . And if the father and mother are contentious people who bicker with his wife, and he knows that his wife is in the right, he should not rebuke his wife so as to please his parents."[72]

It is interesting that the operant principle behind the policy of both Rashba and the author of **Sefer Ḥasidim** of requiring the son to continue to live with his parents as was usually the case in medieval Jewish society, is that the son must fulfill his obligations to his parents.[73] The evidence from responsa literature cited above, suggests that the parents were usually pleased that the couple would live near them and often paid for, or provided, the couple's lodging.[74] Sometimes, the requirement for the couple to live in the same town as the parents was stipulated at the time of the betrothal as a condition for the marriage.[75] But the religious obligation to honor one's parents is clearly one reason for a son choosing to remain in close proximity to his parents. This observation raises a far larger question in light of our discussion of attitudes toward childhood. Can the enlightened attitude of Jewish parents toward their children in the medieval period be understood in part as a function of the halakhic responsibilities that a parent has for a son?

The answer to this question is one that is not easily arrived at. I think however, that a preliminary suggestion can be made. J. L. Flandrin in a work entitled **Families in Former Times--Kinship, Household and Sexuality,**[76] argues that the poor treatment of children and the lack of parental appreciation of children in Christian society until the period of the Reformation may be explained by the lack of a coherent, comprehensive formulation of parental obligations in Church law until that period.[77] The high rate of infanticide through the High Middle Ages is explained by Flandrin as a function of the fact that in popular medieval ideology, children belonged solely to their parents and were thought to exist totally under parental control.[78] Thus, parents felt that they were not responsible to any higher authority when it came to the welfare of their children. While the Bible, in no less a text than the Ten Commandments mandates that children respect and aid their parents, there is no Biblical formulation of parental obligations to their children. Ambrose of Milan and Augustine wrote that parents must nourish their child's body and soul--they must feed their child and provide some measure of moral education.[79] Apparently, these somewhat nebulous teachings did not make a great impression on many medieval parents. It is only in the sixteenth and seventeenth centuries, especially as influenced by the Protestant Reformation and Catholic Counter-Reformation, that parents respond to new religious law which contained more extensive and more specific responsibilities regarding their children.[80] Parental responsibilities are derived not because the parents "own" the child but because proper care and support and training of children is required by Divine law. Parents must, by law, provide religious and moral education for their children, teach their children a means of earning a livelihood and on the simplest level, insure their physical safety.[81] If one sired children, one was obligated to educate them. Moreover, parents were now required to be more vigilant concerning when and whom their children married.[82] These new formulations did ultimately affect Christian parents. Flandrin notes that a move by Christian parents to limit their fertility by means of birth control followed in the wake of the Reformation and counter-Reformation. These limitations may have been initiated because the moralists of the period made parents realize the full extent of their obligations to their children.[83]

We need look no further than the Talmud to see that rabbinic Judaism mandated quite clearly that the father support his son, educate him, prepare him for a trade and find for him a suitable mate.[84] These basic requirements were subsequently added to by a number of medieval authorities.[85] Failure to comply with these requirements constituted a transgression against God, while those who complied with these dicta were vouchsafed Divine reward.[86] These obligations on the father, and to a lesser extent on the mother, could easily develop in the parent a deep sense of commitment to the child's development, aside from the natural feelings of love which the parent has for the child. With all that Jewish law requires of a parent, assuming that medieval Jewish parents on the whole fulfilled these basic requirements, the picture we have drawn of parental attitudes toward children and childhood may well be viewed as a societal extension of the letter of the law. In Christian society, enlightened and improved attitudes toward childhood seem to coincide with the promulgation of legal requirements between parent and child. The evidence for appreciation of childhood by medieval Jewish scholars and laymen may also be viewed as a kind of extra-legal policy adopted by these Jews in the spirit of what they observed as part of Jewish law.

Summary

This study has demonstrated that there is significant evidence for an appreciation of childhood for its own sake among medieval European Jewry. While the evidence is for the most part literary, it reflects, in large measure, the feelings of actual parents and cannot be qualified as the product of scholarly musings. The child in Jewish society was valued as a source of pleasure and as an important resource for the future. The training of the child in matters of morality and religious sensibility should commence at an early age on a level which the child could appreciate. Close bonds between the child and his parents were not loosened by either the educational developments or the child's marriage. An hypothesis to explain these developments has also been suggested. When compared to earlier studies on attitudes toward childhood in general medieval society, the material in this study indicates a much different perspective in medieval Jewish society.

APPENDIX

Nursing Practices in Medieval Jewish Society

In the course of researching the attitudes of parents to children in medieval Jewish society, I came across a variety of sources which deal with nursing practices in that society. Toward a further insight into the social history of western European where, a number of these sources are presented below with a brief analysis.

Gersonides, in his commentary to I Samuel 1, notes that one of the lessons to be learned from the Biblical description of the birth of Samuel to Hannah is that a mother should nurse her own child. Hannah nursed Samuel before turning him over to the service of God (1:25) and similarly, Miriam insured that Moses would be nursed by his mother.[1] R. Menaḥem Ibn Zeraḥ writes, in a more practical tone, that the nursing of a child by its mother is preferable since the child was nourished by the mother's menstrual blood while in the womb; this blood forms the substance of the mother's milk after birth.[2] Most interesting is R. Menaḥem's advice that the mother not begin to nurse until the eighth day after birth because only then is her milk properly consistent. Prior to this discussion, R. Menaḥem gives detailed instructions for selecting a nursemaid (based on certain physical qualities and appearance and on her personality) to insure the high quality of the milk.[3] R. Menaḥem does not specify of what faith the nursemaid must be. He does caution that she should not engage in intercourse during the period of her service since this will detract from the quality of the milk.[4]

It is evident from rabbinic sources that non-Jewish nursemaids were used by Jews in their homes.[5] A non-Jewish **meineqet** in the home of the Tosafist R. Toviah of Vienne became the object of an halakhic discussion between R. Toviah and R. Yeḥiel of Paris concerning the use of a non-Jew to perform certain acts for a Jew on the Sabbath.[6] R. Meir ha-Levi Abulafia ruled in a responsum that a non-Jewish nursemaid may be employed in a situation where the mother wants to remove the child from his deceased father's family household and travel with the child to another city because such travel for a suckling child is dangerous. If the mother insists on leaving, the nursemaid is to be used. Use of a nursemaid, even a non-Jewish one, is preferred by Ramah in this situation where allowing the child to travel with his mother will place the child in danger.[7]

R. Isaac Or Zaruᶜa expresses concern that a pregnant woman should be most careful not to eat non-kosher food because that action, according to a passage in Talmud Yerushalmi, can adversely affect the spiritual persona of the child. Furthermore, he advises that nursemaids (**meiniqot**) not feed the children prohibited foods, "in order that they become good Jews."[8] It would seem clear from the context that this wet-nurse is non-Jewish. The author of **Sefer Ḥasidim** is concerned lest non-Jewish wet-nurses and servants feed children and others in the household non-kosher food.[9] R. Meir of Rothenburg was asked to react to the fact that **meiniqot goyot** were giving wine to young children. He responds that this practice need not be stopped.[10] One might argue that this woman served as a nanny for these children to whom she gave wine. In light of the sources cited above, there is no reason to doubt that she served at some point as a wet-nurse. Moreover, numerous pieces of Church legislation sought to prohibit the use of Christian wet nurses by Jews.[11]

The Talmud recognizes that the child prefers his mother's milk and is best served by his mother nursing him. Indeed, nursing her children is part of a wife's obligation to her husband. A sugya in **Ketubot** (59b) discusses the parameters of this obligation. Included in this discussion is a regulation that if the child recognizes its mother's milk (see Rashi's commentary **ad. loc.**) and a divorce ensues, the divorced mother must nurse the child, with the father providing monetary compensation. The child's health would be adversely affected if the mother was to discontinue her nursing. The observations of various medieval halakhists based on this sugya may contain historically relevant material.[12] A clearly relevant comment is one by R. Isaiah the Younger (Riaz): "Even when a non-Jewish woman has accepted a (Jewish) child to nurse, if the child recognizes her, she must be compelled with compensation, to continue nursing the child lest the child be in danger."[13]

NOTES

[1] The book was published in Paris by Librairie Plon. A second edition was published in 1972. It contains a new introduction by Ariès in which he responds to some of the criticism of his first edition.

[2] The work was translated by R. Baldick and published in New York by Vintage Books. All page references are to this edition.

[3] P. Ariès, **Centuries of Childhood**, pp. 128-29; 9-10. (Hereafter cited as Ariès). Cf. D. Hunt, below, n. 16, p. 34.

[4] Ariès, pp. 33-34; 43-50; 91-92. Cf. D. Wrong's review of Ariès' work in **Scientific American** 208 (1963): 182.

[5] Ariès, pp. 129-31. Cf. L. Stone, **The Family, Sex and Marriage in England 1500-1800** (London, 1977), pp. 112-14. (Hereafter cited as Stone). Like Ariès, Stone wishes to demonstrate the shifts in the attitude toward childhood in European society (in Stone's case specifically in English society) as the Middle Ages gave way to the early modern period. Ariès however, spends more time discussing attitudes toward childhood in the medieval period in order to sharpen his comparisons. Stone's conclusions ultimately dovetail with Ariès' conclusions, both in terms of the nature of the shifts and the timetable. Stone is more sensitive than Ariès in distinguishing between the attitudes of the upper and lower strata of society. See below, n. 12.

[6] **Ibid.**, pp. 100-02; 113-21.

[7] **Ibid.**, pp. 128; 27-29.

[8] **Ibid.**, pp. 38-40. See also Stone, pp. 105-06 and below at the end of n. 14.

[9] L. White, "Technology Assessment from the Stance of a Medieval Historian," **American Historical Review** 79 (1974): 9-10. Cf. Stone, pp. 105-07, 113. For the change in attitude beginning with the late seventeenth century, see pp. 246-48.

[10] Ariès, pp. 140; 145-54.

[11] **Ibid.**, pp. 365-69; 411-13; 315-24. Upper class or upper middle-class children were sent to a boarding school or to live with a tutor in order to acquire an education. Lower down the social scale, children were sent to the homes of others to begin work as apprentices, domestic servants or laborers. See Stone, pp. 107, 109-11. Cf. L. DeMause (below, n. 13), p. 33, and J. L. Flandrin (below, n. 73), pp. 203-04.

[12] **Ibid.**, pp. 405-07 and **passim.** L. K. Berkner, "Recent Research on the History of the Family in Europe," **Journal of Marriage and the Family** 35 (1973): 395-96, notes correctly that Ariès' examples are based almost exclusively on sources that reflect the attitudes of the aristocracy and upper classes in

European society. Quite clearly, attitudes of the lower classes toward children and childhood would be less enlightened. As will be shown, it is appropriate to compare attitudes toward children in Jewish society to the attitudes of the upper class in general society. See M. Güdemann, **Ha-Torah veha-Ḥayyim**, v. 1 (Warsaw, 1897), pp. 186-87, R. W. Southern, **Medieval Humanism and Other Studies** (New York, 1970), p. 11, and the preceding note. Cf. **Tosafot Bava Qamma** 58a, s.v. **'I nami mavriaḥ ari.**

13 U. T. Holmes, "Medieval Childhood," **Journal of Social History** 2 (1968): 164-72. Cf. M. McLaughlin, below, n. 19. While McLaughlin refers only once to Ariès in a note to her article (p. 102, n. 4), it is obvious that the material she assembles is designed to conflict with some of Ariès' conclusions. A more direct attack is mounted by L. DeMause, "The Evolution of Childhood," in **The History of Childhood**, ed. L. DeMause (New York, 1974), pp. 1-73.

14 William Marshall was an English statesman who lived in the latter half of the twelfth century (1146-1219). His biography was written in the thirteenth century by a biographer who was old enough to remember some aspects of William's life. The details of his childhood may have been supplied by family members. See. J. Crosland, **William the Marshall: The Last Great Feudal General** (London, 1962), pp. 8-10. Crosland characterizes the childhood portion of the biography as "ringing true." For background on William being taken as a hostage (as a guarantee for a truce between Stephen and William's father Marshal John) see pp. 19-20. Interestingly, while King Stephen displays a very positive attitude toward childhood as Holmes notes, John himself is unconcerned that his son's life is in danger while he is held captive. John says, "What does it matter? I possess the anvil and hammer with which to produce many more." See below, n. 22.

15 Chrétien de Troyes was a contemporary of William. This reference is from his **Conte du Graal.** See Holmes, "Medieval Childhood," p. 166, n. 11.

16 Stone, p. 108. Holmes argues (pp. 170-72), without much force, that the impending marriage of a child did not necessarily weaken the ties of the child to his parents. On the issue of the age of male and female children at marriage, dealt with by both Stone and Holmes, see also Ariès, pp. 102-03. The consensus of these scholars is that for males, there was often a period of several years between adolescence and marriage. For Jewish society, see below, n. 65.

17 D. Hunt, **Parents and Children in History** (New York, 1970), pp. 39-44.

18 I. H. Forsythe, "Children in Early Medieval Art, Ninth Through Twelfth Centuries," **History of Childhood Quarterly**, v. 4 (1976-77):31-70. See also, in the same volume, L. Demaitre, "The Idea of Childhood and Childcare in the Medical Writings of the Middle Ages," pp. 461-90. Forsythe refers to several additional papers, most notably those delivered at the Tenth Annual Medieval Studies Conference held at Kalamazoo, Michigan in 1975. I have not as yet been able to retrieve those studies.

19 M. McLaughlin, "Survivors and Surrogates: Children and Parents from the Ninth to the Thirteenth Centuries," in **History of Childhood**, ed. L. DeMause (New York, 1974), pp. 101-81. (Hereafter cited as McLaughlin). This volume led to the creation of a periodical called the **History of Childhood Quarterly.** The nascence of this periodical is itself an indication of the revitalized interest of scholars in childhood in history. Following the publication of volume four, the periodical was renamed the **Journal of Psycho-History.**

20 See especially pp. 117-18, 127, 132.

21 **Ibid.**, pp. 135-39. Bartholomaeus Anglicus taught theology at the University of Paris and c. 1225 joined the Franciscan order. His views on childhood are found in his oft-printed encyclopedia, **De proprietatibus rerum.** In this work, Bartholomew cites the views of Greek, Jewish and Arabic scholars on medical and scientific subjects. Vincent's work on the education of noble children was written at the request of Queen Margaret, wife of St. Louis. It was edited by A. Steiner in 1928. See also A. L. Gabriel, **The Educational Ideas of Vincent of Beauvais** (South Bend, 1962).

22 **Ibid.**, pp. 111-12; 120-21. Thus, there is evidence for royal and Church legislation to prevent the "overlaying" of infants by their parents. Cf. Stone, p. 474.

23 The bulk of Ariès' sources are from France and England, with other areas in western Europe being represented as well. As such, we limit the present study to Jewish society in western Europe. While the social history of the Jews in northern France undoubtedly differs in many ways from the social history of Jews in Christian Spain (as but one example), I find no reason to assume a priori that attitudes toward childhood would necessarily be different. I think that my conclusions will bear this observation out. While the intellectual historian must always view Sefarad and Ashkenaz in a comparative light, the social historian may, if the evidence warrants, view these cultures as on the same side of the ledger, with the general society forming the corrective element of the study. This approach will be utilized for Jewish society within the boundaries of medieval Christendom. For Jewish attitudes toward childhood in Arab and mediterranean Moslem lands, see S. D. Goitein, **A Mediterranean Society,** v. 3 (The Family), pp. 229-50. Goitein devotes an entire section to depicting the nuclear family as described in the texts of the Cairo Geniza. There is also an essay on the value of children to parents. On the whole, this section seeks to collect and broadly categorize the material.

24 The commentary was edited by M. Kasher and Y. Blacherowitz as part of their **Perushei Rishonim le-Massekhet Avot** (Jerusalem, 1974). M. Saperstein, who has worked extensively with this commentary, has noted the many discrepancies between the printed edition and the manuscript, Escorial Library of Madrid, Hebrew ms. G.IV.3. See M. Saperstein, **Decoding the Rabbis** (Cambridge, Mass., 1980), p. 21, n. 2. See also I. Twersky, "Yedayah ha-Penini's Commentary on the Aggadah," (Hebrew) in **Studies in Jewish Religious and Intellectual History Presented to A. Altmann,** ed. S. Stein and R. Loewe (Alabama, 1979), p. 75, n. 8. I have checked the section cited here in the

manuscript (fol. 14 r-v) and the discrepancies are minor. The text as it appears in the manuscript is the basis for the translations and citations in this study. In the printed edition, the text is found in the commentary to chapter three, mishnah 14, p. 63.

25 Saperstein, **ibid.**, p. 21, n. 1, and in greater detail, **idem.**, "R. Isaac b. Yeda'ya: A Forgotten Commentary on the Aggadah," **REJ** 138 (1979):17-45. See now the review of Saperstein's book by J. Elbaum in **Tarbiz** 52 (1984) 675.

26 The phrase in the mishnah which R. Isaac comments on reads: " **. . . ve-siḥat yeladim . . . moẓiʾin ʾet ha-ʾadam min ha-ʿolam.**"

27 " **. . . veyesh lo le-qaṭan gaʿguʿim ʿal ha-av kol asher yedabber ʾim ṭov ʾim raʿ.**

28 "**Ki khen ṭevaʿ ha-ʾadam lihiyot ha-ʾav veha-ʾem mishtadlim bivneihem keshe-hem qeṭanim min ha-gadol ha-yodeʿa livḥor ba-ṭov u-maʾos ba-raʿ ve-ʾeino ẓarikh ʿod le-meineqet.**"

29 Cf. the comment of R. Yonah of Gerona (d. 1263) in **Perushei R. Yonah ʿal Massekhet Avot**, ed. M. Kasher and Y. Blacherowitz (Jerusalem, 1969), p. 45: "The conversation of children--this pleasure (**shaʿshuʿa**) tugs at the hearts of people because of their love for the children, and the study of Torah is thereby vitiated," and the comment of R. Bahya ben Asher (c. 1300) in **Kitvei Rabbeinu Baḥya**, ed. C. B. Chavel (Jerusalem, 1970), p. 580: "Constant conversation with them will lead one to frivolity . . . because their words tug at the heart and people are drawn to them." R. Baḥya cites a passage from **Kohelet Rabbah** to show that the father loves the small child even more the older one. The comment of R. Yonah which is a brief and fairly obvious interpretation of the mishnah, may be the product of exegesis rather than a reflection of historical reality. The same observation probably holds true for R. Baḥya's comment although it should be noted that R. Baḥya is writing after R. Isaac b. Yedayah. The development and details of the parent-child relationship, in particular the great parental love, appreciation and interest for the small child, included by R. Isaac b. Yedayah in his comment clearly show that R. Isaac himself had an excellent awareness of the distinct nature of childhood. Moreover, the preaching tone of R. Isaac and the stress laid on parental improvement in this comment render the comment a reflection of, and response to, actual parental attitudes and practices.

Note the different attitude of parents to childhood as expressed by Maimonides in **Moreh Nebukhim** 3:49. One reason given by Maimonides for the circumcision of the child being mandated by the Torah on the eighth day is because, " . . . the love of a father and mother for the newborn child is not as strong as the love for the child when he is a year old. The love for a one year old is not as the love for a six year old. If two or three years were allowed to elapse, prior to the circumcision, the circumcision would be cancelled by the father because of his feelings of mercy and great love for the child." While this formulation may be significant for our discussion, and indeed, McLaughlin (p. 138) considers it as such, it may well be the reasoned opinion of a philosopher and not a reflection of parental attitudes toward childhood in his time. Maimonides describes the lesser love which the father has for the newborn child in the following terms: " . . . **aval bi-zeman leidato otah ha-ẓurah sheba-medammeh ḥalushah meʾod.**" Cf. the formulation of Phillip of Novara cited by McLaughlin, **ibid.** (Maimonides is, in any event, geographically outside the scope of this study).

Baḥya Ibn Paquda's formulation (**Ḥovot ha-Levavot, Shaʿar ha-Beḥinah**, ch. 5, Warsaw edition, pp. 118-20) may also be in this category. Some of his perceptive observations, which are certainly more expansive than those of Maimonides, adumbrate those of R. Menaḥem Ibn Zeraḥ (see below), although Menaḥem's formulation is much more practical. Like Maimonides, Baḥya assumes that parental love and concern grow as the child's rational faculties and abilities develop and progress. It should be noted that Bahya imparts these views of childhood when he discusses the notion that man can better understand the protective relationship between God and man by studying the relationship between parent and child: "The baby is delivered into this world with his senses weak except for taste and touch so his Creator prepares food for him, his mother's breasts turning the blood, which used to nourish him in her womb into milk in her breasts . . . Another of God's graces is in making the nipple as small as the needle's eye, not so wide as to make the baby choke on the milk . . . Then the body grows stronger and the baby starts to discern colors and hear voices, while God puts mercy and compassion into the hearts of his parents so that his upbringing is easy for them, even to the point that his food and drink are more important to them than their own. And all the trouble and pain of his care, like washing, cleaning and fondling him, guarding him against misfortune even against his will, all this seems like a trifle. When he passes from infancy to childhood, his parents do not come to dislike him nor do they grow weary of his many demands and his lack of comprehension of all the trouble in feeding him and cleaning after him. On the contrary, their love and concern for him grow until they reach their peak when he learns to talk in an orderly and reasonable way, when his senses and intellectual powers become stronger, when he starts to learn and differentiate the intelligible things by means of his natural faculties" (trans. M. Mansoor, London, 1973, pp. 162-63). Baḥya continues his discussion in this section by pointing to other organs and bodily functions which further attest to the miraculous Divine order, designed to protect and nurture the human being during his entire lifetime. The effect of the Moslem milieu on Baḥya's position must be considered. See below, n. 57.

30 **Ẓedah la-Derekh** (repr. Jerusalem, 1977), article one, principle three, chapter 14, p. 32a. R. Menaḥem's father fled France in 1306 and settled in Navarre where Menaḥem was born c. 1310. R. Menaḥem later studied in Toledo with R. Yehudah, son of R. Asher b. Yeḥiel (Rosh).

31 His approach to these topics is very similar to that of Bartholomew of England, see above, n. 21. There is also an explicit reference to swaddling of the infant in this text: "The newborn child must be anointed with astringents . . . because the child is soft. His skin must be toughened so that it will not be damaged easily by external agents. Also, he must be swaddled **(she-yehattel be-hittul)** so that his limbs will not become

crooked." Swaddling was a virtually universal practice in medieval society (see McLaughlin, pp. 113-14 and n. 51, and L. DeMause, above, n. 13, pp. 37-38. Cf. L. Stone, **The Family, Sex and Marriage in England, 1500-1800**, pp. 160-62. On the termination of this practice, see Stone, pp. 424-26.). There is no doubt that this practice was common in Jewish society as well. It is also referred to in Baḥya Ibn Paquda's **Ḥovot ha-Levavot** (Warsaw ed., p. 205). Baḥya describes the trust that some men have in God, that He will do what is best for man just "as the mother takes passionate care of her child, cleaning and washing him and binding and unbinding him (=swaddling)." (The translation from the Arabic is Mansoor's [London, 1973], p. 329). In Judah Ibn Tibbon's Hebrew translation, the mother cares for the child, "**be-reḥizato ve-hittulo u-keshirato ve-hatarato.**" Cf. Rashi to **Soṭah** 11b, s.v. **meshapper.** For an example of this practice as depicted in medieval Jewish art, see the depiction of the finding of Moses by the daughter of Pharoah in the early fourteenth century in British Museum ms. Add. 27210, fol.9 (reproduced in **Aspects of Jewish Culture in the Middle Ages**, ed. P. E. Szarmach [Albany, 1979], p. 136), fol. 10v (reproduced in color in B. Narkiss, **Hebrew Illuminated Manuscripts** [Jerusalem, 1969], p. 57), and fol. 15r (reproduced in T. and M. Metzger, **La Vie Juive au Moyen Age**, p. 218).

32 Cf. McLaughlin, p. 118, and **Tosafot Beiẓah** 23b s.v. **ᶜagalah shel qaṭan.**

33 Meiri's comment reads as follows: " . . . This is a suggestion to educate one's son in deportment and ethics according to the child's way, i.e., according to [the way suitable for] the child's age, a five-year old according to his way and a ten-year old according to his way."

34 This text was published and edited by A. M. Habermann in **Qovez ᶜal Yad** 11=n.s. v.1 (1936):47-88. The relevant section is on p. 82.

35 Ariès, pp. 100-06; 396-98.

36 See for example, H. H. Ben-Sasson, **Peraqim be-Toledot ha-Yehudim bi-Mei ha-Beinayim** (third printing, Jerusalem, 1969), pp. 195-205 and J. Katz, **Exclusiveness and Tolerance** (New York, 1962), pp. 41-43; 55-63. As Prof. Katz notes, medieval Ashkenazic households certainly had non-Jewish servants in them. The behavior and interaction of these servants was carefully regulated. Cf. the Appendix, above.

37 **Sefer ha-Berit**, ed. F. Talmage, pp. 25-26. (Translation in F. Talmage ed., **Book of the Covenant** [Toronto, 1972], pp. 32-33). The point is made also, perhaps even more clearly, in a parallel passage in ms. Rome 53 (fol. 22v). The text was first published by J. Rosenthal in **Hagut ᶜIvrit ba-Amerikah**, v. 3 (1974), p. 67. It is conveniently compared to the **Sefer ha-Berit** text by J. Rembaum in **AJSreview** 5 (1980):86-87. The key passage reads: "The **maʾamin** said: I will now establish that Jews practice good deeds, as is readily evident. Behold, the Jews young and old alike, study Torah. They accustom their sons from youth to study and go to synagogue. He removes obscenity from his mouth . . . They guard their daughters from being wanton . . . There is no open unchastity among them."

38 See E. E. Urbach, "Études sur la littérature polémique au moyen âge," **REJ** 100 (1935) 66, and Rembaum, p. 86.

39 See the statement of the student of Peter Abelard reproduced in B. Smalley, **The Study of the Bible in the Middle Ages** (second edition, Oxford, 1952) p. 78, and the position of Berthold von Regensburg described in J. Cohen, **The Friars and the Jews** (Ithaca, 1982), p. 231 and the statement of Giordano da Rivalto in Cohen, p. 238. See also D. Berger, **The Jewish-Christian Debate in the High Middle Ages** (Philadelphia, 1979), pp. 25-27; 257. Cf. Petrus Alfonsi, **Dialogus Petri et Moysi Judaei**, in **Patrologia Latina**, ed. J. Migne, v. 157, cols. 596-97; **Sefer Ḥasidim**, ed. J. Wistinetzki, #1301; Solomon b. Simon Duran, **Milḥemet Miẓvah** (Leipzig, 1856), p. 14 and J. Cohen, **ibid.**, pp. 67 and 147.

40 The relationship between the Tosafists and the German Pietists has been a topic of discussion in some recent literature. See. H. Soloveitchik, "Three Themes in the Sefer Ḥasidim," **AJSreview** 1 (1976):339-54, I. Ta-Shma, "Miẓvat Talmud Torah ke-Veʿayah Ḥevratit-Datit be-Sefer Ḥasidim," **Bar Ilan** 14-15 (1977):104-09, and I. G. Marcus, **Piety and Power** (Leiden, 1981), pp. 102-05.

41 F. Baer, Magamato ha-Datit ha-Ḥevratit shel Sefer Ḥasidim, **Zion** 1 (1938):6-7.

42 J. Shatzmiller, "Doctors and Medical Practice in Germany Around the Year 1200: The Evidence of Sefer Ḥasidim," **Journal of Jewish Studies** 33 (1983): 583-94. On the richness of **Sefer Ḥasidim** as a source for family life and the like within the larger Ashkenazic society, see especially p. 584.

43 It must be noted that just as Ariès (pp. 25-26) and Holmes (above, n. 13, p. 165) have shown that the terms for small child, young child, adolescent etc. in medieval French and other Romance languages were often interchanged, we find in medieval Hebrew texts instances of a twenty year old being called a **yeled** or a two year old being referred to as a **naʿar.** See e.g. **Tosafot Niddah** 14b s.v. **mai lav** and E. E. Urbach, **Baʿalei ha-Tosafot,** v.2, p. 525, n. 17*. This interchangeability does show, to some extent, that the ages and stages of childhood were not as fixed then as they are today. In the case of **Sefer Ḥasidim,** the context in most cases will aid in making judgements.

44 **Sefer Ḥasidim,** ed. J. Wistinetsky (hereafter referred to as **SHP**), section 432.

45 **SHP** 770. See also section 815.

46 **SHP** 102-03. I do not think that the sensitive appreciation of childhood in these sections is necessarily at odds with the attitude expressed in 857. Positive parental attitudes toward childhood do not dictate that the child (young adult) who strays must be held near at all costs.

47 Cf. Rashi's commentary to **ʿAvodah Zarah** 17a, s.v. **avi hadaihu,** where Rashi justifies the custom of ʿUla to kiss his sisters following synagogue services: "He would see the way of people when they leave the synagogue to immediately kiss their

father and mother or an important person on his heel or on his hand (as a sign of giving honor)." In light of the following sources, this text may also reflect historical reality.

48 **Sefer ha-ᵓOrah,** ed. S. Buber, v.2, #133, p. 221 and **Sefer ᵓIssur ve-Heter,** ed. Freiman (repr. Jerusalem, 1973), #127: "Once a child [**tinnoq**] was sitting on the shoulders of my teacher [Rebbi] in the synagogue. When it came time to recite the Shemaᶜ, he instructed that the child be removed from him because the average child is unclean [**setam tinnoq ba-ᵓashpah**] and it is not proper to recite Shemaᶜ near the child." **Shibbolei ha-Leqeṭ,** ed. S. Buber, end of section 15, p. 8) notes that this description was given by R. Isaac b. Judah **(z"l)**. On the possible identification of R. Isaac's teacher in this text as R. Eliezer, see A. Grossman, **Ḥakhmei Ashkenaz ha-Rishonim,** pp. 218-19.

49 **Sefer Or Zaruᶜa,** v.2, **Hilkhot Shabbat,** section 68. See also **Tosafot Ḥagigah** 3a s.v. **littein sekhar le-meviᵓeihen** and **Maḥzor Vitry** (ed. S. Hurwitz), p. 713.

50 See the sources cited in M. Güdemann, **Ha-Torah veha-Ḥayyim Bimei ha-Beinayim be-Ẓarefat ve-Ashkenaz** (Warsaw, 1897), p. 90, nn. 5,6. See also **Haggahot Maimoniyyot** to **Mishne Torah,** "Hilkhot Megillah," end. Cf. Ariès, pp. 125-26.

51 **Ibid.,** p. 90, n. 4. See also D. Goldschmidt, **The Haggadah: Its Sources and History** [Hebrew] (Jerusalem, 1960), p. 11, nn. 7-9. The implications of circumcision rites for attitudes toward childhood will not be dealt with in this study.

52 **SHP** 820.

53 **SHP** 160. Cf. **SHP** 683 for an insight into the disciplining of young children and its effect. The warning of the eleventh century churchman Burchard of Worms, that a mother should not put her child near a fire on which a pot of water is boiling, lest another person come and upset the pot of water and scald the child (found in Burchard's **Decretum,** book 19, article 149, published in J. P. Migne, **Patrologia Latina** v. 140 [1853], col. 1012) is more simplistic and does not reflect an appreciation of childish curiosity.

54 **Tosafot ha-Rosh, Sanhedrin** 19b s.v. **she-pedaᵓo mi-ẓaᶜar giddul banim** (in **Sanhedrei Gedolah,** v.3, ed. B. Lipkin [Jerusalem, 1970], p. 81). The same point is made less clearly in the standard **Tosafot.** Both texts base the joy of having children on a slightly incongruous Talmudic passage, that God rewarded ᶜOved ᵓEdom by granting him six children from one pregnancy. They also sharpen their questions by noting that Abraham also sired additional children from Qeṭurah. This argumentation may diminish the historicity of their sentiments regarding children.

55 We find several additional areas used by Ariès and others to judge the attitude of parents to children. These areas may not be as crucial or as indicative for Jewish society but they are nevertheless worth noting. There is ample evidence for Jewish children playing with toys and other games in this period. The evidence must be evaluated in light of the argument of Ariès and Holmes, referred to above, as to whether the fact that adults

played with the same toys and games vitiates this evidence as a further indication of societal attitudes toward childhood. A responsum found in **Haggahot Mordekhai (Sanhedrin** 722) signed by a certain R. Joseph b. Samuel, censures those adults who play with nuts as part of a game of chance. Among the reasons given for the impropriety of this activity is that only children were permitted to play with nuts and then, only on the first day of Passover. By the same token, a passage in **Maḥzor Vitry** (ed. Hurwitz, p. 291) recommends that women and children who regularly roll apples and nuts not be restrained from doing so on the Sabbath unless the one who admonishes them is sure that his words will be heeded. Cf. **Sefer Roqeaḥ, Hilkhot Shabbat,** #130. Ball-playing and racing are also referred to (**Maḥzor Vitry, ibid.**); **Tosafot Sanhedrin** 26a s.v. **kaddur,** and **Beiẓah** 12a, s.v. **hakhi garsinan; Shibbolei ha-Leqeṭ, Hilkhot Shabbat** #121, ed. S. Buber, p. 94; Semaq #281); Rashi, **Sanhedrin** 77b, s.v. **ke-gon ʾeleh ha-mesaḥaqim be-kaddur**) but the age of the participants is not always clear. Cf. **SHP** #168 (p. 308) and **Tosafot Shabbat** 45b s.v. **hakha** and generally L. Rabinowitz, **A Social History of the Jews in Northern France** (repr. New York, 1979), p. 229. There are also sources which refer to and deal with the singing of lullabies to young children. See **Ẓedah la-Derekh,** cited above, n. 29 and **SHP** #344-47.

With respect to mourning for children who passed away, the death of a small child required the same mourning as the death of an adult and there is no indication that scholars or rabbis tried to downplay a child's death as we find in non-Jewish sources (see above, n. 8). A custom which existed in southern France and northern Spain, that a first born male child was not mourned since as a **bekhor** he was consecrated to God received the censure of such rabbinic authorities as Ribash (**Responsa** [repr. Jerusalem, 1968], #95) and Meiri (**Ḥibbur ha-Teshuvah,** ed. A. Sofer [New York, 1950], pp. 613-14). Meiri notes that in some places the custom was observed only for a boy who died before he reached age thirteen, while in other places the age limit was twenty. In Narbonne, they mourned only the first day for a **bekhor.** Meiri reluctantly accepts the existence of the Narbonese practice because it is an established minhag and cannot be summarily dismissed. Indeed Rabad and R. Asher of Lunel endorse this **minhag,** see **Teshuvot ha-Rabad,** ed. J. Kafih, #212. From Rabad's formulation it would seem that the custom was in effect even for a son who was past age thirteen when he died. A Talmudic ruling (**Moʿed Qaṭan** 26b), prohibiting the mourner from holding an infant during the **shivʿah** period, lest the mourner be brought to frivolity, is cited approvingly by many medieval authorities. Meiri's comment on this Talmudic passage may be significant. A mourner should not hold a child, "**shema yavo li-dei gaʿaguʿa ve-yitganneh ʿal ha-beriyyot.**" Cf. also Nahmanides' **Torat ha-Adam** in **Kitvei ha-Ramban,** ed. C. Chavel, v.2, pp. 12-13. That the Jews did not let the fear of infant or child mortality affect their enjoyment of their children might possibly be adduced from the Biblical interpretation of R. Nissim b. Reuven of Gerona to Genesis 20:2 (**Peirush ha-Ran ʿal ha-Torah,** ed. L. Feldman [Jerusalem, 1968], p. 270).

Finally, a statement about the types of sources available for the study of childhood in Jewish society is now in order. To this point, the vast corpus of Hebrew poetry written in western Europe, both sacred and secular, has proved to be disappointing in terms of providing sources for this study. Evidence from these sources seems to be available through weak inference at best. Consider this passage from a liturgical poem of R. Amittai (in **Shirei Amittai**, ed. Y. David, [Jerusalem, 1975], p. 23), written for the Sabbath **ᶜamidah** in which a **ḥatan** participates (**Qedushta de-Ḥatan**): "From the time that he is born, his parents will educate him in His commandments. At eight days he will be circumcised and then he will be taught the statutes of God and his Torah." As for medieval Jewish art, specifically manuscript illuminations, it has been noted at the outset of this study that lack of technical skills rather than a certain attitude toward childhood may characterize any findings in that discipline. Compare the differing depictions of children in the late 14th century Spanish Kaufmann Haggadah (reproduced in B. Narkiss, above, n. 30, p. 71), with the depictions in a late 14th century German Pentateuch (Narkiss, p. 115) and those in an early 15th century German siddur (p. 119). See also, T. and M. Metzger, **La Vie Juive au Moyen Age**, pp. 226, 230. Note also the thirteenth and fourteenth century depictions of Jesus as a baby reproduced in B. Blumenkranz, **Le Juif Médiéval au Miroir de l'Art Chrétien** (Paris, 1966), pp. 121-23, 127.

Important citations for the study of childhood in general medieval society could be discovered in prose literature, tales, stories, memoirs and hagiography. We simply do not possess works on medieval Jewish figures comparable to the writings describing the life of St. Anselm (see R. W. Southern, **St. Anselm and His Biographer** [Cambridge, 1966]) or the memoirs of Guibert of Nogent (see J. F. Benton, **Self and Society in Medieval France: The Memoirs of Guibert of Nogent** [New York, 1970]). On the absence of a Jewish genre comparable to medieval Christian hagiography, see H. H. Ben-Sasson, "Le-Megammot ha-Kronografiah ha-Yehudit shel Yemei ha-Beinayim u-Vaᶜayotehah," in **Historians and Historical Schools** [Hebrew] (Jerusalem, 1962), p. 29. While we do have medieval Jewish stories and tales (see J. Dan, **Ha-Sippur ha-ᶜIvri bi-Mei ha-Beinayim**, Jerusalem, 1974), these limited sources do not contain much material concerning the appreciation of childhood.

[56] A responsum of Ramah (**Or Ẓaddiqim** #289) may be indicative of child custody procedures in this period. See also the question in R. Joseph ben Meir ha-Levi Ibn Megash, **Responsa**, (Warsaw, 1870), #133, and below nn. 56,67 and **Responsa of Rosh**, 17:7 and 82:2-3. Of course, the trustee or executor, appointed by the **beit din** also had an important role in protecting the interests of his young charge(s). Indeed, many responsa deal with children under the care of the trustee. See e.g., M. Elon ed. **Mafteaḥ ha-Sheʾelot u-Teshuvot shel Ḥakhmei Sefarad u-Ẓefon Afrika**, v.2 (Jerusalem, 1981), pp. 20-21, 73-74, 117, 198-99. The parameters of this institution are outside the scope of this study. See also I. A. Agus, **Urban Civilization in Pre-Crusade Europe**, index, s.v. trustee, and **idem., R. Meir of Rothenburg** (Philadelphia, 1947), v.1, p. 67. See Judah b. Asher, **Responsa Zikhron Yehudah** (Berlin, 1846) #85 which records a question concerning a father who was dying and made a bequest to his unborn child. Cf. J. H. Mundy, "Charity and Social Work in Toulouse, 1100-1250," **Traditio** 22 (1966):256-57 and 266.

[57] See L. Finkelstein, **Jewish Self-Government in the Middle Ages**, (2nd edition, New York, 1964), pp. 168-70, text C.

58 McLaughlin, pp.

59 R. Joseph Ibn Megash, **Responsa** (Warsaw, 1870), no. 71. While R. Joseph flourished in Moslem Spain, where he died in 1141, the content of his responsum in light of the sources cited above in n. 56 is certainly appropriate for our discussion and need not necessarily be viewed as the product of Moslem influence on Jewish society in the lands rules by Islam.

60 See e.g., **Tosafot Ketubot** 50a s.v. **bar shit le-miqra**, S. Assaf, **Meqorot le-Toldeot ha-Ḥinukh be-Yisrael**, (hereafter Assaf) v.4, p. 2, **Daᶜat Zeqenim** to Leviticus 19:23 and **Ẓedah la-Derekh** cited above, n. 29.

61 A representative sampling of these responsa which highlights the fact that the **melammed** (tutor) invariably taught in the home of the student(s) or at least in their town consists of the following sources: **Teshuvot R. Gershom**, ed. S. Eidelberg (New York, 1955), #71-73, responsum of R. Yehudah ha-Kohen, published by A. Grossman in **Alei Sefer** 1 (1975):33, **Sefer Or Zaruᶜa, Pisqei Bava Meẓiᶜa**, #243, **Responsa of R. Meir of Rothenburg**, Prague #385-87, 37, 85, 250, 385, 434, 488, 667, 833; Cremona #2, 3, 125, 191. Note also the halakhic formulations of **Sefer Mordekhai, Bava Meẓiᶜa** 343-46.

62 **Responsa of R. Gershom**, ed. S. Eidelberg (New York, 1955), #71, p. 165-66.

63 See e.g., **SHP** #1484, and Assaf, v.4 (Tel Aviv, 1930), pp. 33-34.

64 **Sefer Ḥuqqei ha-Torah** outlines a program for elementary and advanced education. Most scholars now assume that it is of Provencal origin. See I. Twersky, **Rabad of Posquières** (second edition, Philadelphia, 1980), pp. 25-26 and nn. 25-27. S. W. Baron entertains the possibility that the document emanated from the milieu of the German Pietists. See his **Social and Religious History of the Jews**, v.6 (Philadelphia, 1958), p. 395.

65 **SHP** 822-25, 748-49, 777-79, 1479; Assaf, v.1 (second printing, 1954), pp. 10-11.

66 The responsa from **Sefer ha-Dinim** are found among the responsa of R. Meir of Rothenburg, Prague edition, #906-07. See the translation and analysis of these responsa in I. A. Agus, **Urban Civilization in Pre-Crusade Europe** (second edition, New York, 1969), pp. 402-04.

67 R. Meir ha-Levi, **Responsa (Or Zaddiqim)**, #290.

68 For Ashkenaz, see I. A. Agus, **The Heroic Age of Franco-German Jewry** (New York, 1969), pp. 277-84. Note especially **Tosafot, Qiddushin** 41a s.v. **ʾasur** and **Kol Bo** (Lemberg, 1860), p. 86a. This practice proved beneficial for the couple both economically and socially. For Provence, see **Teshuvot Ḥakmei Provence**, ed. A. Sofer (Jerusalem, 1967), pp. 123-4. For Spain, see A. A. Neuman, **The Jews in Spain**, v.2, pp. 22-24. In late medieval and early modern Jewish society, the average age of children at the time of marriage went up. See J. Katz, **Tradition and Crisis**, p. 139 and above, n. 15a. See also McLaughlin, p. 126, n. 14.

69 This position of Rashba is not found in his published responsa or halakhic writings but is cited in his name by R. Jacob Castro, **Responsa Oholei Yaʿakov** (Leghorn, 1783) #300. See G. Blidstein, **Honor Thy Father and Mother** (New York, 1975), p. 104.

70 R. Solomon Ibn Adret, **Responsa**, v.4 (Salonika, 1863), #168. Cf. **Sheʾelot ha-Rashba ha-Meyuḥasot la-Ramban** (Warsaw, 1883), #102 concerning the impact of a quarrel between a wife and her father-in-law on the couple's domestic harmony.

71 **SHP** 564, p. 371. Cf. **SHP** 1084--on Psalms 128:3 ("Your sons shall be like olive tree seedlings around your table") the author comments: "If a person has older sons (**banim gedolim**), he shall not let them eat in a different house, in order that they not become gluttons."

72 **SHP** 563.

73 See G. Blidstein, **op. cit.**, p. 114.

74 See above, n. 68. It would seem that this type of arrangement was usually implemented to cover the early years of the young couple's married life. See the next note. Parents were often instrumental in helping to settle the young couple's spats and squabbles. See **Responsa of Ramah (Or Ẓaddiqim)** #253 and **Responsa of Ran** (Warsaw, 1882), #15. On the other hand, we find the wife returning to her mother's house to give birth (**Responsa of R. Meir of Rothenburg,** Prague 946) and when she was at odds with her husband. See **Responsa Zikhron Yehudah** #71 and **Responsa of Rashba**, v.1 #692, v.4 #72 and v.8 #102.

75 **Responsa of R. Meir of Rothenburg**, Cremona 217-18. In the late medieval period in Europe, a contract was drawn up before marriage which stipulated that the parents would maintain the young couple in their household for a set number of years. The time period for this maintenance was relatively brief. Cf. J. Katz, "Nisuʾin ve-Ḥayei ʾIshut be-Moẓaʾei Yemei ha-Beinayim," **Zion** 10 (1946):25 and **idem.**, **Tradition and Crisis**, pp. 139-40. For the development of this institution in general medieval society (beginning in Languedoc after 1350), see J. L. Flandrin (next note), pp. 83-84.

76 The book was originally published in French in 1976 under the title: **Familles: parente, maison, sexualité dans l'ancienne régime.** It was translated into English under the title **Families in Former Times--Kinship, Household and Sexuality** (Cambridge, 1979) by R. W. Southern.

77 Flandrin, pp. 130-33.

78 **Ibid.**, p. 136.

79 **Ibid.**, p. 175. Cf. p. 119.

80 **Ibid.**, pp. 137-39.

81 **Ibid.**, pp. 176-77.

82 **Ibid.**, pp. 133-36.

83 **Ibid.**, p. 237.

84 **Qiddushin** 29a-30b; 82a; **Ketubot** 65b.

85 Regarding support and sustenance, see e.g., **Semaq** #277. On parental involvement in selecting a suitable mate while considering the feelings of the child, see the sources analyzed by G. Blidstein, **Honor Thy Father and Mother**, pp. 85-94. The obligation of the father to train his child in religious observances (**miẓvat ḥinukh**) was greatly expanded in the medieval period. For a collection of sources on many facets of this obligation, see Y. Blau, **Ḥanokh la-Naʿar** (Jerusalem, 1980). On the obligations of the mother in this regard see Rashi, **Ḥagigah** 2a s.v. **ʾeizehu qaṭan; Tosafot ʿEiruvin** 82a s.v. **qaṭan ben shesh; Tosafot Yeshanim Yoma** 82a s.v. **ben shemoneh; Tosafot Nazir** 28b s.v. **beno ʾin bitto lo; Responsa of R. Meir of Rothenburg**, ed. Cremona, no. 200.

86 See e.g., **Shabbat** 127a, **Pesaḥim** 113a.

NOTES TO APPENDIX

[1] Levi b. Gershon, **Commentary to I Samuel**, end chapter seven. This is the fourteenth lesson (**toᶜelet**) which Gersonides derives from the opening narratives of I Samuel.

[2] **Ẓedah la-Derekh**, cited above, n. 30. This observation is undoubtedly based on the formulation in **Bekhorot** 6b, "**dam neᶜeḳar ve-naᶜaseh ḥalav.**" Cf. Baḥya Ibn Paquda, **Ḥovot ha-Levavot, Shaᶜar ha-Beḥinah**, ch.5 (Warsaw, 1865 edition, p. 118). An observation similar to that of R. Menaḥem is made by Bartholomew of England, see McLaughlin, p. 115, n. 59, and above, n. 31. In Christian sources, the notion that the mother's milk is blood frothed white is found in the writings of Clement of Alexandria. See **Clement of Alexandria The Instructor, Ante-Nicene Christian Library**, v.4 (Edinburgh, 1867), p. 141. See also F. Talmage, "An Hebrew Polemical Treatise, Anti-Cathar and Auto-Orthodoxy," **HTR** 60 (1967) 328, n. 34 and D. Berger, "Christian Heresy and Jewish Polemics in the Twelfth and Thirteenth Centuries," **Ibid.**, 68 (1975) 294.

[3] Cf. McLaughlin, p. 116, n. 67.

[4] For an halakhic problem raised by the action of a Jewish nursemaid, see **Responsa of R. Meir of Rothenburg**, Prague edition, #864. See also **Responsa of R. Asher b. Yeḥiel**, 17:7.

[5] Cf. L. Stone, **The Family, Sex and Marriage in England**, p. 106. Note that in the higher levels of general medieval society, to which Jewish society has been compared, children were specifically sent out of the home to be nursed, primarily because of parental fears of infant mortality. Cf. the literature cited above in n. 11.

[6] See the text published by I. Elfenbein in **Ḥoreb** 10 (1948):133. On the implications of this source for the use of a non-Jew on the Sabbath, see now J. Katz, **Goi shel Shabbat** (Jerusalem), 1984), pp. 48-50.

[7] **Or Ẓaddiqim**, repr. Jerusalem, 1972, #290.

[8] **Sefer Or Zaruᶜa**, v.2, **Hilkhot Shabbat**, section 68.

[9] **SHP** #1438, p. 348.

[10] R. Meir of Rothenburg, **Responsa** (Lemberg) #150.

[11] There is an abundance of Church legislation which sought to prohibit the use of Christian wet nurses by Jews. A collection of the texts of conciliar legislation and papal formulations, beginning with the Third Lateran Council in 1179 and extending through 1250 for southern France, northern France and England, can be found in S. Grayzel, **The Church and the Jews in the Thirteenth Century** (revised edition, Philadelphia, 1966), pp. 73, 115, 194, 205, 253, 297, 299, 307, 317, 321-23, 329, 333. It would seem that even some needy Jews had non-Jewish nursemaids for their children. See **Sefer ha-Pardes**, ed. H. Ehrenreich (Budapest, 1924), p. 255.

[12] See e.g., **Sefer Or Zaruʿa, Hilkhot Yibbum ve-Qiddushin** #629, **Shibbolei ha-Leqeṭ**, v.2 (ed. M. Z. Ḥasidah [Jerusalem, 1969], p. 111) citing R. Samson of Sens, **Teshuvot Ḥakhmei Provence**, ed. A. Schreiber, pp. 291-92, **Semaq** #277, and especially R. Meir of Rothenburg, **Responsa** (Prague) #863, which contains opinions of both R. Samson and R. Tam.

[13] This statement of Riaz is cited in **Shiltei Gibborim** to **Ketubot** 59b. It is also found in **Pisqei Riaz**, ed. A. Liss (Jerusalem, 1973), p. 201. Cf. **SHP** #346 and **Pisqei Rid** (R. Isaiah of Trani), ed. A. Liss, p. 495.

THE MODERN STUDY OF RESPONSA

Peter J. Haas

i

At the conclusion of his article "Sheʾelot u-Teshubot" in the **Jewish Encyclopedia**[1], Jacob Lauterbach noted that "Responsal literature as a whole has as yet found no literary historian." His assessment, made some 75 years ago still holds valid. There have been few attempts systematically to study this corpus of Jewish material from a literary or historically critical point of view. The result is that this corpus of literature central to classical rabbinic Judaism remains largely unavailable to, and so ignored by, students of religion. I hope in the following to take the first steps toward remedying that situation.

Despite this literature's relative neglect by scholars of religion, an understanding of this corpus is crucial for an understanding of the religious mind of classical Judaism. This is true first of all because these texts comprise the bulk of rabbinic writings from the early Middle Ages onward. No other single rabbinic genre approaches the responsa literature in sheer number. Further, responsa are the literary tool-in-trade of the rabbinate. It is through these documents that the rabbis shape and justify their world and exercise their influence. Rabbis as a group devoted more of their energy to composing these legal texts than they did to composing prayers, catechisms, theologies and the like. As I said, for all these reasons a literary- and historical-critical study of responsal literature is essential for understanding classical rabbinism.

In the pages that follow, I attempt to take the first steps toward creating a literary critical description of the responsa genre. I stress at the outset that I am not concerned with the content of the responsa. That is, I am not interested in describing what Jewish law has to say on this or that topic. I am interested in the structure and development of legal argumentation as an expression of Jewish religiosity. I want to know how rabbis proposed routinely to articulate through law their views on religious and moral issues. So my focus is not on individual texts so much as on the traits of the responsa literature as a whole and on how, and why, these traits change over time.

My own endeavor does not take place in the vacuum. Responsa have been the subject of isolated historical and literary studies since the beginning of modern Jewish studies in the **Wissenschaft des Judenthums.** Many of these studies have been influential in shaping my own thinking. I begin then by reviewing what has gone before. The survey that follows will show that the academic study of responsa has already moved a considerable distance toward an adequate literary critical account. At this point, my effort is to bring these results together and to evaluate where we stand and what work, at this stage, lies ahead.

Before moving forward, I should like to point out more explicitly how the modern critical study of the literature we are about to review differs from the traditional use of responsa. Put simply, traditional rabbis read responsa in order to find out what the law is. That is to say, they take responsa at face value, as a true and accurate articulation of what Torah demands. Arguments marshalled in defense of one position or another are taken as evidence of what Scripture, for example, actually means to say. Opinions that prevail are regarded as true. Critique is possible only within the bounds of the system. Like any system of law, responsa are held to describe a closed self-referential universe which is truly and eternally valid.

The rise of modern Jewish scholarship in the nineteenth and twentieth centuries brought a new range of assumptions, and so a new set of questions, to the responsa literature. Rabbinic legal literature came to be seen not as a divinely inspired corpus of texts, nor as the product of a historical legal and philosophical reflection, but as the result of Jewish cultural creativity. As such these texts became available as sources for the study of Jewish history. Over the next century and a half, at least four avenues of investigation of the responsa literature developed. The first to emerge, not surprisingly, was the least imaginative in its questions. It viewed responsa merely as repositories of historical data: names, dates, the realia of everyday life. Only gradually did interest develop beyond the "facts themselves" to the more abstract questions of how people understood these facts and made use of them to construct meaningful lives. These abstract concerns developed as scholars became aware of the historicity of the Jewish community and its law. Questions were asked as to how Jewish legal sages at various points in history proposed to organize and evaluate human action given the facts at their disposal. Scholars began to investigate the character of Jewish law as a product of human experience. Responsa, naturally, played a major role in this endeavor because these texts represent the work of legal minds as they applied themselves to the particular problems of their day.

This new historical awareness gave rise to a third program of inquiry, namely the interest in the nature of Jewish legal thinking in general. This third agendum seeks to establish the particular convictions and values which give to Jewish jurisprudence its particular shape and character. This approach, too, relies heavily on responsa, although now the field of inquiry is more global, including codes, philosophical texts and other writings. The question is to find the character of mind that transcends individual responsa or corpora of responsa, and encompasses the community's **Weltanshauung** as a whole. It is a question not only of Jewish law, but of what makes Jewish thinking "Jewish."

This last approach, like those before it, is not yet critical of the source material itself. It still takes responsa at face value. It is, finally, interested in content, that is, in what the responsa say. A fourth approach, only now taking shape, takes the very existence of a responsa literature as worthy of investigation, independent of whatever the content of the texts might be. That is, it is concerned with the responsa literature as a mode of expression within Jewish culture. Its major concern is to define the traits of the genre, to trace their trajectory over time and to ask why these traits, and the genre which comprehends them, are meaningful within Judaism. It wants to know why we have responsa at all and what that fact means as regards our understanding of Judaism. My sense is that this last approach has the most promise for directing us to an understanding of Judaism as a religion. Before turning to our constructive work on this level, however, I shall review the other scholarly traditions and evaluate the successes and failures of each.

ii

The earliest **Wissenschaft** scholars regarded responsa as a source for historical data. They worked their way through responsa looking for information regarding Jewish life in medieval European or North African communities. Zunz, for example, who stands at the head of so much modern Jewish scholarship, examines responsa in order to retrieve basic historical data, such as place names[2], market prices[3], and various social and religious customs.[4] We end up, then, with lists of diverse facts, about this and that, gathered from here and there. Zunz shows little interest in linking these facts together to provide a coherent picture of Jewish life. Thus, while these data may be of some interest to historians, they are, as handled here, of no help to students of Judaism. In fact, this approach may be detrimental, in that it suggests that responsa are sources of hard facts about Jewish life and culture.[5] As we shall see, shortly, this assumption is far from assured.

The dangers of this assumption are illustrated in Ben Zion Katz's **History of the Jews in Russia, Poland and Lithuania.**[6] Here Katz attempts to bring together responsa from a particular time and place - in this case northeastern Europe in the sixteenth and seventeenth centuries - as sources for writing a local history of the Jewish community. In fact he does not provide the full responsa at all, but only citations or even summaries of the relevant content. Nonetheless his basic approach is clear. Responsa provide the data we need for writing communal histories.

What is of interest is his reasons for thinking this to be the case. In his Introduction, he lays out his basic assumptions. "Rabbinic literature can be considered an extremely reliable source," he says, "on which no doubt is to be cast, because the questions were also asked by rabbis, so that when they turn to a question . . . they researched it as thoroughly as they could . . . "[7] Thus even though these were not written primarily as historical texts or as records of events, they can serve as trustworthy sources of data. "The facts speak for themselves."[8]

The facts, of course, do not speak for themselves. Katz's "history" ends up being a formless collection of snippets about this and that. The data is mostly trivial and entirely episodic. Even Katz himself is unable to provide any narrative to connect what he has. Clearly what is needed is a critical methodology that can move beyond the trivia referred to in the texts. We would like a program that will get us to the people and events behind the texts. Curiously, it took nearly a century before scholars began to formulate approaches designed to exploit responsa along these lines.

Two early attempts to use responsa in a more controlled and methodologically vigorous way are represented by the work of Jacob Mann and Isadore Epstein. We begin with Jacob Mann. Mann's foray into the responsa literature represents a quantum intellectual leap over Zunz, although it is not without its problems as we shall see. Mann's innovation is to come to the texts with a clear agendum in mind. He is not just looking for this or that. In this case, he is interested in adducing the "internal" life of the Jewish community, that is, the way in which its social life is organized.[9] To get at this issue, he proposes to examine two critical areas: 1) how the community settles internal disputes and 2) how it sees its relationship to the outside world. These questions are particularly apt because they search out issues of structure and perception and they do so in a way well suited to the sources - the adjudication of disputes.

Approaching the material with this agendum in mind, Mann begins to produce interesting results. Through his eyes, we begin to see how medieval Jews actually viewed the world and proposed to operate in it. Yet, as we stated, Mann's program, in the last analysis, is far from satisfactory. Two basic methodological problems remain unresolved. The first concerns the scope of his inquiry. He simply tries to cover too much complex terrain with too little material. His discussion of Jewish attitudes toward non-Jewish courts during the several centuries of the Geonic period, for example, covers only seven pages and some 35-40 responsa entries (many only referenced and never cited).[10] Even worse, almost no other evidence, such as Babylonian archival material, is cited. The result is that a narrow and idiosyncratic base of evidence (Jewish juridical documents) is used to support wide-ranging and detailed conclusions about Jewish communal life. There is a second, more subtle, problem - one that will continue to plague this approach. Put simply, Mann accepts responsa too uncritically. A particular question posed in a responsum is taken to be a true and accurate reflection of a chronic state of affairs. The reader is never reminded that responsa are geared to serve specific communal and religious needs, and by nature deal with unusual, anomolous, and even by hypothetical cases.[11] Further, they are designed to do so in terms of the specific legal categories of rabbinic Judaism. They are not written as historical records. This is not to say that responsa are useless for historical reconstruction, but it is to say that responsa must be used with critical care, at the least in conjunction with other primary evidence. In short, the positivistic bias of Zunz is still in evidence. While Mann does take seriously the context of conflict out of which responsa come, he is too ready to take what they say as what was actually the case, as opposed to what was perceived to be the case or what might have been the case. The way litigants decide to describe conflicts for the purpose of rabbinic adjudication is taken as an objective description of how things really were.

Isidore Epstein takes steps toward solving these methodological problems. He diminishes the impact of our first criticism by narrowing his field of inquiry. In particular, he chooses to deal with individual authors.[12] By so doing, he keeps his data within controllable and coherent limits. That is, we do not have responsa from here and there, early and late, simply thrown together, but rather we have responsa that reflect the view of a single mind over a single lifetime. This narrowing of focus also allows Epstein to advance on Mann's second methodological problem as well. Mann's agglutinative approach works only if we assume that the institutions described in responsa remain essentially unchanged over time. If two responsa a century apart deal with tax courts we can use them to adduce a picture of tax courts only if we assume that the institutions described in responsa remain essentially unchanged over time. If two responsa a century apart deal with tax courts we can use them to adduce a picture of tax courts only if the institution and character of tax courts remain the same over that century - a dangerous assumption. Mann, by considering material spanning centuries, must simply assume that no substantive change occurred. Epstein avoids the problem by taking the author's experience as his constant. This allows him to control for changes in institutions, as well as for responsa which deal with an unusual or imaginary case. It is the author's **approach** to the problem that interests Epstein, not what the actual facts out there might be. By framing his inquiry as he has, Epstein establishes a much more reliable epistemological framework for interpreting responsa. Of particular importance is his insight into responsa as the creative products of individual human minds.

Epstein's two essays were followed some twenty years later by Irving Agus' biographical study of R. Meir of Rothenberg.[13] Agus' conception of the task moves beyond Epstein's in at least two ways. First, he cites the particular texts or passages which he uses as evidence. This allows the reader to see and evaluate the connection made between what the texts actually say and Agus' conclusions about Meir. But more significantly, Agus understands that the literary corpus of a responsa writer is itself of significance for understanding the author. Thus, Agus not only gives us an account of Meir's life and writings, but he publishes Meir's responsa as part of his study. His reasons for doing so are worth repeating:

> I have sought to retain as much as possible all the elements of each query and response that might be of interest to the student of history, sociology, economics, government or law; but above all I endeavored to maintain the unity and the spirit of the Responsum as a clear and definitive literary creation.[14]

The last sentence is significant. Responsa are literary creations. As such, their style and "spirit" reflect the character of mind of their author. Thus through Meir's literary products we confront something of the man himself. Having arrived at this conclusion, howver, Agus does not show us how to make use of it. He simply presents the roughly 800 responsa texts ascribed to Meir, leaving it to the reader to adduce whatever insight this corpus might support.

Agus attempts a much more ambitious project in his **Urban Civilization in Pre-Crusade Europe**[15]. This massive study, Agus states,

> endeavors not only to extract information from a highly complex source, but to develop a proper method and

> technique for a critical study of Responsa as historical sources. An attempt is made to demonstrate the wealth of accurate historical information contained in this genre of literature, and to prove that it thus constitutes the richest and most reliable source of information for the history of European Jewry in the past one thousand years.[16]

In many ways this sounds similar to what Mann had tried to do. In method, however, this study is much more sophisticated. Responsa from a number of writers are grouped according to major theme (travel, real-estate, education, etc.). Within each thematic chapter, the responsa are arranged in approximately chronological order. Agus then presents each text in turn, providing a translation of its relevant parts and then commenting on the meaning and historical import of that text. Since he moves in chronological order through texts concerned with a single topic, he can control for historical development. This is the most careful use of responsa as historical sources we have seen. The texts are categorized, arranged and considered in context. Yet despite its controlled reading of the documents, this project suffers from the same weaknesses as does Mann's seminal study. The historical reconstruction still relies on a narrow base of evidence: Jewish juridical literature. Like Mann, Agus fails to bridge the gap between the kinds of cases brought for rabbinic adjudication and the way they are framed, on the one hand, and the historical realities, on the other. Further, we lose the sharp focus on a single mind and again are asked to consider a broad panorama that transcends generations. Agus' careful consideration of each responsum's context can not solve this problem entirely.

The methodological problems faced by all these scholars, from Mann to Agus, result from the very way in which they frame their questions. It is at bottom a matter of the sources available and what we can know from these sources. If one proposed to use responsa alone as sources for historical research, then it is inappropriate to ask about hard social, political and economic facts. Responsa are not disinterested historical witnesses. They are legal documents which are designed to categorize and adjudicate human actions within the framework of Jewish law.[17] By nature, they thrive on the novel, the unprecedented, even the imaginary. They are not interested in, or meant to deal with the dry facts of life.[18] It follows, if we are to use responsa for historical reconstruction, we need to control for their inherent bias. This means, at a minimum, that responsa are to be used in conjunction with other sources. For example, a study of Jewish transportation in the thirteenth century should take place within a discussion of transportation in the thirteenth century in general. Then responsa can be invoked to highlight the particularly Jewish experience and perspective of matters. Agus' groundbreaking work falls short, as did Mann's, because it fails to control for the intellectual bias of his sources.

Reliance on only this one source of data leads to a second problem, which Weinryb calls "fragmentization."[19] By this he means the temptation to treat a few scattered responsa on a particular theme as an adequate base for historical reconstruction. Agus, for example, provides less than forty responsa on "travel." These responsa represent about ten known authors (about half of the texts collected here are of acknowledgedly unknown or doubtful authorship), spanning nearly three centuries (mid-ninth to mid-twelfth centuries) and representing communities from Babylonia to Moslem Spain to Provence. Even if each text by itself were an accurate and reliable account, we do not have nearly enough texts to form a coherent picture of "Jewish travel in any one time and place."[20]

That the careful use of responsa for historical research can increase our knowledge of Jewish life in the past is not to be denied. All these authors have shown this. But this line of inquiry is inherently limited. Responsa, by themselves, tell us only about how Jewish law deals with certain conflicts. Historical questions that range beyond this area can not turn to responsa alone for answers. So, while responsa are helpful as one kind of historical source, as both Epstein and Agus have shown, it is clear that they cannot be used alone to create a historical sociology of Jewish life.

In light of this critique, we should mention Simha Assaf's **BeOhole Yaakob** (Jerusalem, 1943). Here Assaf brings together a number of essays dealing with specific areas of inquiry in Jewish history: "History of the Rabbinate," "The Jews of Egypt in the Time of Maimonides," "Toward a History of the Jews of the Island of Malta," etc. This collection is significant because in each case the basic skeleton of the argument is constructed out of data supplied by a variety of historical sources. Responsa are used primarily to illustrate a point or to provide details. By using responsa in conjunction with other sources in this way, Assaf avoids the most blatant dangers discussed above. This seems to be a much more fruitful way of using these texts for historical purposes.

iii

If responsa are troublesome sources for historians of Jewish society, they are tailor made for historians of Jewish law. Responsa, after all, are the very literature in which Jewish law is produced and promulgated. It follows that responsa should have higher potential for use as sources for reconstructing the history and evolution of Jewish law than they do for the reconstruction of Jewish social or political history. Some attempts have been made to use responsa in just this way. While there are still methodological problems to be resolved, this approach builds on much firmer ground and correspondingly gives deeper insight into the possibilities for using responsa as historical sources. We turn, then, to the historians of Jewish law.

The immediate problems researchers in Jewish law face is the overwhelming amount of material at their disposal. Orthodox rabbis, who spend a lifetime working as Jewish legal professionals, find it impossible to be expert in more than a few areas. Scholars who wish to deal with Jewish law in general, and in a way informed by modern academic methodologies are in an even more difficult position. The result is that projects in this area are by nature limited in scope.

In general, such projects can be limited in one of two ways. The first is to concentrate on a particular area of law: marriage and divorce, for example. On this view, a single coherent set of legal context is provided. That is, we may end up with a description of Jewish marriage and divorce, but will not see how these rulings relate to contiguous areas of law: women, oaths, property rights and so forth. A second strategy compensates by stressing the synchronic as opposed to the diachronic. That is, it examines a wide range of legal topics as these coexist and influence each other at some particular time. Such a study is like a snapshot, catching how things are together at one moment, but leaving us uninformed as to how they got that way and how they will develop.

Of the first approach, tracing the development of a single theme or topic over a broad span of time, the most outstanding example is David Feldman's **Marital Relations, Birth Control and Abortion in Jewish Law.**[21] In his preface he gives a brief statement which reflects his working hypothesis:

> The "Jewish Law" of the title refers, of course, to the classic legal tradition that begins with Bible and Talmud and courses through to the most recent Responsum, as sketched in Chapter 1. The extent to which this law is operative today differs among the three alignments of Modern Judaism--Orthodox, Conservative, and Reform. The law [halakhah] itself is traced here through the works of its historic spokesmen, in a manner seeking to transcend the position of any one group. For, all three are heirs to the culture, outlook, and values of Judaism's legal-moral tradition reflected in these pages.[22]

Feldman articulates his assumptions well. He assumes an essential unity to Jewish law as it "courses" through the centuries and claims that we can trace the trajectory of this law in a more or less neutral way, fitting all major pieces of Jewish legal literature into an overarching scheme.[23] In fact, Feldman's two hundred pages scarcely catch the full diversity of Jewish speculation on the various topics mentioned in his title. Rather, the book focusses on a few central issues and uses them as a sort of skeleton around which other rulings can be organized. His book presents, so to speak, a caricature of Jewish law in which a few outstanding features are examined closely so that a sense of the whole is conveyed. This is not at all to detract from the magnitude of his accomplishment. It is simply to point out that the nature of the task forces him to use Jewish jurisprudential literature in a highly formalized and somewhat oversimplified way. Nonetheless some solid advances are achieved. Responsa are used competently in conjunction with other legal and moral texts. Further, a sense of the dynamics of the legal themes is established so that each responsum is set within an intellectual context. Finally, our attention is drawn away from how things "really were" to how the framers of responsa perceived and evaluated the world.

Turning to the second strategy, the synchronic, we find a number of studies. Unfortunately, almost all of these deal with Jewish law in Biblical or Talmudic times, that is, before responsa were written.[24] None of these are of particular help in deriving a methodology for studying responsa. But they do speak to the broader field of Jewish law and so yield some useful insight relevant to our concerns. In particular, such studies have explored ways of articulating themes and concepts inherent in the Jewish legal enterprise.

In the end, histories of Jewish law have so far been disappointing. They all end up treating "the law" as a self-contained topic, unconnected to the social experiences of the community. All we have finally are descriptions of basic lines of logical development, as if the work of spinning out the law occurs in a vacuum.

To bring the study of Jewish jurisprudence into the world of the humanities, we should like to show how Jewish law, in its way, reflects broader truths about how human beings relate their perceptual, moral and legal worlds to the physical realities around them. For this we need to take up the questions of values and interpretation. That is, we want to know why the law moves in a certain direction at a particular time. Whose interests are being served and how? It is precisely to these kinds of questions that our next group of researchers address themselves.

iv

In this section, we move beyond purely historical questions to those studies which are concerned with the values and principles that animate Jewish law in general. The authors we are about to examine share a conviction that we can discover such values by studying how individual rabbis in fact apply Jewish law to specific cases. The assumption here is that the content of the legal system is not predetermined. Any number of logically possible interpretations exist. The final choices that are made grow out of complex social and cultural factors acting on the rabbi, often on the subconscious level. The scholar's task is to describe these factors by examining the results they produce. As is clear, responsa are particularly suited to provide just this kind of data.

Our review begins with Eduard Baneth, the first modern scholar systematically to isolate and compare different theories operating behind medieval Jewish legal speculation. In "Sociale Motive in der rabbinischen Rechtsplege"[25] he centers attention on a Mishnaic ruling (Mishnah Ketubot 10:4) that has generated a number of legal disputes. The issue at hand is the division of one's estate among several wives. He shows that each of the five major lines of interpretation reflects a certain principled understanding of what the law ought to do. His conclusion is that the particular interpretation taken up by an author reflects that author's own convictions about the law.[26] This insight is not new. It can be seen behind Epstein's decision to focus his study on an individual author, as we already noted. Baneth's importance lies in the fact that he was the first to demonstrate so clearly that the law can be interpreted in a number of ways and that these ways grow out of different convictions about the law on the part of the individual rabbis. We would have liked Baneth to link the rabbi's choice to economic, social, or religious factors. Unfortunately, he does not push his analysis in this direction. He is satisfied simply to note that diverse possibilities inhere logically in Mishnah's legal ruling, and presumably throughout Jewish law.[27]

Diversity in the law can not only be viewed synchronically, that is, as several possibilities open at one time, but also diachronically, that is, as changing over time. An attempt to study how such development over time occurs is that of H. J. Zimmels. Zimmels topic is the rabbinic attitude toward the Marranos. In **Die Marranen in der Rabbinischen Literatur** (Berlin, 1932), Zimmels proposes to describe these attitudes by examining pertinent responsa from the fourteenth to the eighteenth centuries. This project has two parts. In Chapters One and Two he investigates the rabbis' attitudes toward the converts themselves. In Chapters 3 and 4 he looks at the way the rabbis view the life and culture of the Marranos. The entire work concludes with an appendix containing the translated texts of the responsa used in the study. In providing the reader with the relevant texts, Zimmel anticipates Agus by twenty years.

The conceptual breakthrough occurs in Chapters 1 and 2. Zimmels notes that the rabbinic attitude toward Marranos can be divided into five phases, the earliest, evident already in the fourteenth century, holds that Marranos are Jews in all respects, albeit sinning Jews. Attitudes become progressively harsher throughout the fifteenth, sixteenth and seventeenth centuries. Marranos are gradually "demoted" to being Jews only as regards inheritance (the second stage), then as not Jewish in any respect (the third stage), then as worse than all other non-Jews (the fourth stage). The trajectory finally settles on a slightly more understanding tone in the late seventeenth century (the fifth stage) when some responsa come to regard Marranos as "children imprisoned among non-Jews." What we see is a consistently developing condescension toward the Marranos.

Zimmels makes it clear that responsal law does change over time. Working within the same legal tradition, different rabbis at different times simply see matters differently. His statement of matters should be distinguished from Feldman's similar sounding conclusion. For Feldman, the law undergoes a linear, logical unfolding. Each succeeding generation builds on or develops what has gone before. Zimmels makes no such claim. Each stage is a self-standing and fully logical perspective. What we have is not development, but change. Entirely new ways of seeing matters emerge. By bringing this so clearly into focus, Zimmels' work represents a major advance. It is unfortunate that, like Baneth, he did not attempt to adduce the social or especially the religious reasons that lie behind the changes he so clearly perceives. We see that the law does evolve. We are still in the dark, however as to why and how that change comes about.

One promising attempt to push the analysis in this direction is made by Simon Hurwitz in **The Responsa of Solomon Luria.**[28] Hurwitz is interested in aiding "the student of law in the understanding of jurisprudence."[29] That is, he wants to see how Jewish legal decisions actually are made. To this end he sets before the reader the responsa of Solomon Luria. The choice is an apt one. Luria was critical of Jewish legal thinking as he knew it and hoped to effect some reform. In particular he wanted to move away from the prevailing casuistry and to introduce more scientific methods of legal analysis such as textual criticism.

Here, then, we have a person who is aware of juridical methodology, is able to articulate his dissatisfactions with it, and is struggling to devise new ways of thinking about the law. We have every reason to expect that a review of his work will throw light on the character of the received tradition of legal thinking, on the new directions he pioneers, and on the social, religious and intellectual influences that animate Luria's work. Unfortunately, Hurwitz fails to fulfill these expectations. He merely presents Luria's responsa, without discussing the deeper philosophical issues at stake. Like Agus, he leaves the readers to draw what conclusions they can from the new corpus of responsa at hand.

Only in the sixties do scholars develop theories for linking changes in legal thought, or accepted understandings of the law, to socio-religious factors. In fact, three widely different theories seem to emerge. The first, chronologically, is Jacob Katz's. In **Exclusiveness and Tolerance**, Katz attempts to trace the shifting Jewish legal attitude to social relations with non-Jews.[30] His underlying thesis is that as the social, political and economic context changed, so did the rabbi's view of what the law demands. In particular, as the leaders of the Jewish communities in Central Europe were faced with a more receptive outside world, they began to display more tolerance in their responsa for social interaction with outsiders. The laws which buttressed Jewish exclusivity, laws which once seemed self-evident, come increasingly to be limited or interpreted away. The motive for this changing attitude, Katz points out, is supplied by the surrounding culture.

The opposite theory is put forward by Yedidiah Dinari.[31] Dinari claims that Jewish law develops not because of outside influence, but according to its own internal logic. He takes as his case in point Jewish jurisprudence of the fifteenth century. Here he notices that custom suddenly becomes a much more serious factor in legal thinking. This shift, he claims, is due entirely to forces already operating within the legal system. He is adamant in saying that "secular" social or economic factors play no role, although he is unable to explain why custom does emerge as a major factor at just this time.[32] It is interesting to note that this same renewed attention to custom is occurring at this same time in German jurisprudence, a fact which Dinari himself points out. The conclusion would seem to be obvious. Despite his disclaimer, surrounding cultural norms have more to do with canons of Jewish jurisprudence than Dinari realizes, or wishes to acknowledge.[33]

A third theory seems to be offered by Emanuel Rackman in his review of Moses Feinstein's published responsa.[34] Rackman is impressed by Feinstein's willingness to take bold initiatives to correct what he sees as imbalances in the law. The motive for such change, in Rackman's view, is neither liberal American culture (because Rackman is committed to the integrity and self-sustainability of the entire Jewish legal tradition) nor simply to the logical demands of the law (since Feinstein is breaking new ground), but to Feinstein's own courage in searching for "breakthroughs for the exponents of a truly viable Halacha."[35] In other words, halachic change is a function not of the surrounding culture (as Katz would have it), nor of the law's internal logic (Dinari), but of a rabbi's willingness to bring his own moral sensibilities to bear.[36] We might call this a charismatic, as opposed to a sociological or logical, explanation for perceived changes in Jewish jurisprudence.

What all of this presupposes is that Jewish law is not simply rationally deduced conclusions flowing from certain premises. Rather, all these scholars (Dinari may be an exception) treat Jewish jurisprudence as a cultural phenomenon which reflects the values and convictions of its practioners. Shifts in legal paradigms must be seen as social acts and studied as such. Aaron Schreiber gives this view its most satisfying articulation so far. His claim, borrowing a phrase from McDougal, is that "law is a process of authoritative decisions, not a body of abstract rules and legal doctrines."[37] The authorities, of course, make decisions within a particular context. The task is to understand why they make the decisions they do. Schreiber goes on to say that our study of

> authoritative decisions must take account of changed conditions and new developments in many diverse areas, ranging from social customs, to religious, philosophical, and ethical perspectives, to new instruments of production, forms of credit, ownership devices, and modes of travel. Law, then, must stress its overriding goals and assess existing and projected societal

> conditions, determining which decisions will best attain such goals. This makes it necessary for decision-makers, as well as scholars, to determine precisely what the goals are (along with the relative weights of each, if they clash in a given case), to isolate the basic social postulates and criteria of choice on which the legal system rests, without which the prescribed and applied law of a culture cannot be understood.[38]

A legal decision, to repeat, is a function of the particular social context in which it is made. To understand a particular legal act, it is not enough merely to know what Jewish law has said up to that point. It is necessary also to understand the perceptions of the decision maker as he attempts to shape a meaningful and principled application of the legal tradition to social realities. The focus of attention shifts then to the mind of legal experts.

Despite Schreiber's excellent opening statement, his own work is disappointing. Part of the reason is that he is interested in all of Jewish law. He thus draws material from a number of diverse types of legal literature, including cuneiform tablets, Scripture, Talmud, medieval legal codes, and so forth that cover the width and breadth of Jewish history. While a number of socially determined choices in law are defined, the material is too broad to allow particular influences to be identified. Even when Schreiber turns to responsa, the most likely source for linking up social reality to legal decision-making, we are left unsatisfied. In fact, he devotes only nine pages (out of 424) to responsa, and even this is nothing more than a reprint of Solomon Freehof's general orientation to the literature.[39]

This concern with the social and cultural matrix in which decisions are made continues to be a subject of investigation. Two scholars currently connected with Hebrew Union College continue to explore the social factors which stand behind the shaping of particular decisions found in responsa. The first is Stephen Passamanack, who was the first researcher who explicitly began to ask such questions systematically of responsa material.[40] The process is carried forward by David Ellenson, who focusses especially on the responsa of nineteenth-century German traditional rabbis.[41]

The effect of these studies has been to establish responsa firmly as historical documents. It is no longer possible to see them as describing a literature that undergoes change according to its own ahistorical logic, as Feldman assumes. We now must see them as the products of individual minds, located in concrete historical and cultural contexts. These studies have also revealed that the making of Jewish law is a much more variegated activity than was once thought. The realization that a person like Meiri could approach the laws regarding relations with gentiles with an entirely new attitude, or that custom could come to play a major role in Jewish law at a particular time, concurrent with the rise of customary law in Europe, makes us realize how much a part of European intellectual life rabbinic legal speculation is. Specific legal decisions can be fully understood, it follows, when they are placed within the context in which they are made. We have here the first step toward bringing the study of Jewish law into the horizon of the humanities.

This area of research has changed fundamentally how we view Jewish law. It has clearly demonstrated that legal decisions are the products of individual perceptions as these take shape in concrete historical contexts. We can no longer take seriously the myth that responsa simply spell out what is inherent in the law. Responsa, rather, reflect the creative thought of legal minds struggling to formulate responses to new situations.

This description of matters raises a whole new set of questions about responsa. In particular, it provokes us to ask precisely what responsa do, if they do not do what they claim to do, namely spell out what is already inherent in the law. Why do we have responsa at all? What role do these texts, as a genre, play in the development of Jewish law, or in the making of Jewish legal decisions? Why does the genre have the characteristics it does and not some others? Do these characteristics remain constant, or do they change over time? Such questions shift our interest away from the content of a responsum to its form and function. It is with these questions in mind that we turn to our fourth group of researchers, the literary critics.

V

The goal of the literary critic is to describe the nature of the responsa genre. Yet the variety of texts encompassed by the genre has made it clear to almost all critics that the genre includes several kinds of responsa. Most research in this area thus has concentrated as first step toward tackling the genre as a whole on adducing and describing the subtypes that make up the genre. This work is complicated by two factors. First, is the sheer vastness and technical nature of the literature. It is simply hard to gain access. Second, is the fact that the texts are legal and argumentative, presenting a difficult style to divide into formal literary types. For these reasons it comes as no surprise that the earliest literary critics divided up the genre according to standards devised for other kinds of Jewish literature. It is only with the more sophisticated study of responsal jurisprudence, such as we reviewed in section IV, that it became possible to devise new, and more rigorous methodologies for categorizing the responsa material. Thus the history of this line of research has been one of ever more sophisticated attempts to correctly define the major responsal types, historical settings.

Our review begins with Leopold Zunz, the first modern, university trained scholar to deal with the history of Jewish literature. Zunz's interest was not in responsa, but in what he considered the more literary manifestations of Jewish culture, namely midrash and aggadah. He is important for us because the periodization he established for the aggadah became standard for the history of all Jewish literature. Even scholars who dealt entirely with responsa adopted his basic model. It is thus necessary briefly to examine Zunz's work before turning to studies focussing specifically on responsa.

Zunz's literary-historical program is worked out in **Die Gottesdienstliche Vortraege der Juden.**[42] For the period that concerns us, i.e. from the seventh century on, Zunz defines four epochs.[43] The first, the Geonic, runs from the redaction of Talmud (ca. 500 CE) to the collapse of the Geonic academies in Babylonia (ca. 975). This period concludes with the transference of Jewish academic life from Babylonia to Europe. This next period, which Zunz calls the "First Rabbinic" runs to the middle of the fifteenth century. By this time a number of significant changes have occurred in Europe. Among these are the fall of the Byzantine Empire, the discovery of America, Luther's rebellion against the church, the establishment of the Inquisition in Spain, and the invention of movable type. Taken together, these changes create an entirely new social, cultural and intellectual environment. The corresponding changes in Jewish literature are recognized by positing a new literary-historical epoch: the "Second Rabbinic Period." This period will last until the cataclysmic changes of the eighteenth century--the German Enlightenment and, for the Jews, emancipation. This new political, social and religious reality produces the literature of Zunz's fourth literary epoch: "the Present."

It is worthwhile pausing for a second to consider the effect of Zunz's seminal work on the literary study of responsa. First, as we already noted, he was the first to create a critical history of Jewish literature. He thus presented **Wissenschaft** scholars with a possible way to investigate the evolution of Jewish thought and culture over time, free from the classical rabbinic notion that Jewish thought and culture are a seamless and homogeneous whole. As we shall see, scholars after Zunz find it quite natural to break the responsa literature into these same literary epochs. In addition, Zunz pioneers a method for establishing such a historical grid. He proposes that Jewish literature matches stage by stage the development of Jewish civilization. Jewish civilization, in turn, develops along the trajectory traced by European civilization. It follows that benchmark events in European culture can serve as rough markers for turning-points in Jewish literature. The power of Zunz's achievement is such that generations of later scholars took his basic presuppositions for granted, even if they felt free to tinker with some of his particulars.[44] Zunz bequeathed to later generations, then, not only a history of Jewish literature, but also a theory and method for identifying the chronological units of such a history.

Zunz, as we said, did not deal with responsa. The first scholar to do so specifically was Z. Frankel.[45] Like Zunz, Frankel was concerned first of all to construct a literary history. He apparently did not find Zunz's scheme to his liking, for he devised his own periodization for responsa. He posits five periods in all. These are as follows:[46] 1) Geonic: mid seventh to the eleventh centuries; 2) responsa of the early Spanish and French schools: tenth through twelfth centuries; 3) late Spanish and French schools: thirteenth and fourteenth centuries; 4). responsa of Italian, Turkish and German sages: fifteenth and sixteenth centuries; 5) responsa of Italian, Turkish, German and Polish sages: 17th century on.

Unfortunately, Frankel, unlike Zunz, never makes clear his rationale for dividing the material up in the way he does. A closer examination of his proposed scheme, however, shows that he drew his criteria not from the literature itself, but from the social and political world of the authors, just as Zunz had done. Thus we still have a taxonomic scheme which, in the last analysis, is artificially imposed on the literature. Let us now turn to Frankel's proposal.

Frankel's first period, the Geonic, is most obvious. According to every criteria we can name, Geonic responsa are different from later rabbinic ones: they are written by the academic heads of the Babylonian academies rather than by local rabbis, they are descriptive rather than explanatory, they are short and to the point rather than long and argumentative, they rely on Talmud alone rather than on Scripture and logic, and so forth. The principles of selection governing the rest of his scheme, however, are less clear. Locale appears to be one criterion. His description of each period includes reference to a particular intellectual center: Babylonia in period one; Spain and France in periods two and three; Italy, Turkey and Germany in period four; and Poland in period five. But this by itself does not account for all of his choices. Why distinguish between an early and a late school in Spain and France, for example? Or why, for that matter, link together Italian, Turkish and German responsa? It may of course be quite true that early French responsa are different from late French responsa, or that German responsa are related to Italian ones. But since Frankel never tells us how he arrives at these conclusions, we can not be sure what particular characteristics he had in mind in each case.

Another apparent criterion is date. Each period, as we noted, is defined at least in part by a specific block of centuries. But again there is no explanation as to why those particular dates and not some others. What appears to influence

Frankel is some sense of the kind of responsa produced in each of his periods. That is, place and date are used only as rough markers for setting off what are in fact reigning literary paradigms. This notion of what Frankel is about is confirmed by his discussion of the "spirit" of the responsa in each of his epochs. His discussion is worth quoting at length.

> In the first three periods, philosophical speculation is like a clear and smoothly flowing brook; matters are investigated with intelligence and acumen, overenthusiastic dialectics are still held in check, the powerful logic, which does not stray from the issue, reveals intensive study and imports a scientific character (to the discussion). These same characteristics appear also in the responsa of these periods: they are clear and lucid, such that a reader reasonably familiar with the material can follow them without strain and achieves easily a clear view of the discussion and conclusions of the responsum. In later periods, philosophical speculation becomes like a rushing torrent; throwing out sparks of wit in all directions. The overall construction is daring, although often the foundation is weak and it is only through careful joining that it is able to support the superstructure. And while the responsa of this period also sparkle with astonishing and ingenious arguments, clarity often is lost. (Such responsa) not rarely leave one with a feeling of uneasiness, of doubt as to the legitimacy of making legal distinctions on the basis of such overwhelming dialectics.[47]

In other words, each cultural center displays a particular intellectual style which the responsa reflect. The great shortfalling of Frankel is that he is unable to build on his insight. Instead of developing his idea that we have different kinds of responsa, Frankel falls back on the positivist criteria of name and date. Because of this, Frankel is finally not able to give us a literary history in the strict sense of the term.[48] He gives us a chronology. His monograph in fact ends up to be little more than a listing of prominent responsa writers, arranged according to date and place of activity.

Before turning to the most recent scholar to propose a general chronology of the responsa literature, namely Jacob Lauterbach, we need briefly to examine two "scientific" studies of responsa published in the late nineteenth century by Joel Mueller. The first, entitled "Letters and Responsa in the pre-Geonic Jewish Literature," was appended to the fourth annual **Report of the Lehranstalt fuer die Wissenschaft des Judenthums.**[49] A few years later Mueller published his **Introduction to the Responsa of the Babylonian Geonim.**[50] These two projects are important because they represent the first attempt by a modern scholar systematically to investigate the responsa of a particular literary type. Our hope is that Mueller will be able to provide that literary characterization of responsa types that Frankel did not. As we shall see, this eludes Mueller as well. In fact, Mueller gives up some of the ground Frankel had gained.

In "Letters" Mueller takes up a topic alluded to, but never developed, by Frankel. Frankel claims in **Entwurf** that responsa go back to Biblical times. This process continues on into late antiquity, according to Frankel, where it is seen in the question-and-answer procedure reported in the Talmud. It is this intellectual tradition which finally develops into the mature responsa literature as we know it. Frankel is of course aware that no actual responsa from pre-Geonic times actually exist. He thus limits his discussion to the post-Talmudic responsa.[51] Mueller is now prepared to walk through the door opened by Frankel. He proposes to study the pre-Geonic responsa literature. He in fact hopes to trace the literary heritage of responsa (he is careful not to call them responsa **per se**) all the way back to the reign of King David.[52]

To make this claim even minimally plausible, Mueller must account for the fact that responsa as such do not appear before the Geonic period. He does so by pointing to the Tannaitic ban against writing down the law.[53] This artificial restraint, he claims, prevented actual responsa from being composed in the first few centuries of the Christian Era. When the ban was lifted in Talmudic times, legal briefs again were written. The rabbis, no longer having a received scribal tradition as regards these texts, copied the most suitable model at hand, contemporary Roman legal briefs (the **responsa prudentium**) such as we find in the Digest.[54] These texts evolve into the classical rabbinic responsa as we know them. The point of all this is to establish the existence of a corpus of a pre-Geonic legal advisory literature, even though no actual specimens survive.[55] When true responsa emerge in the Geonic period, we must see behind them, Mueller claims, a long period of development. We can be sure, then, that a pre-Geonic "responsa" literature existed. Because it has been entirely lost, however, we can say nothing about its form or style.

In his second essay, the **Introduction**, Mueller turns to the Geonic responsa, that is, to the earliest actual responsa texts that we have. These texts now present him with a problem. We have just seen that he posits a continuous literary tradition from at least Talmudic times. Yet the responsa from Geonic times are often only one or two sentences long, and almost never have the elaborate argumentative structure that is characteristic of later texts. In short, they do not at all appear to be part of a long literary development that culminates in classical responsa. Mueller must explain this apparent disjuncture. He does so by claiming that the Geonic responsa, when written, were as complex as classical responsa. Later redactors, when trying to create manageable collections, summarized or abbreviated the texts at hand.[56] In fact, these redactors, or subsequent editors, so mutilated the received Geonic literature that even the names of authors attached to individual texts are no longer to be trusted.[57] Thus the Geonic texts as we know them do not accurately reflect the style or format of the literature as the Geonim produced it.

Mueller's work represents curiously both progress and retrogression in the study of responsa. He does note that the Geonic responsa are quite distinct in form from the rabbinic responsa. In fact, he makes it clear that the differences are significant. The conclusion should be that we can not lump Geonic and medieval responsa together as a single literary type. Each has its own literary and intellectual characteristics which can be described and evaluated. But Mueller avoids this rather obvious conclusion. The reason is his conviction that the responsa literature has a single monolithic history from Biblical times to the present. In the interest of preserving this unity, he discounts all the evidence he has carefully amassed about the differences between Geonic and classical responsa.

It is of course possible that Geonic responsa were edited, as Mueller says, but he never substantiates this claim; he merely asserts it. Nor is he able to provide a convincing argument as to why the rabbis, who were meticulously careful about the preservation of holy texts, would show such lack of regard for the Geonic responsa, the basis of their own halachic work.[58] Mueller's summary dismissal of the evidence at hand shows an astonishing suspension of critical scholarship.[59] This is his first major step backwards.

This uncritical attitude toward textual differences leads to a second retreat as well. In attempting to encompass all responsa (even the imaginary pre-Geonic ones) in one definition, Mueller creates such a broad genre that it becomes meaningless as an analytic tool. At times, Mueller seems to consider responsa to be nothing more than the literary expression of the universal human need for legal thinking. The result is that the unique character of the actual literature is lost. Mueller makes it impossible for us to achieve the distance necessary to render an account of this literature which, in his words "dominates for a considerable time all Jewish writing."[60]

The most significant advance in the study of responsa as literature up to our day is that of Jacob Lauterbach. His entry in the **Jewish Encyclopedia** cited at the beginning of this paper is a milestone. He not only recaptures the territory lost by Mueller but makes impressive advances. He is also the last scholar to deal with the full sweep of the literature. He thus sets the stage for all future research on the genre. We therefore examine his article in detail.

In his encyclopedia entry, Lauterbach posits six periods: 1) the Tannaitic-Amoraic, 2) Geonic, 3) first rabbinic (Spanish and French of the eleventh and twelfth centuries), 4) second Rabbinic (Spanish and French of the thirteenth and fourteenth centuries), 5) third Rabbinic (fifteenth through eighteenth centuries), and 6) fourth Rabbinic (nineteenth century on). His dependence here on Frankel is clear. His second, third and fourth periods are taken over without change. The fifth period is essentially a combination of Frankel's fourth and fifth periods. Lauterbach's only initiative in this regard is to introduce the Tannaitic-Amoraic epoch, (possibly under the influence of Mueller) and to distinguish "modern responsa" from the late medieval ones.

As regards periodization, then, Lauterbach has not materially advanced beyond Frankel. In fact his inclusion of a Tannaitic-Amoraic level in respona literature can be seen as a step backwards. Even his criteria for dividing the literature are little more than expansions on Frankel's previous efforts. But Lauterbach has at least reaffirmed the existence of periods within the literature.

Lauterbach's real advances come in his discussion of the responsa materials within each period. Here he has entirely new and important things to say. It is in fact frustrating that Lauterbach did not take his own observations more seriously. One has the impression that the periodization came first and the study of the texts second, rather than the other way around. A good example is his discussion of the second period, the Geonic. This period ends, Frankel argues, in the tenth century when the Geonim in Babylonia lose influence in the West. This date is determined by a number of external factors, including the political fortunes of the Abbasid caliphate and the beginning of the renaissance in Christian Europe. Yet Lauterbach admits that the responsa literature itself suggests a different date altogether. He notes that during the early Geonic period responsa are written exclusively by the heads of the academies in Mesopotamia. By the later part of this epoch (i.e., mid-ninth century on), responsa are being written also by local European authorities.[61] This change in locale and pattern of authority means that later responsa function differently than older ones. There are in fact also some literary shifts which occur at this time, as Lauterbach notes. Later responsa are more "discursive," for example, than are the earlier Geonic responsa. They are more likely to be written in Hebrew or Arabic rather than in Aramaic. All this suggests that we should recognize an "early" and a "late" Geonic period. Having noted these changes, however, Lauterbach ignores their implication. He chooses instead to stick with the by now traditional schema of Zunz and Frankel, calling for a single Geonic period, ending in the tenth century.

Important insights occur in his discussion of the next three periods as well. It is well worth our while to review some of these. The third period--the first Rabbinic--covers the early

Spanish and Southern French writers. The basic characteristic of responsa during this period, Lauterbach claims, is that the Spanish works are tighter and more "scientific" while the French are more dialectic and casuistic. We thus see two different "schools" or theories of law operating in neighboring civilizations. These distinctions gradually disappear and a new "universal" responsa form appears. This new form is characteristic of period four--the "second Rabbinic." In this new period, the Spanish responsa become much more dialectic, showing Christian European influence, while the French writers are becoming more empirical and scientific, betraying Spanish influence. This period then produces a new breed of responsa which draws on the strength of both the Old French and the Old Spanish traditions.

Lauterbach notes that during the following period--the third Rabbinic--we find not so much a shift in the literary style, as a change in the function of responsa. European responsa of the previous periods (the first and second Rabbinic) dealt with the full range of rabbinic intellectual endeavor: law, Scriptural exegesis, aggadah, folklore and medicine. In the third Rabbinic period, he claims, responsa are restricted largely to legal matters. As a result, the responsa literature of this period is much more legalistic or "pilpulistic" in tone. It becomes a specialized tool of the legal expert. There are other signs of this shift in function: their argumentation becomes much more conservative and cautious, they are arranged in collections which parallel the organization of the great legal code, the **Arbaʿa Turim.** In short, responsa come to function as one component of a larger legal system.

Lauterbach here has significant things to say about the character of responsa as we move from period to period. He is in fact the first scholar clearly to note that there are important formal and substantive differences among responsa of different times and places. Through his eyes we see the fundamental choices available to authors, and it becomes clear that responsa do indeed reflect social and cultural assumptions and values. Lauterbach is not yet able to relate what he finds in responsa to the values and myths of rabbinic culture. But he does leave us with a new appreciation of the richness of the literature, and a sense for the broader questions that can be asked. It is unfortunate that since Lauterbach, there have been no serious attempts to carry his work forward or to deal critically and in a comprehensive way with the issues he raises.

There has, however, been some credible work done on Geonic responsa by Simha Assaf. Besides publishing collections of Geonic texts, he has devoted some energy to adducing the context within which Geonic responsa were written. His conclusions reveal that even Geonic responsa display stylistic variation and literary development.[62] Earlier responsa were shorter and more to the point. Later Geonic responsa are more apt to enter into investigations of the question from several angles. Some, such as the "Letter" of Sherira Gaon, are virtual books in themselves. But even finer distinctions can be made. Assaf claims (p. 215) that he can even distinguish different styles among the various authors, although he does not elaborate. Assaf's conclusions are not without problems. He claims, for example, that the responsa were written by scribes, not the Geonim themselves, yet are stylistically linked to the Geonim who sponsor them.[63] He also claims both that the geonic materials were meticulously preserved and that the copyists often abbreviated them (p. 217). Yet Assaf at least alerts us to the fact that even the Geonic responsa hardly constitute a single monolithic corpus.

Two more recent essays should be mentioned to complete our survey, although neither materially advances the state of the question. The first is Freehof's introduction to his **The Responsa Literature**, published in 1955. The second is the entry under "Responsa" in the **Encyclopedia Judaica** written by Israel Ta-Shma and Shlomo Ṭal. We shall look briefly at each.

Freehof's aim is "to give a general description of the responsa literature: its development, the great contributors to it, how it reflects Jewish history, the stirring controversies which it records, and even some of the strange and curious items which it contains and which serve to illustrate the spiritual depth and geographical extent of its influence."[64] Clearly this is not meant to be a scholarly analysis of the literature. It is, as Freehof admits, designed to introduce laypeople to this branch of rabbinic literature. His survey is therefore necessarily brief and oversimplified. He notes, as do all writers, that a major stylistic shift occurs between the eleventh and the thirteenth centuries. Beyond this his division of the material into epochs is fairly routine. He notes several centers of responsa activity: Germany and Spain (to the fifteenth century), Turkey and Poland (sixteenth and seventeenth centuries), and finally Hungary and Galicia (nineteenth century). In each case he does provide some historical data to explain why each center flourished when it did. The survey is too brief, however, to allow us to see in any detail what differences these historical factors make on the actual literature.

The second essay which I wish briefly to describe appears in the new **Encyclopedia Judaica.**[65] The editors have divided this entry between two contributors. Israel Ta-Shma covers the responsa of the Geonim and the "rishonim" (i.e. rabbinic scholars before the publication of the massive legal code, the **Shulkhan ᶜArukh** in the sixteenth century). Shlomo Tal reports on responsa from this period to the present. On the editorial level, then, a clear theory of the nature of the genre is operating. It assumes three major epochs: the Geonic, that of the Rishonim and that of the sixteenth century to the present. The Geonic, as we have seen has become a well-established period. The single break posited here: that between the "Rishonim" and the later period is new. It is based on what at least contemporary Orthodox see as a standard watershed in the history of Jewish law--the publication of the **Sulkhan ᶜArukh.** We have already seen that the publication of an earlier code, the **Arbaᶜa Turim,** provided a legal framework in which responsa came to operate. On the surface, then, the use of this later and more widely accepted code seems natural. On closer examination, however, the choice is not so apt. Surely the publication of this code was of major significance in the history of Jewish jurisprudence. In fact it eventually influenced the way responsa collections were organized. But it had no immediate impact on how responsa were written or on the epistemology of Jewish legal speculation. We have already seen that the responsa literature itself reveals lines of internal development that are independent of the appearance of the **Skulkhan ᶜArukh.** Thus making the publication of this code a major turning point in the development of the responsa literature completely ignores the efforts of Frankel, and later of Lauterbach, to establish a taxonomy on the basis of the literature's own evidence. In terms of methodology, this represents a clear step backwards.

vi

We conclude by drawing together what our review has revealed. First we note that responsa can not be accepted uncritically as accurate historical sources, despite the rather naive assurances of Ben Zion Katz. Responsa are designed to fulfill a specific religious, social and legal function. They describe events in terms of a pre-conceived grid of reality. This is not to say, to repeat once again, that none of the data in responsa are useful for historians. It is to say, however, that responsa reflect the mental world of the rabbis, not, in the first instance, what really happened. Our conclusion was that a more sophisticated way of approaching the responsa is to examine them as evidence of how the rabbis perceive and evaluate the world. This would not only circumvent the naive historical positivism of the nineteenth century--but would be more appropriate to the nature of the texts themselves.

This conclusion led us to examine the scholarship devoted to the history of Jewish law and jurisprudence. This approach proved more useful. Research along these lines reveals Jewish jurisprudence to be an expression of the community's intellectual life. We begin to see how particular issues or values come to the fore at certain junctures. We watched as social or cultural changes influenced rabbis to adjudicate cases in certain ways. In short, we became aware that Jewish legal speculation is a social artifact, closely bound up with the perceptions and values of individual authors living in particular historical contexts. But insofar as this new awareness focussed our attention on the historicity of individual texts, it ignored the character of the enduring enterprise of writing responsa. That is, we found we could account for shifts in legal thinking but could not yet show how these affected, or were expressed in, the responsa genre. We wanted to know why the responsa form continues to be a compelling format for Jewish legal discourse, how shifts in legal thinking influence the form responsa discourse takes, and in what ways the writing of responsa shape how the law is conceived.

It was with these questions in mind that we turned to the literary historians. We found the preliminary results encouraging. The literature turned out to be far from homogenous. There are epochs and areas with their own styles and epistemologies, thus making the writing of a critical literary history possible. It became clear that by comprehending the parts, each in turn, we could better understand the whole. Our major disappointment here was that no questions were asked once the parts had been discovered, laid out and labelled. We gained no further understanding of the genre as a whole, of its place in rabbinic culture, or of the nature of the Judaism that gives it rise. Inquiry ended when the immediate results were in hand.

What remains is a clear sense of the direction in which further work lies. The first task is to complete the categorization and description of the various types of responsa. On the basis of these findings we can then turn to defining the nature of the responsal system as a whole. Beyond that lies the final labor of adducing what this kind of literature, and the convictions upon which it rests, has to tell us about how the rabbis attempt to organize their universe.

NOTES

[1] **Jewish Encyclopedia,** XI:240-250.

[2] "Ueber die in hebräisch-jüdischen Scriften vorkommender hispanischen Ortnamen" in **Zeitschrift fuer die Wissenschaft des Judenthums** (Berlin, 1823), pp. 121, 132ff.

[3] **Zur Geschichte und Literatur** (Berlin, 1845), pp. 175-176.

[4] **Ibid.,** pp. 183ff.

[5] Cf. Freehof's discussion in **The Responsa Literature,** p. 194. "On the other hand, there is one reason why the responsa are an exceptionally good source of historical information. The questions that come up in the literature were submitted for legal discussion; it was necessary therefore for their facts to be precise and their circumstances sharply delineated . . . If, therefore, there is any record at all in the responsa of an event of this nature, it can be trusted as factual and need never fall under the suspicion of being literary embellishment . . . " This is a good example of the positivistic use of responsa we find in Zunz.

[6] **Leqorot hayehudim berussia, polin veliṭa,** Berlin, 1899, repr. Jerusalem, 1970.

[7] p. 1.

[8] p. 3.

[9] "The Responsa of the Babylonian Geonim as a Source of Jewish History" in **JQR 7** (1916-1917), pp. 457-490; 8 (1917-1918), pp. 339-356; 9 (1918-1919), pp. 139-179; 10 (1919-1920), pp. 121-152, pp. 309-365; 11 (1920-1921), pp. 433-471. Repr. in **The Responsa of the Babylonian Geonim as a Source of Jewish History** (New York: Arno, 1973).

[10] **Ibid.** 10:1, pp. 137-144. The problem of sources is compounded by the nature of the preserved Geonic responsa. These are often quite short, sometimes only a sentence or two. They also usually lack reference to the petitioner and even the author. It is possible that some of these were edited by their collectors. This makes the materials in our extant collections even more questionable as historical sources.

[11] The deeper problem here is what we might call "naive realism." This is the view that events and facts occur out there and that the law is applied to them. This is not self-evidently the case. The events themselves take on structure and meaning through the very act of being considered legal problems. Thus it is methodologically inaccurate to take a case as reported into the legal system and as an objective description of what really happened. See Zunz's comment in note 5.

[12] **The "Responsa" of Rabbi Solomon ben Adreth of Barcelona** (Routledge, 1925); Repr. in **Studies in the Communal Life of the Jews of Spain,** 2nd ed. (New York: Hermon, 1968), p. xi. A second

study, entitled **The Responsa of Rabbi Simon b. Ẓemah Duran** was published by Oxford University in 1930. A similar kind of study is Abraham Hershman's **Rabbi Isaac ben Sheshet Perfet and his Times** (N.Y., JTS, 1943). Hershman, however, does not display the analytical sophistication of Agus. While his biography of Perfet (completed in 1931) is competent, he does not convey a solid sense of Perfet as a rabbinic mind. His discussion of Jewish communal life, Chapters 11-16, reminds one of Mann's work thirty years earlier. Hershman does have a contribution to make in his analysis and dating of the individual texts in Perfet's corpus. For this, see pp. 5-8 and especially his Appendix, pp. 217-236.

13 **Rabbi Meir of Rothenburg: His Life and Words as Sources for the Religious, Legal and Social History of the Jews of Germany in the Thirteenth Century**, 2 vol. (Reprinted, New York: KTAV, 1970).

14 **Rabbi Meir of Rothenburg** (New York: KTAV, 1970), pp. xii-xiii.

15 2 vols, pub. by Yeshiva U. Press, New York, 1965.

16 **Ibid.**, pp. x-xi.

17 Cf. Jacob Katz, "Al halacha v-derush kimqor histori," ("Concerning Halacha and Homiletics as Historical Sources") in **Tarbiz** 30:1 (Oct. 60), p. 63.

18 See B. D. Weinryb, "Responsa as a Source for History (Methodological Problems)" in H. J. Zimmels, ed. **Essays Presented to Chief Rabbi Israel Brodie on the Occasion of his Seventieth Birthday** (London: Soncino, 1967), p. 409.

19 **Ibid.**, p. 404-406.

20 cf. Isaiah Sonne, **Contempoary Jewish Record** VI (1944), p. 421.

21 New York: Schocken, 1968. The only other academic study of this kind that I know of is I. Epstein's "The Jewish Woman in the Responsa" in **Response** 18 (Summer, 1973), pp. 23-31.

22 "Preface," p. vi.

23 Feldman's book is not really as neutral and detached as it might at first seem. In the final analysis his reading of the tradition is that of liberal Orthodoxy, a point Solomon Freehof brings out in his review of Feldman's book in **The Journal of Religion** 49 (Oct. 69), p. 373.

24 Some examples are M. Katz, **Protection of the Weak in the Talmud** (N.Y., 1966); Hayyim Nahmani, **Human Rights in the Old Testament** (Tel Aviv, 1964); David Amran, **The Jewish Law of Divorce According to Bible and Talmud** (Phila: Stern & Co., 1896); Israel Levitan, **Jewish Law of Agency with Special Reference to the Roman and Common Law** (N.Y., 1923).

25 In **Festschrift zum 50 jährigen Bestehen der Hochshule für die Wissenschaft des Judentums** (Berlin: Philo, 1922), pp. 49-100.

26 This point is spelled out in terms of modern philosophy of law by Ronald Dworkin in R. M. Dworkin, "Is Law a System of Rules?" in R. M. Dworkin, ed. **The Philosophy of Law** (Oxford: Oxford U. Press, 1977), pp. 38-65.

27 Freehof presents as examples a number of cases which generated heated controversy among rabbinic authorities of the time. See "Widespread Debates" in **The Responsa Literature,** pp. 147-190.

28 New York: Bloch, 1938.

29 **Ibid.**, p. ix.

30 First printing, London: Oxford, 1961.

31 Yedidiah Dinari, "HaMinhag VeHaHalacha Betshuvot Ḥachmei Ashkenaz ba-meʾah ha-15" (Custom and Law in the Responsa of German Sages of the 15th Century) in **Sefer Zikaron le Benyamin DeVries** (Jerusalem, 1968), pp. 168-198.

32 **Ibid.**, p. 197.

33 **Ibid.**, pp. 197-198.

34 "Halachic Progress: R. Moshe Feinstein's **Igrot Moshe**" in **Judaism** 13:3 (Summer 64), pp. 365-373. Moses Feinstein is an East European rabbi who, as head of the Metivta Tiferet Jerusalem Academy in New York, is a major voice in American Orthodoxy.

35 **Ibid.**, p. 366.

36 A similar view of how change is introduced into Jewish law was put forth 35 years earlier by Solomon Zucrow, **Adjustment of Law to Life in Rabbinic Literature** (Boston: Stratford, 1928). In this book he urges Orthodox rabbis to use their influence to make Jewish law more consonant with modern times.

37 Aaron Schreiber, **Jewish Law and Decision-Making** (Philadelphia: Temple, 1979), p. 5.

38 **Ibid.**

39 **Ibid.**, pp. 366-375.

40 See for example his "Cannons of Controversy" in **HUCA** (1977), pp. 265-300.

41 See for example his, "The Role of Reform in Selected German-Jewish Orthodox Responsa: A Sociological Analysis" in **HUCA** LIII (1982), pp. 357-380.

42 Originally published in 1832 by A. Asher, Berlin. A second edition, containing the author's corrections, was published by Dr. N. Bruell in Frankfurt a.M. in 1892.

43 A summary of his chronology for midrash from its beginning in the Biblical period to the end of the Geonic period is given in the beginning of Chapter 19. The remainder of his chronology is developed in Chapters 22-24.

[44] Albeck, in his introduction to the Hebrew edition, remarks, " . . . for this book remains a model and example for those which will come after it, and its influence and importance are unabated. But the influence of the book was not at first along the lines the author had in mind, namely in the direction of emancipation and Reform. . . The book's influence and importance are rather in its mode of research and in the foundation it has laid for the periodization of the aggadic literature, and rabbinic literature in general." Albeck, **Haddrashot Beyisrael,** (Jerusalem: Mosad Bialik, 1974), pp. 19-20.

[45] Zacharias Frankel, **Entwurf einer Geschichte der Literatur der nachtalmudischen Responsen,** (Breslau, 1865).

[46] **Ibid.,** pp. 11ff.

[47] **Ibid.,** p. 13-14. Frankel declares that his third period, that of the later Spanish and French schools, represents the full flowering of the responsa literature "because it is rich with a variety of questions and the most interesting conclusions (p. 27). The sharp contrast Frankel draws between these "ideal" responsa and the responsa of his own day is noteworthy. Frankel may have intended this work to contain an oblique critique of the rigidity and aridity of East European Orthodox rabbis.

[48] A similar critique is advanced by Abraham Geiger in "Ein Curiosum" in **JZWL** 3 (1865), pp. 174-178.

[49] "Briefe und Responsen in der vorgeonaeischen juedischen Literature" in **Vierter Bericht ueber die Lehranstalt fuer die Wissenschaft des Judenthums** (Berlin: 1886).

[50] **Mafteaḥ le-Teshuvot HaGeonim** (Berlin: 1886). This volume bears a German titlepage which reads "Einleitung in die Responsen der babylonischen Geonen."

[51] **Entwurf,** p. 8.

[52] **Letters,** pp. 3-4.

[53] Mueller considered this ban to be a temporary aberration. See his discussion in "Letters" pages 4 and 8.

[54] "Letters," pp. 11-12.

[55] "From the mid-fourth century on, until Geonic times, we have virtually no mention of responsa . . . But a phenomenon which appears in later writings allows us to suggest that at that time, when the chain of oral tradition was threatened, the exchange of epistles kept teachers and students, leaders and the people in communication. No responsa of the saboraim survive, but with the earliest Geonim we find the epistolary style come to full bloom, dominating the literature. "Letters," p. 12.

[56] **Introduction,** p. 3.

[57] **Introduction,** p. 4.

[58] It is of course true that a certain amount of editing and censorship did take place during the collection and publication of responsa. This was true even for the responsa of the

classical medieval sages. See Shmuel Weingarten, "Teshuvot SheNignezu," **Sinai** 29 (1951), pp. 90-99.

59 Geonic responsa found in the Geniza display the same stylistic features as the responsa found in the later rabbinic collections. This is a devastating rebuttal to Mueller's claim.

60 "Letters," p. 14.

61 **Jewish Encyclopedia**, XI, p. 242.

62 Cf. his **Tequfat HaGeonim veSifrutah** [The Geonic Period and its Literature] (Mossad HaRav Kook, 1967), pp. 211-220.

63 Cf. **Ha-ʾim Katvu HaGeonim et Teshuvotehem raq beKalah deAdar?** (Did the Geonim Write Their Responsa Only During the Assembly of Adar?) in **Ibid.**, p. 256.

64 Solomon Freehof, **The Responsa Literature** (Phila.: JPS, 1955), p. 18.

65 **Encyclopedia Judaica** (Jerusalem: Keter, 1972), XIV: 83-95.

YIDDISH AND THE SETTLEMENT HISTORY OF ASHKENAZIC JEWS*

Alice Faber and Robert D. King

0. Prefatory Remarks

Identification of the roots of Ashkenazic Jewry and of its native language Yiddish is a vexing problem both for Jewish and for general history. Surprisingly, we know less than one might suppose about the settlement history of European Jewry. Speculations and surmises abound, but previous scholarship reveals very little that can be called the definitive "truth." It is the purpose of this paper to summarize research we are conducting that may ultimately tilt the balance away from speculation toward a more factual understanding of what happened.

We begin by considering the comparative method in historical linguistics, a tool that allows linguists studying a group of genetically related languages to reconstruct some aspects of the internal structure of the predecessor language of the group, making it possible to discuss relative closeness of languages in a meaningful way. Thus, an examination of the Indo-European language family reveals a group of Slavic languages (Russian, Ukrainian, Polish, etc.), a group of German languages (German, English, Norwegian, Dutch, etc.), and a group of Romance languages (Latin, French, Spanish, Rumanian, etc.), as well as other groups such as Celtic, Indo-Iranian, and so on.

These relationships entail hypotheses about historical and cultural connections. If we assume that all of the Romance languages sprang from **one** ancestor, then the present-day spread of these languages must be due to some combination of migration and cultural assimilation. In this particular case, the combination of factors is relatively straightforward. Latin spread throughout Europe with the Roman legions. And the number of speakers of Latinate (Romance) languages increased as a result of the assimilation of Celts and Germans, among others, into Roman/Christian culture. Similarly, in more recent centuries, French, Spanish and Portuguese spread as a result of colonial expansion during the Age of Imperialism. Again, these languages gained strength through the assimilation of outsiders (Native Americans, etc.) to culturally dominant languages.

It is clear that, on the basis of the linguistic comparisons alone, much of what results from application of the comparative method is speculative. Confirmation of linguistic hypotheses based on the comparative method comes from historical records. But it is not always the case--indeed, lamentably it usually is **not** the case--that records bearing on hypotheses derived from the comparative method will be available. This lack of independent confirmation is not a fault of the method itself. New records may be discovered; new archaeological sites may be uncovered. Like all scientific hypotheses, hypotheses regarding language relatedness are based as much on conceivable evidence as they are on presently existing evidence. A potential problem arises only to the extent that hypotheses about historical relatedness based on the comparative method contradict what is known from (or assumed on the basis of) external historical evidence.

We feel that the study of Yiddish presents just such a problem. In Section 1 of the paper, we outline the generally accepted historical view of Jewish migration patterns in Europe. Then, in Section 2, we summarize a comparison of Yiddish with other German dialects. The results of this comparison suggest that Yiddish comes from a dialect of the German east; Bavarian and, to a lesser extent, East Central German, gave us Yiddish. In Section 2 we will also discuss attempts to relate certain idiosyncratic features of the liturgical Hebrew used by Yiddish speakers to characteristics of the various European languages. Our results are difficult to reconcile with the "textbook" account of Jewish migration patterns in Europe during the Middle Ages, summarized in Section 1. Then, in Section 3 we outline some of the directions in which our research is taking us in our attempts to resolve the conflicts between Section 1 and Section 2.

1. Migration Patterns of Jews in Europe

Jewish settlement in Europe is generally assumed to have begun during the Roman Empire. However, there is little documentary evidence supporting this assumption, and much of what we know is purely accidental. Jewish epitaphs have been found in catacombs under Rome from around the beginning of the Common Era (Leon 1960:45). Rome was apparently a focus from which Jews settled the rest of the Empire, reaching as far north as Cologne.[1] The earliest known concentrations in Europe north of the Pyrenees (it seems generally to be assumed that the community in Spain did not interact in significant ways with the developing Ashkenazic community) were in the Rhine valley, in modern France and Germany. There, in Mainz, Troyes and Speyer, Jews lived under episcopal protection and religious studies flourished.

However, in 1096, in the wake of the First Crusade, the situation turned ugly. Mobs, sometimes incited by Christian clerics, sometimes acting under their own impetus, attacked Jews, offering the choice of conversion or death. Despite the fact that these attacks were condemned by the Church and by some civil authorities, they continued. To avoid the mobs, Jews moved east, probably only a village or two at a time.[2]

Coupled with the rise of a bourgeois middle class was an increased government intolerance of Jewish economic activity. Expulsions from one territory or another were common, although Jews often returned after a short time to those communities from which they had been expelled. Even then, significantly fewer returned than were expelled. Many moved east. Then, expulsion took on a more national flavor. In 1290, Jews were expelled from England, and in 1306, from Ile de France. Other areas soon followed suit. The refugees again moved east.[3]

It is around this time that the first references to a Jewish community in Poland are found. Poland, as a developing country, needed people, especially people who were neither noble nor serf, and Jews were initially welcomed. Also welcomed at this time were German merchants, many of them associated with the Hanseatic League. The Polish Jewish population grew rapidly, from 50,000 in 1500 to as many as 500,000 in 1648 (estimated by Dubnow 1916:66n), on the eve of the Chmielnicki massacres. Much of this growth was due to immigration of refugees from persecutions further west.

What we have given here is the "received" view of Jewish migration to the Slavic east. It is important to remember that historical documentation for the various parts of this account is sparse indeed; the account rests more on inferences from a few events and known facts than on a foundation of solid knowledge.

2. The Linguistic Evidence

2.1 Yiddish as a German Dialect

From the lexicon alone we establish immediately that Yiddish is, at bottom, a German dialect. Most Yiddish words (between seventy and ninety percent, depending on style, country, religious background, ideological orientation, and so on) derive from the Germanic component. The language has a heavy lexical influence from Hebrew-Aramaic, a moderate and geographically variable influence from Slavic, and a small handful of very old words from Romance. Grammatically, virtually everything about Yiddish (except its word order) is German: its verb system, its gender system, its processes of pluralization, and so on.

Our task here is to apply the comparative method to the Yiddish dialects (Northeastern, Central and Southeastern Yiddish) and see what "Proto-Yiddish" looks like. That Proto-Yiddish, in this sense, will closely resemble a German dialect is clear at the outset; the question is **which** German dialect Proto-Yiddish most resembles.

Without going into detail, it becomes apparent early in our application of the comparative method that many of the major German dialects can be discarded as candidates for identification with Proto-Yiddish. The Low German dialects of northern Germany have contributed nothing of importance to the formation of Yiddish (Yiddish undergoes the Second or Old High German consonant shift). Similarly, we find no trace in any of the modern Yiddish dialects of linguistic features found in most of the other major dialects of Germany, e.g. Alemannic (Switzerland and southwestern Germany), Alsatian, Rhine Franconian, or Moselle Franconian (spoken in southwestern Germany). That similarities between Yiddish and these German dialects exist is obvious, but this is true of **any** two German dialects taken from anywhere, say Pennsylvania German and the Swiss German dialect of Appenzell (though of course there is not a close relationship between the two: they both just happen to be German dialects). We find, for example, absolutely no trace in Yiddish of the "ur-Alemannic" characteristic retention of long high vowels--a feature that serves as a major part of the definition of an Alemannic dialect.

Leaving the details of application aside, a linguist would soon determine that Yiddish has important points of similarity with only two German dialects: East Central German and Bavarian. East Central German refers to the group of dialects spoken in the eastern provinces of Germany colonized relatively late in the Middle Ages and at the expense of Slavic-speaking populations; this dialect once was spoken as far east as parts of present-day Poland (Thuringia, Saxony, Silesia). Bavarian, or Bavarian-Austrian as it also is called, was originally spoken not only in present-day Bavaria and Austria, but over most of what once constituted the Austro-Hungarian Empire (that is, over parts of present-day Czechoslovakia and Hungary.[4]

The principal East Central German features found in Yiddish are:

1. Non-affricate reflexes of Germanic **p-**, **pp-**, and **-p** (Standard Yiddish examples are **ferd** 'horse,' **epl** 'apple,' **kop** 'head;' compare German **Pferd, Apfel, Kopf**).

2. Middle High German diphthongs **ie, ü̯e, uo** (MHG **knie** 'knee,' **grüene** 'green,' **buoch** 'book') which show up both in East Central German and Yiddish as monophthongs (Yiddish **kni, grin, bukh**).

3. Retention of the vowel in the unstressed prefixes **be-** and **ge-** (Standard Yiddish **bakumen** 'received,' **gehat** 'had').

The most important points of agreement between Bavarian and Yiddish are:

1. Apocope (MHG **bluome** > Yiddish **blum** 'flower,' **tage** > **teg** 'days,' etc.).

2. Loss of the rule of final devoicing (compare MHG **rat** 'wheel' with Standard Yiddish **rod**).

3. A direct causal relationship between (1) apocope and (2) loss of final devoicing (see King 1980).

4. Early and complete unrounding of front rounded vowels (MHG **über** > Yiddish **iber** 'over').

5. Retention of an ancient and archetypically Bavarian pronominal dual **ets-enk** ('you,' nominative and dative/accusative) in certain dialects of Central Yiddish.

6. Lack of umlaut in the present tense of verbs (compare Standard Yiddish **du trogst** 'you carry' and **er trogt** 'he carries' with German **du trägst** and **er trägt**).

7. Loss of vowel length. A phonemic contrast of long and short vowels is found in almost all German dialects; its absence is exceedingly rare. Both Bavarian and all dialects of Yiddish except Central Yiddish lack phonemic vowel length.

8. The diminutive system. Both Bavarian and Yiddish have the **l**-diminutive: **tish** 'table,' **tishl** 'little table.' This diminutive is common among Upper German (Bavarian and Alemannic) dialects. What is not common, however, in German dialects is the existence of an intensive diminutive (or, as it sometimes is called, an iminutive) having the shape **-ele**. Thus: **tish, tishl**, and **tishele** 'very little table.' Both Bavarian and Yiddish have the two degrees of diminutive in the same phonological shapes, and with the same regularity of patterning.

We do not think it can be seriously disputed that of all the German dialects that have left an imprint on Yiddish, Bavarian has played the leading role by far, with East Central German in second place, and with **no other** German dialect having significant impact. In particular, **linguistically speaking**, the Rhineland was **not** important for the formation of Yiddish. No linguist reconstructing backward from present-day Yiddish dialects would end up in the Rhineland. The reconstruction would lead to Bavarian and East Central German, the two German dialects spoken farthest east in the medieval German-speaking territory.

2.2 Yiddish and Liturgical Hebrew

In a certain sense, it is impossible to find a clear demarcation between Yiddish and Hebrew in Europe in early times. Max Weinreich (1954) has discussed what he terms "Merged Hebrew," the Hebrew-Aramaic lexical items that have been absorbed into Yiddish; in some instances, these items differ from native Germanic words only in their lack of a convincing Germanic etymology. At the same time, the pronunciation of liturgical Hebrew, in medieval Europe as well as in any other Jewish community, is clearly susceptible to influence from the everyday language. Thus, it is commonplace that American Jews use the vowels **ow** and **ey** found in most dialects of English instead of Hebrew **o** and **e**. The explanation for this phenomenon is to be found in the study of "foreign accents" in general, a topic well outside the scope of this paper.

While the association of native language sound systems with changes in liturgical Hebrew pronunciation is clear, the learning of Hebrew in medieval Jewish communities differed in one important way from the learning of, say, French in modern American schools: each generation of American schoolchildren that studies French is expected at least to attempt to adhere to the norms of French pronunciation. In contrast, children learning Hebrew in Europe were expected to conform not to an externally determined pronunciation norm but to the Hebrew pronunciation of preceding generations in the same region.[5] It is thus possible to find in the liturgical Hebrew of a given region the effects not only of the presently coterritorial languages but also of those languages that were coterritorial at some time in the past.

We can thus look for phenomena in Ashkenazic liturgical Hebrew that betray the influence of various European languages. We can also examine transliterations of Hebrew words in Latin letters and of European words in Hebrew letters. To the extent that the phenomena we isolate occurred in limited areas at specified times, we can infer that by a particular time the Jews had passed through the area in question in sufficient numbers that the language of the region influenced Hebrew pronunciation. We will discuss in this section three features of Ashkenazic pronunciation and the light that they shed on the migrations of Ashkenazic Jews.

2.2.1 Sibilant Phonemes

While Biblical Hebrew orthography distinguished four sibilants (שׁ ,שׂ ,ס , and ת), most dialects of European Hebrew have reduced the system to two sounds (**s**, representing the latter three, and **š**), in accord with the sound system of Yiddish. In the Yiddish and liturgical Hebrew of some parts of Lithuania, however, a further merger took place, so that the two sounds were not distinguished. The single remaining sound was pronounced differently than either the **s** or **š** of other Yiddish dialects (Bin Nun 1973:366). The origin of this **sabesdiker losn** (so called because of the pronunciation in these dialects of the Standard Yiddish **shabesdiker loshn** "Sabbath speech") is unclear: it is one of U. Weinreich's (1963) riddles of bilingual dialectology (see also U. Weinreich 1952). Associations have been claimed both with early Ashkenazic liturgical Hebrew (Gumperz 1942:111), with early modern Polish (U. Weinreich 1963:354) and with medieval German (Bin Nun 1973:367). If Gumperz' claim that the Yiddish phenomenon is directly attributable to highly idiosyncratic pronunciation habits of early medieval French Jews could be substantiated, that would lend support to the textbook view in which the latter community provided the demographic core for eastern European Jewry. It is therefore worth scrutinizing this claim in further detail.

It is now reasonably well (although not universally) accepted by scholars of medieval French and German that neither of those languages used a sound like the modern English **š**. Instead, they used two sounds that to speakers of modern English would be interpreted **s**. In the pronunciation of one (/ṣ/), the tongue tip would have approached the roof of the mouth (apical s̭). In the pronunciation of the other (/s/), the part of the tongue just behind the tip would have made the closest approach, nearly touching the roof of the mouth and then withdrawing slightly (dorsal **s**). Historically, the /s̭/ developed from an early stop /t/, via an affricate /t^s/, maintained in initial position in German but elsewhere becoming /s/. It is altogether conceivable that the development of the affricates and the loss of the affrication except word-initially, giving fricatives, were distinct processes, separated by a time span of several generations.[6] It is only in light of these crucial facts about medieval French and German that the Hebrew spelling of words from these languages can be interpreted.

While it is clear that the Hebrew letter ס, assumed to represent **s**, is virtually never used, and Hebrew ש, assumed to represent š, is used for both French/German **s** sounds,[7] it cannot be inferred that ס and ש were pronounced identically in medieval Hebrew. What probably happened is that Hebrew /š/ (ש) had the same tongue configuration as French/German /ṣ/, while Hebrew /**s**/ (ס), a non-affricate, had a tongue configuration not used in the European languages. It would thus not have been necessary to use ס to write European languages (see Faber 1982 for more detail).

The line of reasoning utilized in the preceding paragraph can be clarified with a modern example. Both modern French and modern German use a vowel sound not used in English in which the tongue position of **i** and the lip position of **u** are combined. This sound is spelled **ü** in German and **u** in French. Now, suppose that someone, for whatever reason, wanted to use German spelling conventions to represent English pronunciation. The word 'I' might be written **Ei**, the word 'cow' might be written **kau**, but it would be difficult to write the word 'give' because German has no conventional way to spell the sound **v** at the end of a word. It should be obvious that the German spelling of 'give' would provide an even worse approximation of English pronunciation than does English spelling. It would furthermore be illegitimate to infer from the **absence** of the letter **ü** in the Germanized English that German did not actually use the sound represented by that letter, substituting for it **u** or **i**.

If it cannot be demonstrated that failure to differentiate ס from ש was a general feature of early Rhineland Hebrew, then Gumperz' (1942:111) assertion that Lithuanian **sabesdiker losn** is a direct continuation of that failure cannot be maintained. But the origin of **sabesdiker losn** remains to be explained. Several points are clear; others are less so. While in this century, **sabesdiker losn** is restricted to Lithuania, in the past it was found in a wider area. Until at least the seventeenth century, failure to differentiate **s** and **š**, called **mazurzenie** in Polish, was a stereotypical feature of Jewish Polish (Neil Jacobs, personal community), and, presumably, of Polish Yiddish and liturgical Hebrew. If Uriel Weinreich's (1963:354) suggestion that **sabesdiker losn** originated under the influence of **mazurzenie** is correct, then the phenomenon could have originated as early as the thirteenth century, when **mazurzenie** is first documented (Stieber 1968:67-68). Bin Nun (1973:367) provides an alternate explanation, one which is compatible with Weinreich's. He attributes the development of **sabesdiker losn** to developments in medieval German. When the medieval sounds /ṣ/ and /s̭/, described above, were changing to the modern /š/ and /s/, it is possible that, in some dialects, the two sounds merged. This suggestion would be strengthened if it were the case that other German dialects than Yiddish that were spoken in Poland developed along the same lines. In any case, if a tendency to merge /s/ and /š/ developed in some Yiddish dialects, it would have been strengthened under the influence of **mazurzenie.** However, it is impossible to speculate about where in Germany these Yiddish speakers lived before migrating to Poland. Thus, the phenomenon of **sabesdiker losn,** however worthy of study in its own right, cannot contribute definitively to the understanding of Ashkenazic origins.

2.2.2 Beged Kefet

While study of **sabesdiker losn** in Yiddish cannot contribute to the understanding of Ashkenazic origins, the study of some characteristics of liturgical Hebrew can be of use. It is well known that the pronunciation of certain Hebrew letters varies depending on whether they are written in fully vowelled texts with a central dot, called a **dagesh,** or without such a dot. The following letters can take this **dagesh:** ב, ג, ד, כ, פ, and ת, hence the name. In modern Israeli Hebrew, only the letters ב, פ, and כ have the dual pronunciation. With **dagesh,** they are pronounced /b/, /p/, and /k/, respectively, and without **dagesh** they are pronounced /v/, /f/, and /x/. When the symbol **dagesh** originated it presumably reflected variation in the pronunciation of ג, ד, and ת as well. On the basis of the traditional pronunciations in Jewish communities throughout the world, it is safe to say that the **dagesh**-less pronunciation of these letters was, respectively, /ɣ/, /ð/, and /θ/.

A little oral experimentation will show that the articulatory difference between each pair of sounds like /b/-/v/ (stop-spirant) is minimal. In all cases, air escapes relatively freely from the mouth during the pronunciation of the sound spelled without a **dagesh,** while air flow through the mouth is blocked momentarily during the pronunciation of sounds spelled with the

dagesh. Linguists utilize this pattern by formulating a general rule of **spirantization** in Hebrew. The two spirantization patterns discussed so far, the Biblical Hebrew and the modern one, are listed below.

Biblical		Modern	
b-v	p-f	b-v	p-f
d-d	t-θ		
g-ɣ	k-x		k-x

The liturgical Hebrew of Ashkenazic Jews is characterized by still a third pattern.

Ashkenazic	
b-v	p-f
	t-s
	k-x

How the Ashkenazic system developed out of something like the Biblical system is a question of no small import. Sampson (1973) attributes the different pattern to influence from the sound system of German, which does not contain the sounds /ɣ/, /ð/ and /θ/. The similar sounds /g/, /d/, and /s/ were substituted for these sounds by speakers who were unable to pronounce the more "authentic" /ɣ/, /ð/, and /θ/.

What Sampson's account leaves unclear, however, is why /ð/ and /θ/ were not affected in parallel fashion: Why was /ð/ replaced by /d/ and not /z/? Why was /θ/ replaced by /s/ and not /t/? The answer to these questions, an answer not provided by Sampson, who includes only modern German in his discussion, comes from consideration of some changes in German pronunciation that took place around the seventh century CE. These changes are generally discussed under the rubric of the Old High German consonant shift. In the part of the change that is relevant here, /p/, /t/, and /k/, when following a vowel sound, changed to /f/, /s/, and /x/, respectively (Bach 1965:101). The difference between the Biblical Hebrew and the Old German changes lies in what /t/ changed to, /θ/ in Hebrew and /s/ in German. Thus, the substitution of /s/ for /θ/ in Ashkenazic Hebrew can be interpreted as having been under the influence of the German pattern.

The German consonant shift did not occur uniformly in the entire German speaking area. The /k/>/x/ change occurred in the largest area, /p/>/f/ in a more circumscribed area, and /t/>/s/, the change of interest here, in a still smaller area. Maintenance of the original stops is a characteristic of Low German dialects (Northern Germany); in most Upper German dialects, the change operated to completion (South Germany); and Central German dialects exhibit a gradient. The area in which there is the greatest vacillation as regards this change is the High German-Low German border area, the Franconian dialect area, bordering France. It is precisely this area that the textbook account of Jewish migrations (see Section 1) claims was the home of the ancestors of Ashkenazic Jews at the time the Old High German shift was taking place. From the borrowing of the /t/-/s/ alternation pattern in liturgical Hebrew, we can infer that in the seventh century there were sufficient Jews living in the area affected by the change to bring about the borrowing. By the seventh century, the /t/>/s/ change had reached its northernmost boundary (Bach 1965:107), southeast of the line connecting Koblenz with Trier. Thus, there must have been a substantial Jewish population southeast of this line by the seventh century. A population speaking a variant of Old French (Loez) moving into German speaking territory after the completion of this change would not necessarily have modified its Hebrew pronunciation,[8] although these individuals would, when they learned German, of course have adopted the newer pronunciation. This too suggests, albeit not conclusively, that the Jews from the Rhineland were at some point submerged in a numerically larger southern German population.

The explanation in the preceding paragraphs accounts for the substitution of /s/ for /θ/ in the spirantization pattern of Ashkenazic Jews. It is still necessary, however, to deal with the non-spirantization of /d/ and /g/. M. Weinreich (1980:383) notes that /d/ and /t/ both spirantized in the Loez (Old French) area. He further infers that these sounds must also have had spirant variants in western Germany, basing his inference on the presence of transparent borrowings from Hebrew in the Swabian and Hessian dialects of German reflecting the change. These forms are Swabian **yus** 'ten,' from Hebrew **yud 'y**, 10, and Hessian **yuss** and **lames** 'thirty,' from Hebrew **lamed 'ℓ**, 30'. According to

Weinreich, the /θ/ and /ð/ were lost in Ashkenazic liturgical Hebrew when the early German /θ/ and /ð/ changed to Old High German /t/ and /d/.

Weinreich's account is at best somewhat incomplete. While the facts presented up to this point indicate a lack of parallel behavior for /d/ and /t/, his explanation makes inferences about /t/ from evidence for /d/. Furthermore, no explanation is provided for the failure of /g/ to spirantize in Ashkenazic liturgical Hebrew, although an explanation parallel to that offered for /d/ is possible: Pre-German /ɣ/ changed to /g/ when /ð/ changed to /d/ and, thus, German provided no model for a continuation of the spirantization of /g/ in Hebrew. On the other hand, /b/ continued to be subject to spirantization, due to the merger of the spirantized variant with /w/ early in the Christian Era.

2.2.3. Vowel Systems

Still another aspect of Ashkenazic Hebrew pronunciation that may provide evidence for the source of Ashkenazic Jewry is the pronunciation of the vowels. Today, Ashkenazic Hebrew differs from the Israeli standard, ultimately based on the Sephardic tradition, in pronouncing distinctly all seven vowels of the Tiberian vocalization system.

Vowel Name	Hebrew Symbol	Phonetic Symbol	English/French Example
ḥiriq	אִ אִי	i	**beat**
tsere	אֵ	e	**ne**
segol	אֶ	ɛ	**bet**
pasaḥ	אַ	a	**father**
kamats	אָ	ɔ	**caught**
ḥolam	אוֹ אֹ	o	**eau**
kubutz	אֻ	u	**pool**
shuruq	אוּ		

In modern Israeli Hebrew, as in the Sephardic tradition, **tsere** and **segol** are not differentiated, and **kamats** is pronounced sometimes as **pasaḥ** and sometimes as **ḥolam**.

While the seven-vowel system described above is found in modern Ashkenazic Hebrew, there is persuasive evidence that, prior to the thirteenth century, the same pronunciation of liturgical Hebrew was used north of the Pyrenees as was used in Spain. This evidence comes primarily in the form of Yiddish words of Hebrew etymology in which the Yiddish pronunciation reflects **pasaḥ** rather than the grammatically expected **kamats.** Some of these words are **dag** 'fish,' **klal** 'generalization,' **dam** 'blood,' **yad** 'pointer,' and **nadn** 'dowry.' M. Weinreich (1980:356) gives a longer list, noting that some of these items occur only in fixed expressions. It is important to note that, while individual explanations can be found for the apparent deviant behavior of some of these items, the simplest explanation overall is that the seven-vowel pronunciation system reflected in the Tiberian vocalization was imported into the Ashkenazic community sometime after the thirteenth century. Further evidence of an earlier five-vowel system comes from vocalized manuscripts in which interchanges of **kamats** and **pasaḥ** as well as of **tsere** and **segol** indicate that the two pairs were not consistently differentiated in the speech of the copyists. Weinrich (1980:367) notes that there is no evidence for a pronunciation of **kamats** as [ɔ] in France prior to the expulsions of the fourteenth century. Furthermore, by the turn of the sixteenth century, the Tiberian reading tradition had already been established in eastern Europe (p. 368).

Weinreich suggests (1980:373) that the Tiberian reading tradition was brought to eastern Europe via Byzantium and southern Italy by Babylonian scholars who emigrated with the decline in the twelfth century of the great academies of Babylon. Evidence for such a migration is found in the relative preponderance of oriental (Babylonian) names in the lists of martyrs in the thirteenth and fourteenth centuries: only a handful of oriental names are found in the memorial lists from cities like Nuremberg and Worms, while relatively large numbers are found within a one hundred mile radius of Rothenberg in Bohemia (pp. 375-376).

2.3 Summary

A general tendency is discernable in the three examples discussed in Section 2.2. In all three cases a discontinuity is observed between the early Hebrew pronunciation used in the Rhineland and the later pronunciation used in eastern Europe. Because the Rhineland community has been assumed to have formed the demographic core of the eastern European community, it has been necessary to seek linguistic or sociological explanations for the development of the later pronunciations out of the former. For the most part, these explanations have been unsatisfactory. However, if the assumption of demographic continuity is not made, the analytical problem evaporates. What we find in eastern European Jewry is the result of the merger of two originally distinct communities. While the new community clearly maintained in large measure the cultural and religious traditions of the Rhineland component, it maintained the liturgical pronunciation of the numerically larger southeastern component, the latter having been augmented and influenced by migrants from Babylonia. While positive demographic evidence for this scenario is sparse, the scenario nevertheless provides a unified account of the linguistic facts, an account which is bolstered by the analysis in Section 2.1 of Yiddish as a Bavarian (southeastern) German dialect with an admixture of East Central (eastern) German.

3. Problems and Alternatives

We find the received view outlined in Section 1 problematic because it does not readily accord with the hypotheses derived from our comparison of Yiddish with other German dialects (Section 2.1). If the bulk of Polish Jews trace their ancestry to Jews from the Rhineland, their Yiddish (assuming that the language began to develop before the migrations outlined above) should resemble Rhine Franconian and Alemannic dialects of German rather than Bavarian. And, if Yiddish began to develop after the Jews were already in Poland, under the influence of the dominant German culture imported by the Hanseatic merchants, Yiddish should resemble a Low German dialect. The same problem arises if we posit a more southerly migration from the Rhineland to Poland, via Bavaria. If a Rhineland Judeo-German (Loez) had developed prior to these assumed migrations, is it likely that **all** traces of the Alemannic or Rhine Franconian components would have been buried by Bavarian? And, if Rhineland Jews spoke the Low Alemannic or Franconian of their Gentile neighbors, why would they have abandoned that in favor of a Bavarian-Hebrew/Aramaic fusion language? The second alternative is contrary to linguistic commonsense, the first merely inconsistent with the facts.

A high degree of Hebrew/Aramaic literacy in the Rhineland community can be inferred from the existence of "popular" commentaries like Rashi's written almost completely in Hebrew. At the very least, Hebrew lexical items would have been inserted in the Loez (Judeo-French) speech of Hebrew-Loez bilinguals. Regular use of such a "mixed language," much like that observed among American Jews who, as part of their religious identification, are at home in Hebrew/Aramaic religious texts, means that the speech of the Rhineland Jews could not have been exactly like that of their Gentile neighbors. Given that, the only reason we can see for systematic replacement of western forms by Bavarian forms is numerical preponderance of speakers of an eastern German dialect.

Our attempts to resolve this set of paradoxes has led us to a large body of literature that has not been incorporated into the "textbook" Jewish history outlined in Section 1. Much of it is inconsistent with this approach, as is our linguistic treatment. That evidence will be summarized in the rest of this section.

3.1 Demography

The most obvious sticking point for the traditional account is the numbers themselves. If the figures given above for Jewish population increase in Poland, first cited by Dubnow (1916:66n), are correct, where did all those people come from? A ten-fold increase in population over the course of a century and a half presupposes both a high birth rate and a large base of potential immigrants. In 1490, there were 20,000 Jews in the Papal territory surrounding Avignon, 80,000 in the Holy Roman Empire (including Switzerland and the Low Countries), and 120,000 in Italy (Baron 1952, XII:25). At the same time, according to

Baron, there were 30,000 Jews in Poland/Lithuania and 20,000 in Hungary. Jews were never actually expelled from Avignon or from Italy. And, given the conditions under which many refugees left western Germany during the Middle Ages, it is altogether likely that many of them did not survive.

Two approaches to this problem are current. One is essentially to revise the figures. The other is to provide other sources than the Rhineland for the bulk of Ashkenazic Jewry.

3.1.1. The Figures

The study of the demography of medieval Europe is fraught with difficulties. Conclusions are tentative at best, because crucial information is often lacking. It may be possible to make statements about a given community on the basis of parish records of births and deaths, or on the basis of tax rolls. However, this sort of information is often unavailable for Jewish communities. Frequently, the community itself was taxed, as a whole; it may or may not be possible to determine from extant records what the rate of taxation was or how many individuals were subsumed in a given payment. It is often difficult to determine whether it was individuals or households that were being taxed. In either case, the possibility that some part of those theoretically liable for a given tax were in practice exempt from that tax must be considered, as must the possibility of undercounting by the community itself in order to decrease the tax burden. In fact, much of medieval demography consists in finding appropriate multipliers: How many individuals lived in the average house? What percentage of a given population was exempt from taxes? And what percentage of the population managed to avoid being counted?

Weinryb (1976:115) bases his treatment of Polish/Jewish population on reassessments of the ratio of individuals to hearths. He figures that there were 10,000-12,000 Jews in Poland in 1500, 80,000-100,000 in 1600, and 150,000-170,000 in 1648. But Abramsky (1976), in a scathing review of Weinryb, rejects these revisions, insisting that the earlier figure of 25,000 Jews in Poland in 1500 is well-founded.[9] Weinryb suggests, in addition, reasons why the Jewish population in Poland might have increased at a greater rate than the Gentile population, despite the plague, famine, and pogrom that characterized Jewish life in

Poland in the late Middle Ages: (1) Jewish males were not subject to military service, (2) normative Jewish tradition has nothing comparable to the impetus for Christians to join religious orders requiring celibacy, and (3) Jews, even in rural areas, placed a premium on relatively early marriage, rather than requiring a wait until the couple could be self-sufficient.

Jewish communities themselves would probably not have undertaken censuses, for fear of divine retribution like that following the Biblical census commissioned by King David (I Sam. 24). The census, which, according to the Biblical record, took nine months to complete, showed a fighting population of 1,200,000. The plague, sent by God to punish David, killed 70,000 in a single day.

3.1.2. Alternative Sources

Weinryb (1976:19-20) lists eight theories about the origin of Polish Jews.

(1) Scythian migrations, beginning around 600 BCE.
(2) Migration from Babylon and Persia, beginning at the start of the Common Era.
(3) Migration from Greece and the Byzantine Empire.
(4) Migration from the Caucasus of tribes originating there after the destruction of the First Temple (c. 600 BCE).
(5) The Khazar hypothesis.
(6) A pan-Slavic origin for early Polish/Russian Jews, who were completely assimilated to Slavic culture until the beginning of German migrations.
(7) Jewish settlement along trade routes between Western Europe and the Black Sea.
(8) Flight from persecutions in western Europe (see Section 1 above).

Of these alternatives, the best known, apart from the "textbook"(8) above, is the Khazar hypothesis, most recently propounded by Arthur Koestler (1976). Space limitations do not allow us here to do justice either to Koestler's suggestions or to the (we feel) compelling reasons for rejecting them. We will merely point out some of the linguistic considerations militating against his hypothesis that eastern European Jews are descended from a Turkic tribe, the Khazars, that converted to Judaism in the eighth century CE. If a large body of Turkic speakers[10] had moved into an area where old Slavic and Low German were current, it may well be that some kind of fusion language conceptually akin to Yiddish would have developed. Given the lack of certainty as to the exact affiliation of the Khazar language, it is difficult to make precise suggestions as to what that fusion language would have been like. However, pan-Altaic phenomena like vowel harmony and subject-object-verb word order would undoubtedly have been present, as would a substantial number of identifiably Altaic lexical items. None of these features--**not one**--is found in Yiddish, and it is interesting to note that Yiddish has regularized the "un-Turkic" subject-verb-object word order, even in those subordinate clauses which, in other German dialects, maintain the verb at the end of the sentence.

Another linguistic argument against Koestler's thesis of Khazar origin for Polish Jews is that the Karaites, a sect of Jews that rejects post-Biblical Jewish tradition, claim descent from the Khazars. There are Karaite communities in Troki and Poniewiez in Lithuania, Luck and Halicz in the Ukraine, and in Crimea.[11] The Karaites maintain a language, Qaraim, that belongs to the Qypchag subgroup of Turkic. This is the only Turkic language that has lost the pan-Altaic feature of vowel harmony (Menges 1968:181).[12] In addition, Qaraim syntax follows that of Hebrew (p. 63). Thus, the Altaic verb-final word order is replaced, for the most part, by Semitic verb-initial or verb-medial orders.

The point of mentioning the Karaites in this context is simply that their maintenance of a Turkic language for over a millennium of contact (some of it hostile) with rabbanite Jews speaking Yiddish, and with Gentiles speaking Polish, Russian, Ukrainian and Lithuanian makes it hard to believe that there would be no Turkic traces whatsoever in the language of putative descendants of close relatives of theirs. Given Koestler's thesis and the close relationship that would therefore have to be posited between the Karaites and the rest of Ashkenazic Jewry, the only way to differentiate the two groups would be on the basis of nearly total language maintenance on the one hand and

total language loss on the other. It is commonsense to assume that the Karaites are in general the only Jewish descendants of the Khazars.[13] The others were absorbed by the Quman and Pecheneg conquerors (Menges 1968:32) and they left no modern descendants (Krueger 1961:8).

Because of the lack of documentation concerning Jewish migration into Poland, most modern historians list possible points of origin without making any detailed claims as to the relative weights of the contributions from different sources. So, Weinryb states that the most likely geographical sources were Germany/Austria and Bohemia (1976:27). Less significant contributions came from Italy, Caffa (Crimea) and Byzantium. Baron (1952, III:206) states:

> After the decline of the Khazar Empire . . . refugees from the devastated districts, including Jews, sought shelter in the very lands of their conquerors. Here they met other Jewish groups and individuals migrating from west and south. Together with these arrivals from Germany and the Balkans, they began laying the foundations for a Jewish community . . .

Patai and Wing (1975:87) make a clear distinction between origin of the population of a community and origin of its cultural traditions, a point to which we will return below:

> Jews came to Poland approximately from the tenth century on, mainly from the Ashkenazi west, from Byzantium in the south, and from Khazaria in the east. Within a few centuries, Ashkenazi culture became dominant among them, replacing all other cultural influences.

The kind of geographical information presented above is not sufficient to illuminate the central question of this paper, the source of Ashkenazic Jewry. But the linguistic and political geography of Europe was different during the Middle Ages from what it is now. Bavarian German, despite the implicit identification with a particular province of modern Germany, extended over medieval Bohemia and Austria as well. So, immigrants to Poland from Bohemia, for example, might have brought with them some variety of Bavarian German.

3.1.3. Arguments Against a Western European Source

1. The Black Death. Tied to the "textbook" claim that the bulk of Ashkenazic Jewry descends from migrants from western Europe are two assumptions. One is that, for whatever reason, Jews were spared some of the ravages of the Black Death in 1347-1350. Thus, despite the pogroms to which they were subjected before,[14] during and after the plague, they survived the episode disproportionately to their representation in the German population and were thus able to contribute disproportionately to the Polish population.

Present scholarship shows this picture to be simply false. Baron (1972:19) notes that it is always risky to extrapolate from figures given for plague deaths in one area to another area. In different villages around Cambridge, England, the death rate ranged from 47% to 70%. Dinur (1969:70) notes that almost all of German Jewry was "wiped out" during the period of the Black Death, either from plague or from pogrom. Guerchberg (1948), in an extensive study of treatises about the plague written between approximately 1350 and 1450, shows quite clearly that no mention of a differential death rate between Jews and neighboring Gentiles appears until the mid-fifteenth century. Prior to that time, it had been assumed that the death rate was, if anything, higher among Jews than among non-Jews. One Chalin de Vinarion wrote in 1382 that Jews and Spaniards are very susceptible to plague, because of their "sordid lives." The death rate that he observed among Jews was one in five, but it was lower among non-Jews (Guerchberg 1948:37). The fact of a high death rate among Jews was used by the German theologian Karl Megenberg as an argument against the popular calumny that the Jews had caused the plague: if, he asked, the Jews had caused the plague, why hadn't they been better able to avoid dying of it (Guerchberg 1948:21)? Guerchberg suggests that the myth of a lower death rate originated in an attempt to counter the most cogent defense available against the charge that the Jews had caused the plague (p. 39).

2. The Rouen Community. The second claim tied to the "textbook" approach to Jewish migration in Europe is that the eastward movement began relatively early, around the time of the First Crusade in 1096. So, when Jews were actually expelled

later from European countries, the bulk of the population had already moved. This assumption is necessary, given the lack of evidence for a massive Jewish population movement in later centuries, similar to that following the expulsion from Spain in 1492.

The claim, integral though it is to traditional discussions of the history of Ashkenazic Jewry, is not consistent with more recent treatments of French-Jewish history (e.g., Blumenkranz 1972). Jewish settlement in France, especially western France, probably began much earlier than had previously been suggested. And much of this settlement consisted of isolated families in rural areas. Furthermore, a more detailed analysis of what is known of population movements within France suggests that the earlier notion of a linear eastward movement of the Jewish population "center of gravity" is oversimplified and simplistic to the point of being wrong. This is not the place fully to document such a claim, but several points are worth noting: (1) At least some of the refugees from Crusader atrocities in northern France went to England (Blumenkranz 1972:16). Earlier accounts may therefore have double-counted their numerical impact on the eastern European population, once as refugees from the Crusaders and once as refugees from Ile de France after the expulsion of 1306. (2) Much of the Jewish population shift in the twelfth and thirteenth century in France was from rural to urban areas, and not from west to east (Blumenkranz 1972:18). (3) While many of the 100,000 Jews[15] expelled from France in 1306 did go to the Rhineland and Alsace, others went north to Hainaut (modern Belgium) or southeast to Hungary (p. 18), where they presumably joined an already ancient community (cf. Baron 1952, III:211-213). Blumenkranz reports that, as late as 1433, some Hungarian Jews used French as their primary language.

A further difficulty with the claim under discussion is that it is not generally supported by the meager toponymic evidence at our disposal. Much knowledge of medieval Jewish population geography comes from the place names mentioned in the Responsa literature. However, knowing the name of a place in which Jews lived and knowing where that place is (or was) are two different things. Golb (1976, 1977a, 1977b) forcefully illustrates the difference. Given the consonantal nature of the Hebrew orthography, the difference in spelling Between Anjou אניו/anyu/

and Monieuz מניו /monyu/ is simply the difference between א /ʾ/ and מ /m/. In poorly preserved manuscripts, it is sometimes difficult, if not impossible, to distinguish the two. And, once a name is accurately deciphered, confusion still occurs: the town Vienne, south of Lyons, is often misinterpreted as referring to Vienna (Golb 1976:96).

Golb also emphasizes that the phonetic form of many place names during the Middle Ages differed radically from the modern versions. Thus, modern maps may be of little or no help in identifying possible locations of place names found in medieval documents. The latter point is amply illustrated by Golb's identification of Rouen as a major center of twelfth and thirteenth century Jewry in France. He began with the place name RDS, commonly assumed to refer to Rhodez in Provence. Careful examination of a single manuscript in which the name appeared convinced him that a final ם **(m)** had been erroneously read as a ס **(s)**; the correct reading was therefore RDM רדם. It is easy to confuse ר **(r)** and ד **(d)** in manuscripts, and Golb found many references to DRM דרם 'the south,' presumably Provence. Furthermore, DRS דרס also appears in some manuscripts, and has been interpreted as referring to Dreux, a village near Paris. Golb suggests that all of these variants should be read as RDM רדם, corresponding to Rotom, the early medieval name for Rouen. After Jews left Rouen, some of the variants were introduced by copyists who had no knowledge of the earlier name for Rouen and who were trying to make sense of an unfamiliar place name.

After determining that all of the variants should be interpreted as RDM רדם Rouen, Golb presents a collation of documentary evidence suggesting that Rouen was a center for medieval Hebrew scholarship surpassing Paris and Troyes (1977a:258). In fact, it was in Rouen that the Spanish Jewish scholar Abraham ibn Ezra settled in 1150, before moving on to London. Late medieval maps of Rouen show the main synagogue on the site now occupied by the Palace of Justice. Striking confirmation of Golb's surmises came when, in the course of repairs to the Palace of Justice, a large Romanesque **bes midrash**[16] was uncovered, across the street from the plot on which the synagogue had been located.

We dwell on the example of Rouen for two reasons. First of all, it illustrates the extremely tenuous chain of reasoning on which most demographic statements about medieval Jewry rest. Further painstaking paleographic work like Golb's could force other, perhaps more drastic, revisions of our map of Jewish settlement in medieval Europe. Second, and more specifically, it illustrates that vibrant Jewish communities were maintained in Normandy, and perhaps also in Ile de France, until the expulsions of the early fourteenth century. This is hard to reconcile with the constant trickle of refugees drifting eastward that is required by the textbook approach.

The demographic factors presented thus far suggest that the textbook approach to European Jewish history is inadequate. The population base in western Europe simply was not large enough to provide a source for eastern European Jewry. Nor did the population center of gravity start moving eastward early enough to be compatible with that approach. Furthermore, much of the population base that was present in western Europe perished during the Black Death and the concomitant pogroms.

We have little hard evidence for early Jewish settlement in southeastern Europe; although several suggestive details are available, they are not sufficient to allow us to conclude that there was a large community. For example, by the tenth century, there were Jewish communities of some repute in Regensburg and Prague. M. Weinreich speculates that at least some Jews of this area had migrated from Thessaloniki up the Danube and through Austria and Hungary into Bohemia; others had crossed the Balkans, travelled by sea up the Adriatic coast, and crossed the Alps at Carinthia, proceeding from there to the Danube (1980:83). However, he later contradicts this (1980:333), suggesting that Jewish Regensburg was settled by traders from Mainz around the end of the tenth century. In any case, there were Jews in Bohemia, speaking Old Czech, prior to the growth of Jewish population in eastern Europe (Jakobson and Halle 1964), and words of Old Czech etymology dominate the semantic field of ritual slaughtering and butchering in Yiddish (M. Weinreich 1980:543-545).

The twelfth century traveller, Benjamin of Tudela, relays hearsay reports of non-observant Jews living somewhere in the wilds of Walachia (modern Rumania):

> Here are the confines of Walachia, the inhabitants of which are called Vlachi. They are 'as nimble as deer'

> and descend from the mountains into the plains of Greece, committing robberies and making booty. Nobody ventures to make war upon them, and they do not profess the Christian faith. Their names are of Jewish origin and some even say that they have been Jews, which nation they call brethren. Whenever they meet an Israelite, they rob but never kill him, as they do the Greeks. They profess no religious creed.
>
> Asher (1840:48)

Additional evidence consists in the main of chance epigraphic records which are extremely difficult to interpret. Baron (1952, III:206-) and others judiciously refrain from reaching conclusions not licensed by the data available. It would certainly be premature, however, to conclude from remains that are by no means overshadowed by other non-Jewish traces and relics that there was no early Jewish settlement in southeastern Europe. Certainly, though, whatever Jews there were in southeastern Europe at an early date did not contribute to the culture and traditions of eastern European Jewry to the extent that the Rhineland Jews did. We want to emphasize that this lack of cultural remains is not, by itself, evidence against an early Jewish population concentration in southern Germany/ Austria/Bohemia.

3.2 Alternative Sources of Evidence

In this section of the paper we will present non-demographic evidence for Jewish settlement patterns. In many instances, the proposals that we make will be speculative; evidence of a certain sort may well be relevant but not currently available.

3.2.1. Archaeology. The value of archaeological evidence in investigations of the history of Jewish settlements should be clearly evident from the discussion of the Rouen **bes midrash.** Such facts are valuable not only as confirmation of epigraphic evidence concerning Jewish communities but also for the discovery of previously unknown communities. Two instances are known to us of synagogues being uncovered by digs at sites where there was no particular reason to suspect a large Jewish community. One of these is a synagogue in Dura-Europos, on the upper Euphrates

River in modern Syria. It was destroyed around 250 CE (Hopkins 1979), after having been enlarged to accommodate a larger congregation. There is no documentary evidence for the existence of a Jewish community at Dura-Europos (Smallwood 1976:509); nevertheless, there seemingly was a large community. The other synagogue was found at Stobi, in southern Yugoslavia.

> A Jewish community of some wealth existed in Stobi at least by the 3rd century when Polycharmus, 'the father of the synagogue,' built a synagogue nearly in the center of the city. The synagogue was rebuilt again on what was evidently an even more lavish scale early in the following century. A mosaic floor with geometric designs was added and the walls of the main room were covered with frescoes. The synagogue was destroyed in the late 4th century and a Christian basilica was erected upon its ruins.
>
> Wiseman (1973:17)

We suspect that the two synagogues described above are not unique. We further suspect that other synagogues have been excavated and not recognized; early in the Common Era, church and synagogue architectural styles were similar enough that incompletely preserved synagogues were thought by their excavators to be churches, and **vice versa.** There are two other possibilities that must be reckoned with. For both Dura-Europos and Stobi, it is clear that the Jewish communities were wealthy, economically capable of building lavish synagogues. There were doubtless many less fortunate communities, limited to worshipping in an individual's home rather than in a special purpose building. As it is by features like the nook for Torah scrolls that a synagogue is recognized, buildings without these features might never be identified as synagogues. Thus, there would be no reason to suspect the existence of a Jewish community. The second possibility is that, as is the case today, there existed in the early centuries of the Common Era Jewish communities whose members were not particularly well versed in Jewish tradition and observance. Such communities would not be likely to have left artifacts by means of which they could be identified as Jewish by modern scholars. Still another possibility is that sites as yet unexcavated will reveal more hitherto unsuspected Jewish communities.

Also to be considered under the heading of archaeology is the study of cultural artifacts, movable objects found at excavations or otherwise attributable to a particular time and place. Barbara Kirschenblatt-Gimblett (personal communication) has tentatively determined that the locus of origin for Torah faceplates as early as the tenth century CE was Bavaria. These pieces are found in other places in Europe, suggesting a center for religious craftsmanship in Bavaria.

3.2.2. Genetics. It is well known that there are certain genetic mutations found exclusively or almost exclusively among Jews. The best known of these is the mutation that causes Tay-Sachs disease among Ashkenazic Jews, especially those of Lithuanian ancestry. Aside from mutations with such debilitating effects, there are other identifiable genetic differences among individuals. Many of these manifest themselves in the structure of blood proteins, producing the difference among A, B, AB and O blood types, and between Rh-Positive and Rh-Negative, among others.

There has been a substantial amount of investigation of Jewish genetic characteristics because of their bearing on the validity of the concept "Jewish Race." It is often claimed, for example, that Jews tend to be more similar physically and genetically to the non-Jews in the countries in which they live than they are to Jews in other countries. Patai and Wing (1975:50) attribute this similarity to rape during persecutions, claiming that there was very little voluntary interbreeding until the modern age.

Mourant et al. (1978) present a comprehensive review of the genetics literature concerning the question of Jewish-Gentile genetic differences. On the basis of a large number of studies of blood proteins and other genetic characteristics, they conclude that "the Ashkenazim were essentially European Jews, closely related to the Sephardim" (p. 45). They also suggest an eastern migration track from Palestine to Europe (p. 49), which is consistent with the first four of the migration theories presented by Weinryb (pp. 28-29 above): Scythian origin, migrations from Persia and Babylon starting at the beginning of the Common Era, migration via Greece and the Byzantine Empire, and immigration of tribes that settled in the Caucasus (north of the Black Sea) after the destruction of the First Temple. Their results are not consistent with a large Turkic (or Khazar) genetic component in Ashkenazic Jewry.

Geneticists often refer to something called the "founder effect" in discussions of genetic mutations. In a large community, a random recessive mutation that is fatal to someone who inherits the variant from both parents is not likely to spread among the population. However, in an extremely small community, the same recessive mutation is likely to spread to a larger proportion of the community. Studies of Tay-Sachs and other genetic diseases common in Ashkenazic Jews support the view that Jewish communities in eastern Europe shrank to small sizes and then grew extremely rapidly (Mourant, et al. 1978:58). Although they do not say so explicitly, their discussion only makes sense if this growth was via increased birthrate and not via increased immigration.

Mourant and his colleagues make an additional suggestion, one that we do not yet know how to interpret. They state (1978:52) that the genetic separation between Ashkenazic and Sephardic Jews is not much more than one thousand years. We do not know if the methods that Mourant and his colleagues used are powerful enough to differentiate initially shared genetic characteristics from characteristics that are shared as a result of subsequent contact and intermarriage. In other words, we do not know if intermarriage between Ashkenazic Jews and Sephardic Jews who settled in eastern Europe after the expulsion from Spain in 1492 is sufficient explanation for the apparent separation depth.

4. Conclusion

In this paper, we have presented linguistic evidence suggesting a southeastern German origin for the Yiddish language, and, by extention, a southeastern German origin for Yiddish speakers, Ashkenazic Jewry. Because of the conflict between our hypothesis of southeastern origin and the accepted historical accounts of how Jews ended up in eastern Europe, we were forced into a demographic investigation. We found no evidence supporting the accepted, textbook accounts. Nor did we find much evidence supporting our claim that Ashkenazic Jewry can be traced back to southeastern Germany. But there was much more evidence against the textbook theory than there was against our hypothesis. Thus the question of the origin of eastern European Jewry is still open. However, we can draw some subsidiary conclusions, perhaps best thought of as morals.

A. Paleography is important. Before documents can be interpreted, they must be read, and read accurately.

B. It is important to distinguish between the cultural contribution of a subgroup of the population and their numerical weight within the population as a whole. We mean to cast no doubt whatever on the contributions to Ashkenazic culture made by the original Jewish settlers in the Rhineland; it is absolutely incontrovertible.

C. No solution to the question of the origin of Ashkenazic Jewry will be reached without an interdisciplinary approach, encompassing the fields of archaeology, cultural anthropology, demography, genetics, history, linguistics, and paleography.

D. Inference from coincidence is not valid in research of this sort. In the centuries immediately preceding the rise of Polish Jewry, Jewish communities in the following areas shrank drastically or disappeared completely: Khazaria, the Rhineland, northern Italy and the Iberian peninsula. There is no a priori necessity that the antecedents of Ashkenazic Jewry be found in any one of these groups; only a thorough, unprejudiced investigation has a chance of providing answers.

There is a great historical puzzle here that lies at the bottom of our concern. It is expressed most eloquently by Cecil Roth (1966:302-3).

> Was the great Eastern European Jewry of the 19th century preponderantly descended (as is normally believed) from immigrants from the Germanic lands further West who arrived as refugees in the later Middle Ages, bearing with them their culture? Or did these new immigrants find already on their arrival a numerically strong Jewish life, on whom they were able to impose their superior culture, including even their tongue (a phenomenon not unknown at other times and places--as, for example, in the 16th century, after the arrival of the highly cultured Spanish exiles in the Turkish Empire)? Does the line of descent of Ashkenazi

> Jewry of today go back to a quasi-autochthonous Jewry already established in these lands, perhaps even earlier than the time of the earliest Franco-German settlement of the Dark Ages? This is one of the mysteries of Jewish history, which probably will never be solved.

It is too early to ask for a definitive solution to this "mystery" of Jewish history, but linguistics may help to advance us toward that solution. We have presented in this paper a body of evidence suggesting that our hypothesis of a southeastern German origin for Ashkenazic Jewry is more plausible than other hypotheses positing Khazar/Caucasus or Rhineland origins for the bulk of the Ashkenazic population. We do not however have sufficient evidence to claim that our hypothesis is the best possible one, although our faith in the linguistic methodology on which it is based leads us to believe that it is. It is our hope that others will join us in subjecting our hypothesis to a rigorous and unprejudiced investigation.

NOTES

* We would like to thank our colleagues who have commented on the ideas reflected in this paper throughout their evolution. Of course, we alone are responsible for any errors we may have committed. The work reported on here was supported in part by a grant from the University Research Institute of the University of Texas at Austin in 1980 and a grant from the Division of Sponsored Research of the University of Florida in 1981. We are grateful for this institutional support. This article is reprinted here with permission (see Preface).

1 Early Jewish settlement in Cologne is known only because of letters to the Jewish leaders there from the Emperor Constantine (Baron 1952, III:489). Baron also notes that his statements about early settlement are made with "considerable diffidence" because of the paucity of Jewish sources reflecting settlements (III:251, n. 61). Surprisingly and inconsistently, of all the sources that we referred to, only Baron (III:207) makes the equally plausible suggestion that Roman encampments in the **Balkans** were also accompanied by Jewish settlement.

2 For more detailed discussion of Jewish settlement history in Europe, see Max Weinreich (1980:1-246).

3 We have deliberately not given figures here, because of the wide range reported in the literature. Richardson (1960:216) claims that there were a maximum of 3,000 Jews in England on the eve of the expulsion in 1290. Baron (1952, XII:7) thinks that there were 10,000, Arkin (1975:65) 15,000, and Ben-Sasson (1978:463) 16,000. Similar variation is found in figures given for France.

4 On the general question of the German provenience of the Yiddish dialects, see Gerzon (1902), Birnbaum (1954), Bin Nun (1973:77-85), Mieses (1924:271), and M. Weinreich (1980:418ff.).

5 Only with the revival of Hebrew as a modern, spoken language has this changed. In many, but by no means all, Hebrew schools, children learn Hebrew in the same way that they learn French or Spanish in the public schools (and as effectively, we might add).

6 This description has been simplified for the benefit of readers unfamiliar with linguistic terminology. For more detailed description and for a review of the literature documenting these claims, see Fought (1979).

7 French/German **ts** was, of course, represented by Hebrew צ.

8 Although the linguistic conditions under which the Hebrew and German changes took place are similar (generally speaking, following a vowel sound), the grammatical structures of the two languages differ crucially. In Hebrew, root consonants vary in their position in the word, depending on their grammatical form. So, the imperfect **tixtov** תִּכְתֹּב and the perfect **kosavti** כָּתַבְתִּי both represent the root k-t-b. In this example, the /t/-/s/ and /k/-/x/ relationships are perfectly clear, and anyone who learns

Hebrew must learn to cope with the pattern. In contrast, the corresponding German pattern was not maintained as a rule because it created no morphophonemic alteration. Once older **dat** had changed to **das** (Yiddish **dos** דאָס), there was nothing left to suggest a /t/-/s/ relationship.[7]

[9] Estimates for the Jewish population of Poland in 1500 range from Weinryb's low of 10,000-12,000 to Dubnow's high of 50,000. Most estimates fall in the 25,000-30,000 range. Cf. note 2.

[10] The question of the positioning of the Khazar language within the Altaic language family is a difficult one, due to the lack of epigraphic remains within the area of the Khazar Empire. Historical discussions of this empire focus on its relationship with the Volga Bulgars. The latter group left enough epigraphic material that its language can be identified as a precursor of modern Chuvash. Kruger (1961:8) states that the Khazars are "believed by most to have been linguistically related to the Bolgars, but left no modern descendants." Others (Menges 1968:31 and Poppe 1965:36) are less willing to commit themselves to this point of view, in the absence of linguistic evidence. On the authenticity of the Khazar conversion, see most recently Golb and Pritsak (1982), a definitive work, also Pritsak (1955).

[11] Karaites had settled in Crimea by the tenth century CE (Mann 1972:289). The oldest Karaite settlement in Lithuania is Troki; it may have been established as early as 1218, by settlers from Crimea, but Mann prefers a later, mid-fourteenth century date (p. 556). The Karaite charter for Troiki is older than the Rabbanite one for neighboring Vilna.

[12] The vowel distinctions have been neutralized in favor of a more slavic palatal/plain consonant contrast.

[13] We have no quarrel with the position that some Jewish Khazars were absorbed into the Ashkenazic community, but we strongly doubt that Ashkenazic Jewry has a Khazar core.

[14] Guerchberg (1948:3) makes clear that plague-related persecutions of Jews **preceded** by some months the actual outbreaks of plague in parts of northern Europe.

[15] This is Blumenkranz' figure, with no attribution. Baron (1952, XII:12) states that pehaps as many as 100,000 Jews were affected by the expulsion. Nahon (1961:71) attributes the 100,000 figure to Graez. Nahon himself gives a figure of 72,480 Jews in Royal France on the eve of the expulsion. Other figures in the literature are even lower: Arkin (1975:73) says that at most 40,000 Jews were expelled.

[16] While it is clear that the structure in question was a Jewish communal building of some sort, that it was a **bes midrash** is not universally accepted. Nahon (1977) suggests that it may have been another synagogue; there is certainly no a priori reason that a large and vibrant community would not have had more than one synagogue.

REFERENCES

Abramsky, Chimen
1976 "An Opportunity Missed." **Soviet Jewish Affairs** 4:95-100.

Arkin, Marcus
1975 **Aspects of Jewish Economic History.** Philadelphia: Jewish Publication Society.

Asher, A., ed. and trans.
1840 **The Itinerary of Benjamin of Tudela.** London.

Bach, Adolph
1965 **Geschichte der deutschen Sprache.** Heidelberg: Quelle and Meyer, 8th ed.

Baron, Salo W.
1952- **A Social and Religious History of the Jews.** 16 Volumes. Philadelphia: Jewish Publication Society.
1972 **Ancient and Medieval Jewish History,** ed. Leon A. Feldman. New Brunswick: Rutgers University Press.

Ben-Sasson, H. H., ed.
1978 **A History of the Jewish People.** Cambridge: Harvard University Press.

Bin Nun, Yehiel
1973 **Jiddisch und die deutschen Mundarten.** Tübingen: Max Niemeyer.

Birnbaum, Solomon A.
1954 "Two Problems of Yiddish Linguistics." **The Field of Yiddish,** I, ed. Uriel Weinreich, 63-72. New York: Linguistic Circle of New York.

Blumenkranz, Bernhard
1972 **Histoire des Juifs en France (Franco Judaica, 1).** Toulouse: Eduard Privat.

Dinur, Benzion
1969 **Israel in the Diaspora.** Philadelphia: Jewish Publication Society.

Dubnow, S. M.
1916 **History of the Jews in Russia and Poland,** Vol. I. Philadelphia: Jewish Publication Society.

Faber, Alice
1982 "EarlyMedieval Hebrew Sibilants in the Rhineland, South Central and Eastern Europe." **Hebrew Annual Review** 6.

Fought, John
1979 "The Medieval Sibilants ofthe **Eulalia-Ludwigslied** Manuscript and Their Development in Early Old French." **Language** 55:842-858.

Gerzon, Jacob
1902 **Die jüdisch-deutsche Sprache.** Frankfurt: J. Kauffmann.

Golb, Norman
1977a "The Forgotten Jewish History of Medieval Rouen." **Archaeology** 30:254-263, 314-325.
1977b "L'édition de nos TOSAFOT à Rouen à la fin du XIII siècle." **Revue des Etudes Juives** 136:545-549.

Golb, Norman, and Omeljan Pritsak
1982 **Khazarian Hebrew Documents of the Tenth Century.** Ithaca: Cornell University Press.

Guerchberg, Seraphine
1948 "La controversie sur les prétendus semeurs de la Peste Noire, d'après les traités de peste de l'époque." **Revue des Etudes Juives** 107:3-40.

Gumperz, Yehiel
1942 "The Shin and its Metamorphoses." **Tarbiz** 13:107-115 (in Hebrew).

Hopkins, Clark
1979 **The Discovery of Dura-Europos.** New Haven: Yale University Press.

Jakobson, Roman, and Morris Halle
1964 "The Term Canaan in Medieval Hebrew." **For Max Weinreich**, 147-172. The Hague: Mouton.

King, Robert D.
1980 "The History of Final Devoicing in Yiddish." **The Field of Yiddish**, IV, ed. M. I. Herzog, B. Kirschenblatt-Gimblett, D. Miron and R. Wisse, 371-430. Philadelphia: Institute for the Study of Human Issues.

Koestler, Arthur
1976 **The Thirteenth Tribe.** New York: Random House.

Krueger, John
1961 **Chuvash Manual.** The Hague: Mouton.

Leon, Harry J.
1960 **The Jews of Ancient Rome.** Philadelphia: Jewish Publication Society.

Mann, Jacob
1972 **Texts and Studies in Jewish History and Literature.** New York: Ktav.

Menges, Karl
1968 **The Turkic Languages and Peoples.** Wiesbaden: Harrassowitz.

Mieses, Matthias
1924 **Die jiddische Sprache.** Berlin-Vienna: Benjamin Harz.

Mourant, Arthur E., Ada C. Kopec, and Kazmiera Domaniewska-Sobczak
1978 **The Genetics of the Jews.** Oxford: Clarendon Press.

Nahon, Gerard
1961 "Contribution à l'histoire des Juifs en France sous Philippe le Bel." **Revue des Etudes Juives** 121:59-83.
1978 "Le problème de la location de la synagogue médiévale de Rouen à propos d'une fouille récente." **Revue des Etudes Juives** 137:453-462.

Poppe, Nicholas
1965 **Introduction to Altaic Linguistics.** Wiesbaden: Harrassowitz.

Pritsak, Omeljan
1955 **Die bulgarische Fürstenliste und die Sprache der Protobulgaren.** Wiesbaden: Harrassowitz.

Richardson, Henry G.
1960 **The English Jewry under Angevin Kings.** London: Methuen.

Roth, Cecil et al.
1966 **The World History of the Jewish People.** Second Series, Vol. 2. New Brunswick: Rutgers University Press.

Sampson, Geoffrey
1973 "One Fact Needs One Explanation." **Lingua** 34:231-239.

Smallwood, E. Mary
1976 **The Jews under Roman Rule from Pompey to Diocletian.** Leiden: Brill.

Stieber, Zdislaw
1968 **The Phonological Development of Polish,** trans. Elias J. Schwartz. Ann Arbor: Department of Slavic Languages and Literatures.

Weinreich, Max
1954 "Prehistory and Early History of Yiddish: Facts and Conceptual Framework." **The Field of Yiddish,** I, ed. Uriel Weinreich, 73-101. New York: Linguistic Circle of New York.
1980 **History of the Yiddish Language,** trans. Joshua Fishman and Shlomo Noble. Chicago: University of Chicago Press.

Weinreich, Uriel
1952 "Sabesdiker Losn in Yiddish: a Problem of Linguistic Affinity." **Word** 8:260-267.
1963 "Four Riddles of Bilingual Dialectology." **American Contributions to the 5th International Conference of Slavicists,** 335-359. The Hague: Mouton.

Weinryb, Bernard D.
1976 **The Jews of Poland: a Social and Economic History of the Jewish Community of Poland from 1100 to 1800.** Philadelphia: Jewish Publication Society.

Wiseman, James
1973 **The Excavations at Stobi.** Austin: University of Texas Press.

NEW LIGHT ON THE LIFE AND WRITINGS OF LEON MODENA[1]

Howard Adelman

Introduction

Leon Modena was born in Venice in 1571 and died there in 1648. A legendary Leone da Modena was created by the leading nineteenth century Jewish historians and continues to live in most Jewish history books. The names are similar.[2] Indeed the two men are the same, but the life and writings of the historic Leon Modena have not received adequate treatment because of the imposing presence of the legendary Leone da Modena in most presentations of Jewish history. This paper will discuss the reasons for the creation of the legendary Leone da Modena and then present a brief summary of the career of the historic Leon Modena.

The Legendary Leone da Modena of the Nineteenth Century

In the early 1820's, Isaac Reggio (1784-1855) of Gorizia, a scholar sympathetic to the Reform movement, became attracted to Leon Modena's **ʾAri Nohem**, a pioneering critical study of Kabbalah and kabbalistic texts.[3] In it Modena had mentioned a work entitled **Ben David** in which he attacked the kabbalistic doctrine of **gilgul**, the transmigration of souls, and Reggio tried to locate a copy of it. In his search, he read that Modena had written an autobiography, **Ḥayye Yehudah**, in which he supposedly had retracted his views opposing **gilgul**. The reason for this had been that he had witnessed the death of a neighbor's six month old son who before dying had reportedly recited Hebrew prayers, from which Modena allegedly concluded that the soul of an old sage had transmigrated into the infant's body. This account, which had been published in 1774 by Hayyim David Azulai (1724-1806), an itinerant Lurianic kabbalist, fundraiser, and bibliographer from Jerusalem,[4] troubled Reggio greatly because it would have undermined Modena as an authority for views against Jewish mysticism.[5] Accordingly, Reggio offered a number of contradictory and tendentious arguments designed to explain away Azulai's account. First, Modena could not have changed his mind about such an essential kabbalistic doctrine; however, even if he had done so, this was not really an essential doctrine of kabbalistic belief. In addition, Modena might not have heard the infant correctly because he was old and his hearing was weak. Or, the child may have really been four years old and able to say the prayers. Finally, Reggio declared that Modena never wrote his autobiography.[6]

Contrary to Reggio's emphatic denial of the existence of Modena's autobiography, it was soon discovered,[7] but it did not contain the alleged change of views on **gilgul** which Azulai had reported.[8] After reading the autobiography, Reggio again demonstrated his contempt for history, unless it was in the service of his ideology, by writing that the details of Modena's life were of little interest, "**mah bekhakh?**," "so what?" Thus Reggio did not relate much of the contents of the autobiography lest revealing its full contents diminish Modena's standing as a leading rabbi and authority against Kabbalah.[9]

Reggio continued his laudatory studies of Modena and other scholars who had read the autobiography also remained silent about the details of Modena's life.[10] In 1841 the traditionalist scholar Samuel David Luzzatto (1800-1865) published the first report that Modena had been a gambler who had lost large sums of money. To this he also added without any justification that Modena had not done an adequate job of proofreading an edition of the Rabbinic Bible.[11] Luzzatto, who owned hundreds of letters written by Modena, chose these issues to diminish Modena's character for two different reasons. First, he was involved in strife over similar issues with a friend of his, the Galician scholar, Solomon Rapoport (1790-1867).[12] Second, Luzzatto had been in Parma where he had read a manuscript called **Ḳol Sakhal**, a tract written against rabbinic Judaism attributed to a Jew from Spain from about 1500. Modena had copied this, perhaps had translated it from Spanish to Hebrew, and had written a refutation of it, part of which is still extant, called **Shaʾagat Aryeh.** Believing that Modena was also really the author of **Ḳol Sakhal,** Luzzatto concluded that Modena hated rabbinic Judaism.[13] With an eye to discrediting the views of **Ḳol Sakhal,** Luzzatto thus tried to demolish Modena's character in personal matters.[14]

Luzzatto's remarks, however, had the opposite effect because they prepared the ground for the widespread acceptance of a twisted interpretation of **Ḳol Sakhal** by Reggio who published it in 1851. In his introduction Reggio wrote that knowledge of Modena's character and life **would** help the reader to judge his opinions.[15] Thus Reggio betrayed his initial **a priori** assessment of Modena as honest and his subsequent refusal to disclose all the details of Modena's life. One specific way he did this was by exaggerating the extent to which Modena had gambled by adding up out of context all his losses, by incorrectly reporting that Modena had written a dialogue against gambling when in fact it was in favor of gambling, and by writing that Modena had written against a ban on gambling approved by the rabbis when in fact Modena objected to its promulgation by the lay leaders without rabbinic approval.[16] Reggio used gambling to establish Modena's hypocrisy to show that Modena was also capable of writing against rabbinic Judaism when serving as a rabbi. Reggio, therefore, used this alleged hypocrisy to enhance his own reconstruction of Modena's religious views while Luzzatto had used it in the opposite manner to detract from such a polemical use of Modena.

Reggio then offered a series of "proofs," as it were, to show that Modena had really written **Ḳol Sakhal.**[17] For example: (1) So-called Hebrew neologisms, such as **baruch hashem** used in reference to God and **Ner Yisrael** applied to Maimonides, appeared in **Ḳol Sakhal.** Since Modena also created neologisms in his writings, he therefore wrote **Ḳol Sakhal.** (2) The author of **Kol Sakhal** showed that the morning prayers can be said late in the morning. Since Venetians like to sleep late, then Modena, who was from Venice, wrote **Ḳol Sakhal.**

The publication of **Beḥinat Haḳabbalah** produced a major controversy about the views expressed in **Ḳol Sakhal** as well as those of Reggio in the notes. Three basic responses followed Jewish religious denominational lines. The most traditional scholars, for the most part, who had been Reggio's friends, remained silent out of embarrassment for his radical views.[18] The radicals and Reformers applauded Reggio's discovery because it validated their claims about the need for constant adjustments in Jewish religious laws.[19] Those in the emerging group in the middle, the positivist-historical school, condemned the book and some even attributed it to Reggio instead of Modena.[20] But since there was clear evidence that **Ḳol Sakhal** had existed before Reggio,[21] most Jews now considered Modena to have been the author of the work.[22] The possibility that the author of **Ḳol Sakhal** was really of Iberian origins was not considered a serious possibility.

The paradoxical position of proving Modena was a hypocrite to establish him as a precursor of Reform Judaism was carried to an extreme by Abraham Geiger (1810-1874), the leading reform rabbi, ideologue, and scholar. In 1856, Geiger advanced the thesis that Modena fought secretly for religious freedom in an age of repression.[23] Geiger used many aspects of Modena's life and writings to show that although he functioned publicly as a famous rabbi, in private he raged against the Talmud. For example, Modena's attack on Kabbalah was designed to undermine rabbinic authority;[24] his anthologies of midrashim were really attacks on rabbinic beliefs;[25] his ownership of a manuscript by Abner of Burgos (c. 1270-1340), an apostate, was proof of his agreement with it;[26] and an attempt to answer a heretic in Hamburg attributed to him was really an opportunity for him to express his own anti-rabbinic views.[27]

Geiger's major rival in many matters of historical interpretation, Heinrich Graetz (1817-1891), wanted to show that Modena's views did not reflect such a specific program of reform. Rather than harboring secret views against the rabbis, Modena simply suffered from a serious personality disorder. Based on no new historical sources, Graetz, writing in the 1870's, belittled the accomplishments of Modena which Geiger had praised. Graetz painted Modena as an impoverished hack devoid of any principles. Rather than being hypocritical and hence a reformer, Modena was just inconsistent and whimsical.[28]

The Historic Leon Modena

New materials on the life and thought of Modena have become available in the century since Graetz wrote. These have not yet been used to create a picture of the historical Leon Modena which differs radically from that of the legendary Leone da Modena. In reality an examination of these sources shows that Leon Modena devoted his life to serving the Jews of his generation, to enriching Jewish literature for future generations, and to defending the principles of rabbinic Judaism from threats on many sides.

Modena spent his youth in Ferrara, Cologna, and Montagnana and had little contact with the city of Modena.[29] As a precocious student of Jewish and secular subjects and a talented speaker, early in life Modena demonstrated an interest in religious polemics in defense of Judaism.[30] Set on a rabbinic career, he would have to create his own opportunities for many years until he was ordained as a rabbi in 1609 shortly before he turned forty.[31]

Modena found an outlet for his rabbinic skills in Venice as a preacher.[32] On the Sabbath, 300-600 people at three or four locations would hear his sermons which would be discussed as far away as Prague.[33] In addition to his heavy reliance on biblical and rabbinic verses, Modena tried to create a balance between the refined philosophical sermons of the rabbis of Renaissance Italy and the simple pietistic works of popular preachers. He was proud of his structural innovations based on classical rhetorical devices and his ability to keep his audience's attention.[34] He attributed some of his success to his brevity. If they wanted a half-hour sermon, then he would speak only twenty minutes.[35]

To earn his living before he was ordained, Modena used his rabbinic skills in his capacity as a legal clerk for the Venetian rabbinate.[36] Modena also served as a teacher of Hebrew and rabbinics for students of all ages.[37] He also worked regularly in the Venetian Hebrew publishing industry as a proofreader, expediter, and author of dedicatory poems and endorsements for books.[38] A side-line included writing letters for his students to their parents and friends. Many of these have been mistakenly identified by scholars as Modena's own childhood letters, thereby once again distorting the picture of the historic Modena.[39]

In his published books, Modena demonstrated his skills as an author, teacher, and popularizer of rabbinic teachings. In **Sod Yesharim**, Modena prefaced magic tricks, folk remedies, and Jewish riddles to a curriculum of biblical and rabbinic studies to make it attractive to young students. In **Tzemaḥ Tzaddiḳ**, he embellished a Hebrew translation of the most popular Italian book of the period, **Fior di Virtu`**, with many citations from traditional Jewish sources, polemical remarks about Christianity, and, incidentally, a misogynistic view of women.[40] In **Galut Yehudah**, he tried to overcome church laws against translating the Bible into Italian by providing a translation of difficult words from the

Bible for the benefit of students and teachers in Jewish schools.[41] For a growing number of Jews who could not understand Hebrew, Modena made the first complete Italian translation of the Passover Haggadah.[42] In **Lev ʾAryeh**, he presented in Hebrew a system of memory improvement, based on those popular in Venice, as a preface to a work on the 613 religious commandments of traditional Judaism.[43] In his play, **LʾEster**, on the life of Queen Esther he used current dramatic standards to bring traditional rabbinic sources to the attention of the Jews.[44] To the major source for rabbinic materials in Counter-Reformation Italy in which the Talmud was banned, the anthology **ʿEin Yaʿakov**, Modena contributed an index, a supplementary collection, and a commentary.[45] Modena's devotion to rabbinic learning and his educational program for the Jews of Italy, therefore, found expression in the books he wrote.

Modena also created enthusiasm for Jewish culture with his musical innovations.[46] In Ferrara, Modena supported a major musical performance which took place in the synagogue on Friday evening the Fifteenth of Av, perhaps the first musical celebration of this ancient Jewish holiday which is still observed with song and dance festivals.[47] From his ordination until his death, Modena held an elected position as cantor, rather than as a rabbi as is generally assumed, in the Italian Synagogue in Venice.[48] He also worked on the first publication of Hebrew music, the compositions of Salamone de' Rossi (c. 1570-1639), **Hashirim ʾAsher Lishlomo**, and directed a Jewish choral society in Venice.[49]

Yet today Modena is most remembered for his polemics against Christianity, Jewish heresy, and Jewish mysticism. The central issue in these three activities was Modena's defense of rabbinic Judaism against attacks which originated in Christian circles.

Modena's contacts with many distinguished Christians from all over the world made him particularly aware of the issues which concerned discussions of Judaism and Christianity.[50] For example, he wrote the **Historia degli riti Hebraici**, an important Italian treatise in defense of Judaism, and served as an advocate for Jews who had been slandered before the ruling powers for aspects of their beliefs or practices.[51] Despite his close relations and tactful writings, Modena was not above private invective against Christianity such as that which is found in his marginal notes to his manuscript by Abner of Burgos.

Aware of his ability to defend Judaism, Jewish leaders called upon Modena to respond to a rising number of Jewish heretics who challenged rabbinic authority. This movement came to Modena's attention when the rich Venetian Jewish lay leaders, many of Iberian descent, tried, with the support of the Venetian government, to limit the authority of the rabbis by controlling the age of their ordination and their power of excommunication.[52] This movement against the rabbis attracted many former marranos in the port cities of Venice, Hamburg, and Amsterdam, including Dr. David Nahmias,[53] Uriel da Costa, Hector Mendez Bravo, Dr. David Farar[54] and many others whose names are not known.[55] Modena's interest in **Ḳol Sakhal** was part of his effort to read and to be able to respond to tracts written against rabbinic Judaism. Another example of Modena's commitment to rabbinic tradition is the statement in a letter that the alternate readings of the rabbis take precedence over the written text of the Bible and that anyone who does not follow them is subject to excommunication.[56]

The polemical activity to which Modena was most committed was criticism of recent trends in Jewish mysticism: the spread of the new school of Lurianic Kabbalah, the tendency to consider Kabbalah as part of Jewish dogma at the expense of Jewish law and philosophy, and the influence of Christian utilization of Kabbalah on Jewish apostates.[57] He collected books on Kabbalah and circulated his views.[58] These studies culminated in a trilogy of works which remained unpublished during his lifetime: **Ben David,**[59] **ʾAri Nohem,**[60] and **Magen Veḥerev.**[61] One example must suffice to show Modena's intentions. In private notes in the margins of Azariah de Rossi's **Meʾor ʿEynayim** Modena wrote that mention of the vowels in kabbalistic texts may be proof that these texts may be later than kabbalists claim, rather than proof of the antiquity of the vowels.[62] Since the late origin of the Hebrew vowels was used by Christian polemicists against the integrity of the Hebrew Scriptures, it is significant that Modena never used this argument against Kabbalah in his writings which he circulated in public.

Despite all his activities, sometimes numbering up to twenty-six types of work at one time,[63] Modena's income was hardly ever enough to support his family.[64] He therefore turned to gambling for income as well as for relief from the grief of having lost three adult sons: One died by inhaling fumes released by alchemy experiments, another was murdered by a Jewish gang over a woman of questionable morals, while the third spent most of his life in exile in the Levant and in South America.[65]

Conclusion

In his autobiography, the first in Hebrew, whose original manuscript has recently been rediscovered,[66] Modena recorded many of the details of his unhappy but productive life. **Ḥayye Yehudah** is testimony to Modena's candor about his life's successes and failures. Had this book been lost, nineteenth century ideologues would have been robbed of the basis of their attempts to create the legendary Leone da Modena to help them in their controversies, and historians, in search of an understanding of Jewish history, would have lost an illuminating source about a personality from the past--the historic Leon Modena.

NOTES

[1] This paper was originally presented at the annual meeting of the Association for Jewish Studies, Boston, December 20, 1983. It represents some of the findings of a recently completed doctoral dissertation at Brandeis University. For a more detailed discussion of Modena's life and times, see Mark R. Cohen's forthcoming edition of **Ḥayye Yehudah** in English translation. For their editorial help in preparing this presentation, I would like to thank Professors Benjamin Ravid and Leonard Ehrlich and Arnold Adelman, my Doktorvater, my Schwiegervater, and my Vater.

[2] In Italian he always used the name Leon Modena. Leon was a shortened form of the Italian name Leone. When he transliterated his name in Hebrew, it always appeared as "Leon," JTSA MS 8593, 21b-22a, 156b-160a. There was, however, no relationship between his last name in Italian and his Hebrew name, Yehudah Aryeh mi-Modena. The Hebrew mi-Modena was an affectation borrowed from the Italian practice of placing "da" or "di" in the names, M. Schulvass, **The Jews in the World of the Renaissance,** E. Koss, tr. (Leiden, 1973), 32-37. However, it did not transfer to the Italian name in Modena's case. After thirty years of writing "Leone da Modena," Cecil Roth wrote in 1959 that he regretted having done so because, as Modena had asserted in his autobiography, the "da" was superfluous, **The Jews in the Renaissance** (Philadelphia, 1959), 337.

[3] Reggio had a copy of **ʾAri Nohem** as early as 1820 and had written about its contents to Moses Kunitzer who published his letter in **Sefer Hamatzref,** I (Vienna, 1820), #62-70, pp. 40a-45 and in 1830 his own manuscript copy of **ʾAri Nohem** was still in the possession of Kunitzer. I. Reggio, "Mikhtav 24," **Kerem Ḥemed,** I (1833), 87-89; to Samuel Leib Goldenberg, January 22, 1830 (27 Tevet). See also "Mikhtav 20," **Kerem Ḥemed,** II (1835), 135; Thursday, June 9, 1831 (Sivan 28).

[4] H. Azulai, **Shem Hagedolim** (Vilna, 1853), **yod,** #14, pp. 44-45. Kunitzer's response to Reggio included a reference to Azulai's report that Modena had changed his views on Kabbalah in his old age.

[5] On a visit to Venice in 1754 Azulai had seen a copy of Modena's **ʾAri Nohem** and perhaps also a copy of his autobiography and made quick hostile references to each in his journal, H. Azulai, **Sefer Maʿagal Ṭov,** A. Freimann, ed. (Jerusalem, 1921), 8-9.

[6] I. Reggio **ʾIggrot Yashar,** I (Vienna, 1834), #13, pp. 81-86.

[7] Volume one of Reggio's letters had gone to press in 1834 and that same year the manuscript of **Ḥayye Yehudah** was discovered in the collection of Jacob and Isaac Trêves of Venice. At least three copies of it were made and circulated soon after its discovery.

8 Although more research is necessary on this difficult passage, it is possible that Azulai did not maliciously create a false citation and Modena did not change his views on transmigration. It is likely that twenty-five years after he glanced at **Ḥayye Yehudah**, after having read other works with descriptions of similar events, including one in **Sefer ᵓElim** by Joseph Solomon Delmedigo who was mentioned regularly by Modena in **ᵓAri Nohem** and one in **ᵓAri Nohem** itself, Azulai confused some of the details of these stories with Modena, D. Ruderman, "Three Contemporary Descriptions of a Polish Wunderkind of the Seventeenth Century," **Association for Jewish Studies Review**, IV (1979), 143-164; **ᵓAri Nohem**, chapter 17 and final chapter. In **Shem Hagedolim** Azulai demonstrated knowledge of several of the works cited by Ruderman. On Azulai's views on Kabbalah, see M. Benayahu, **Rabbi Ḥayyim Yosef David Azulai**, I (Jerusalem, 1959), 134-141.

9 Reggio saw a copy of **Ḥayye Yehudah** in the hands of Uri Hay Saraval, **ᵓIggrot Yashar**, II, (Vienna, 1836), #18, p. 73 and eventually acquired his own copy of it, **Mazkeret Yashar** (Vienna, 1849), 35.

10 These included Solomon Rapoport (1790-1867), **ᵓIggrot Shir**, E. Graeber, ed. (Przemysl, 1885), #6, pp. 70-72; Hayyim Michael (1792-1846), **ᵓOr haḤayyim** (Frankfurt, 1894), 440; Mordecai Ghirondi (1749-1853), **Toldot Gedole Yisrael** (Trieste, 1853), p. 176, #113; p. 54, #9; p. 244, #49; p. 26, #65.

11 S. Luzzatto, "Literarisch-historische Mittheilungen," **Israelitische Annalen**, III (January 1, 1841), 6, note 4. It is clear from Modena's autobiography that one of his responsibilities for the Rabbinic Bible of 1617 had been to hire a proofreader and thus he was not personally responsible for the errors which had crept in, **Ḥayye Yehudah**, A. Kahana, ed. (Kiev, 1911), 34.

12 S. Luzzatto, **ᵓIggrot Shadal**, E. Graeber, ed. (Przemysl, 1882), #300-1, pp. 738-743, 744-746; S. Rapoport, **ᵓIggrot Shir**, (Przemysl, 1885), #14-15, p. 109-120; I. Barzilay, **Shlomo Yehudah Rapoport and his Contemporaries** (Tel Aviv, 1969), 101-107; M. Margolies, **Samuel David Luzzatto: Traditionalist Scholar** (New York, 1979), 39-40, 142-156.

13 Luzzatto, **ᵓIggrot**, #401, p. 980 (May 25, 1846). Luzzatto gave the impression that he had read this manuscript during a trip to Parma although he did not say when:

> The matter is clear, above all suspicion, that the **Ḳol Sakhal** also is the work of Rabbi Yehudah Aryeh. That rabbi was a hater of the sages of the Mishnah and the Talmud more than the Karaites. He was more Reform than Geiger. This was 220 years ago! And in Italy!!

14 If Luzzatto had been in Parma after 1841, then the hostile view he had developed of Modena may have influenced his judgment concerning Modena's authorship; see also Luzzatto, **ᵓIggrot**, #403, p. 993.

15 I. Reggio, **Beḥinat Haḳabbalah** (Gorizia, 1851), i-v.

16 This responsum on gambling was first published as a fifteen page pamphlet by Modena on February 11, 1630. It was

reprinted in Isaac Lampronti's **Paḥad Yitzhak** under the entry "Ḥerem." The version included in Modena's own handwritten collection of responsa was published in **Ziḳne Yehudah**, S. Simonsohn, ed. (Jerusalem, 1956), #78.

17 Reggio, **Beḥinat Haḳabbalah**, 74-86.

18 These included Luzzatto, "El Yosef Lattes," **Pardes**, III (1896), 120; Rapoport, **S. L. Rapoport's hebraeische Briefe an S. D. Luzzatto**, E. Graeber, ed. (Przemysl, 1885), #37, 208; E. Zweifel, **Shalom ʿal Yisrael**, IV (Zhitomir, 1869), 23; I. H. Weiss, **Zikhronotai** (Warsaw, 1895), 152-186.

19 Adolf Jellnick, "Kurze Anzeigen," **Der Orient**, XII (1851), 590-594; I. Reggio, **Yalḳut Yashar** (Seitz, 1854), 171-178; Meir Letteris, "Vezot Teshuvati leYashar," **Wiener Vierteljahrs-Schrift**, II (1853), 9-11; Joshua Heschel Schorr, "Davar Be'ito," **Heḥalutz**, II (1853), 37-43; "Maʾamar Magen Vetzinnah Leharav Yehudah Aryeh Modena," **Heḥalutz**, III (1856), 146; Solomon Rubin, "Mikhtavim 'el Yashar," **Kochbe Jizchak**, XXX-XXXI (1864), 35-41, 66-70; David Einhorn, "Buecherschau: Leo de Modena," **Der Israelitische Volkslehrer**, IV (1854), 97-101.

20 Bernhard Beer, "Die nuere juedische Literatur und ihre Bedeutung," **Monatsschrift fuer Geschichte und Wissenschaft des Judentums**, II (1853), 87; cf. I. Reggio, "Literarische Nachrichten," **Allgemeine Zeitung des Judentums**, VIII (1854), 120-1; Eliezer Leeser Rosenthal, M. Roest, **Catalogue der Hebraica und Judaica aus der L. Rosenthal'schen Bibliothek**, II (1875), 37.

21 I. Reggio, "Literarische Nachrichten," 120-1; **Yalḳut Yashar**, 182; "Schreiben des herrn Reggio," **ʾOtzar Neḥmad**, I (1856), 127. Graetz's views, which will be discussed below, can be viewed as an extention of this school of thought.

22 A good, thorough refutation of Reggio's so-called proofs was not available for a century and is to be found in E. Rivkin, **Leone da Modena and the Ḳol Sakhal** (Cincinnati, 1952), 100-107. Rivkin's study made its first appearance in **The Jewish Quarterly Review**, XXXVIII-XL (1947-1951).

23 A. Geiger, **Leon da Modena: Rabbiner zu Venedig (1571-1648), und seine Stellung zur Kabbalah, zum Thalmud und zum Christenthum** (Breslau, 1856); A. Geiger, "Zu Leon da Modena," **Hebraeische Bibliographie: Hamazkir**, VI (1863), 23; "Schreiben des herrn Dr. A. Geiger in Breslau an herrn Ignaz Blumenfeld in Wien," **ʾOtzar Nehmad**, I (1856), 130; L. Geiger, **Abraham Geiger: Leben und Lebenswerk** (Berlin, 1910), 340-342.

24 Geiger, **Leon da Modena**, 10-16.

25 Geiger, **Leon da Modena**, 17-23. This view was reiterated by most who wrote about Modena, e.g., I. Zinberg, **A History of Jewish Literature**, IV, B. Martin, tr. and ed. (New York, 1974; from the Yiddish of 1929-1937), 147-151. Important critiques of Geiger's interpretation are found in Rivkin, **Leon da Modena and the Ḳol Sakhal**, 108-111 and B. Safran, "Leon Modena's Historical Thinking," typescript of a paper presented at a conference on the Jews of the seventeenth century, Center for Jewish Studies, Harvard University, 1982.

26 Geiger, **Leon da Modena**, 23-25. An examination of this manuscript shows that Modena made several hostile remarks about Abner and his views in the margins. Further, in his introduction to the manuscript, he wrote that after many years he had considered burning it because he had not yet refuted it, Parma, Biblioteca Palatina, MS 2440 (533), 1a-1b, 14a, 53a, 96b.

27 Geiger, **Leon da Modena**, 25-29; "Zu Leon da Modena," 23-24.

28 H. Graetz, **Geschichte der Juden**, X (Leipzig, 1868), 130-141; **History of the Jews** (Philadelphia, 1895), 65-74.

29 These activities are described in great detail in his autobiography.

30 Modena wrote that these interests began by the time he was ten years old, Parma MS 2440 (533), 1a-b; also quoted in Reggio, **Beḥinat Haḳabbalah**, xiii-xv; **ᵓAri Nohem**, 6.

31 Modena acknowledged receipt of his ordination on Kislev 9, 1609, Guensburg-Moscow MS, 356.7, 78-79. He was in Florence serving as a rabbi and this enabled him to return to Venice to function as a rabbi.

32 **Ḥayye**, 25, 34, 47; Isaac min Haleviim, "Introduction," **Magen Veḥerev**, A. Geiger, ed. (Breslau, 1856), 11a-b; Blau, **Kitve**, #89, BM Or. 5396, 129a-b; **Ziḳne**, "Introduction," #78.

33 **Ziḳne**, #22.

34 BM Or. 5396, 122b.

35 **Ziḳne**, #82, 89. He also used kabbalistic allusions to appeal to his audience, **Ziḳne**, #55.

36 Much of the collection of letters attributed to Modena by L. Blau, **Kitve haRav Yehudah ᵓAryeh mi-Modena** (Budapest, 1905, 1906; Strassburg, 1907) and the manuscript on which it was based, BM Or. 5396, consisted of letters Modena wrote in his capacity as legal clerk for Samuel Judah Katzenellenbogen, Joseph Pardo, and Benzion Zarfati.

37 In addition to teaching primary students most of his life, some of Modena's students became famous, including Azariah Figo, Saul Levi Morteira, Barukh Luzzatto, Joseph Hamitz, and others, Blau, **Kitve**, #182. Despite the times when he was weary from this work, he cherished his students and wrote about them with pride.

38 Most of the books for which he wrote dedicatory poems are listed in his autobiography. It is interesting that he did not record many of the kabbalistic books on which he had labored.

39 Blau, **Kitve**, #50, 51, 52, 53, 54, 55, 56, 58, 59, 60. The manuscript indicates clearly that these were written for others. He also wrote that he had only begun to save his own letters in 1588 at the age of seventeen, BM Or. 5396, 135b. Other often quoted letters, including one about a fight and one requesting tickets to a boat race during a solemn religious

period, were also written for others, #86 and 122; cf. BM Or. 5396, 26b and 79b.

40 The one chapter Modena did not include in his translation was the chapter on amorous love in which much attention was paid to the physical pleasure of love between a man and a woman, **Fior di Virtu`**, chapter 5. A comparison of Modena's sixth chapter with the seventh in **Fior di Virtu`** shows that Modena had eliminated many of the praises of women and the criticisms of men which the original had taken from classical texts.

41 Venice, 1612.

42 Venice, 1609.

43 Venice, 1612.

44 Venice, 1619; see A. Piatelli, "'Ester,' l'unico drama di Leon da Modena guito fino a noi," **Rassegne Mensile di Israel**, XXXIV (1968), 163-172.

45 Venice, 1634.

46 L. Modena, **The Diwan of Leo de Modena**, S. Bernstein, ed. (Philadelphia, 1932), #72, 73, 74, 86, 141; **Hayye**, 39, Isaac min Haleviim, **Medaber Tahfuhot**, J. Blau, ed. **Hatzofe Me-ʾeretz Hagar**, III (1912), 76-77.

47 **Ziḳne**, #6; Salamone de' Rossi, **Hashirim ʾAsher Lishlomo** (Venice, 1622); BM Or. 5396, 130b-131b.

48 Modena's career as cantor is well documented in the records of the Italian synagogue, JTSA MS 8593 and 8594.

49 C. Roth, "L'accedemia musicale del ghetto veneziano," **Rassegne Mensile di Israel**, III (1928), 152-162; E. Werner, "The Eduard Birnbaum Collection of Jewish Music," **Hebrew Union College Annual**, XVII (1943-4), 397-428; I. Adler, "The Rise of Art Music in the Italian Ghetto," **Jewish Medieval and Renaissance Studies**, A. Altmann, ed. (Cambridge, 1967), 345-349.

50 These included Henry Wotton (1568-1639), Giulio Morosini (1612-1683), Andreas Colvius (1594-1671), William Bedell (1577-1644), Samuel Slade (1568-c. 1612), Jean Plantavit de la Pause (1576-1651), Jacques Gaffarel (1601-1681), Gabriel Naude (1600-1653), William Boswell (d. 1649), John Selden (1584-1654), Gaston duc d'Orleans (1608-1660), Henri duc de Rohan (c. 1572-1638), and many others.

51 C. Ancona, "Attachi contro il Talmud di Fra Sisto da Siena e la riposta, finora inedita di Leon Modena," **Bollettino dell-istituto di storia della societa e della stato veneziano**, V-VI (1963-1964), 313; **Hayye**, 63, 67.

52 **Diwan**, #66, 64, 28; Blau, **Kitve**, #65; Haleviim, **Medaber**, 180-182.

53 **Ziḳne**, #41, 80, 75; Jacob Heilpron, **Naḥalat Yaʿakov** (Padua, 1623), #12.

54 **Ziḳne**, #33.

55 **Zikne**, #34, 54, 77, 86, 94, 24, 21; Blau, **Kitve**, #154-156, BM Or. 5396, 145b-147b.

56 BM Or. 5396, 121a-b, 72a.

57 **Zikne**, #33, 35, 55, 131.

58 He compiled a bibliography of anti-kabbalist writers and another one of kabbalistic authors, Library of the Jewish Community of Ancona, MS 7.

59 Modena wrote **Ben David** in 1636 but it was first published in **Ta'am Zekenim**. E. Ashkenazi, ed. (Frankfurt, 1854), 61a-64a.

60 Modena wrote **'Ari Nohem** in 1639, but it was first published by Julius Fuerst in 1840 in Leipzig and by Nehemiah Libowitz in 1929 in Jerusalem.

61 Modena began to write this in 1645 but never completed it and the unfinished portion was first published in its entirety by S. Simonsohn (Jerusalem, 1960).

62 Azariah de Rossi, **Me'or 'Eynayim** (Mantua, 1573), Parma 983, 179b; cf. G. B. de Rossi, **Libri stampati di letteratura sacra ebraica ed orientale della biblioteca del dottore G. Bernardo de Rossi . . . divisi per classi e con note** (Parma, 1812), 45.

63 **Hayye**, 64, these were not successive full time jobs.

64 From scattered statements in his autobiography and letters it is possible to estimate his yearly income from all sources to have been between 100 and 200 ducats, somewhere between that of a journeyman and a master mason. Similarly, based on his yearly rent of about 44 ducats and dowries of about 1,000 ducats which he could not really afford, Modena appears to have been struggling to keep a place in the lower middle class, Blau, **Kitve**, #63, BM Or 5396, 37a, **Hayye**, 59, 31, 47; Haleviim, "Introduction," **Magen Veherev**.

65 Modena described his gambling, his financial crises, and the deaths of his sons in his autobiography.

66 N. Aloni and E. Kupfer, "Kitve-yad 'ivriim nosafim be "Ambrosiana" beMilano shelo nikhlalu birshimat Bernheimer," **'Areshet**, IV (1966), 234-261; A. Luzzatto and L. Ottolenghi, **Hebraica Ambrosiana** (1972), 100-101.

MAIMONIDES ON MIND AND METAPHORIC LANGUAGE

David R. Blumenthal

Introduction

Language was always the issue. Maimonides made it so. He devoted most of the first part of the **Guide for the Perplexed** to a discussion of words and then to an analysis of the theory of predication. And, like a play within a play, he indicated that he would use language ambiguously, ambivalently, in multiple-layered meaning, and in outright obfuscation.

Mind, too, was always the issue. Maimonides established that right in the first chapter of the **Guide.** What humans thought and how they thought mattered; in fact, it was of the utmost consequence. Right thinking was of the essence; it was not a spurious by-product of right behavior.

Much has been written on Maimonides' views of language, especially in this century. Equally much has been written on Maimonides' intellectualism. The nature of great thinking, though, is that there is always more to understand. This article, an essay in exegesis, tries to make a modest contribution to this discussion.

In Chapter One of "Hilkhot Yesode ha-Torah," Maimonides sets forth what one can say and believe about God. Having stated this in philosophic language in paragraphs 1-8, Maimonides confronts, in paragraphs 9-12, the traditional anthropomorphic and anthropopathic language about God. The key paragraph is 9, for there language and mind meet. This article deals, therefore, with that paragraph, explicating and expounding the subtlety and nuance of the concept of mind and the language that mind uses about God.

The Text

9. If this is so, what is [the meaning] of that which is written in the Torah: "and under His feet" (Ex. 24: 10), "written with the finger of God" (Ex. 31:18), "the hand of God" (Ex. 9:3), "the eyes of God" (Gen. 38:7), "the ears of God" (Nu. 11:1), and words similar to these?[1] All [these] are according to

the human mind[2] which recognizes only bodies; hence "the Torah speaks in the language of human beings."[3] All are images.[4] For it says: "I shall surely sharpen the blade of My sword" (Dt. 32:41)[5]--does He possess a sword?! Or does He kill with a sword?! Rather, [this is] a metaphor and all [these] are metaphors.[6] The proof[7] for the matter is: one prophet says that he saw the Holy One, blessed be He, "His garments were as white snow" (Dan. 7:9) while another saw Him "[coming with] blood-red clothing from Baṣra" (Is. 63:1).[8] Moses our Rabbi himself saw Him at the Sea as a hero waging war and at Sinai as a representative of the community wrapped [in a prayershawl].[9] This teaches that He has no likeness or form; rather all [these] are in prophetic visions and reveries. As to the true reality of the matter, the human mind does not comprehend it, nor can it apprehend it or examine it. This is what Scripture says: "Can you find the depth of the divine? Can you find the ultimate of the Almighty?" (Job 11:7).

Commentary[1*]

1. These terms are also dealt with in the **Guide** as follows: feet (I:28), finger (I:46,66), hand (I:46), eyes (I:44), and ears (I:45). **Guide**, I:46, lists other organs ascribed to God including bowels. Cf. also **Comm.**, 229 (feet) and 149 (finger). For other terms such as "the mountain of God," "the courtyards of God," "the bliss of God," "the Temple of God," etc., cf. **MT**, Teshuva 8:4.

2. Maimonides used the Hebrew root **yd^c** to generate a series of verbs and nouns which were crucial to his conception of religion and law. These special meanings are over and above the usual meaning of this root, "to know" or "to have knowledge." I think we can distinguish five principal meanings and several sub-meanings in Maimonides' use of this root.

The first principal meaning is "Intelligences." To convey this Maimonides uses only the plural form **dē^{c}ōt**, often with a qualifying phrase: "the **dē^{c}ōt** which have no matter like the angels" (Yesode ha-Torah 4:8); "the **dē^{c}ōt** which are separated from matter" (ibid., 4:9); "the separated **dē^{c}ōt**" (Teshuva 8:3). There are two other references of some interest: "standing before Him Who is the perfection of the **dē^{c}ōt**" (Yesode ha-Torah

2:2, drawing on Job 36:4) and "by the exercise of the intellect [mind] of the God of **dē^{c}ōt**" (Teshuva 3:2, drawing on I Sam. 2:3). In each of these cases, there can be little doubt that "Intelligences," in the full technical sense of the term (cf. e.g., **Guide**, II:4), is meant.

The second principal meaning is "positive philosophical or scientific knowledge." To convey this Maimonides uses various verb and noun forms.

There are three verb forms, each meaning "to have positive philosophical or scientific knowledge":
(1) **lēda^{c}**: Yesode ha-Torah 1:1 (on God's existence); ibid., 1:10 (on God's essence); ibid., 2:2 (general); ibid., 4:11, 13 (on Ma^{c}aseh Merkavah and Ma^{c}aseh Bereshit); ibid., 7:1 (on prophecy); Teshuva 5:5 (twice, on God's knowledge);
(2) **le-dē^{c}āh**, (a noun used as a verb, see below) Shemiṭa ve-Yovel 13:13 (in the context of worship);
(3) **lā-da^{c}at**, Melakhim 12:5 (in an eschatological context).

There are four separate noun forms:
(1) **yedī^{c}at**: a verbal noun meaning, "having positive philosophic or scientific knowledge of," as in Yesode ha-Torah 1:6 (on God's existence); ibid., 1:7 (on God's oneness); Tefillin u-Mezuza 6:13 (of God as the efficient cause of the universe, with **Guide**, I:16);
(2) **madda^{c}**: meaning, "conviction" as in "Sefer Madda^{c}"; meaning, "scientific knowledge" as in Shevu^{c}ot 5:22 (on astronomy), A.Z. 11:1 and Teshuva 5:4 (on the sciences); and meaning, "philosophic knowledge" as in Teshuva 3:8 (on prophecy) and Shemiṭa ve-Yovel 13:13 (in the context of worship);
(3) **dē^{c}āh**: meaning, "positive philosophical or scientific knowledge" as in: Teshuva 9:2 (twice), Melakhim 12:5, and Shemiṭa ve-Yovel 13:13 (used as a verb), drawn from Is. 11:9 with parallels in **PM**, Pereq Ḥeleq; **Maqala fi Teḥiyyat ha-Metim**, 6; **Guide**, III:11; cf. also **MT**, Sanh. 2:1 (on the qualities of a judge) and Yesode ha-Torah 7:7 (on the qualities of a prophet);
(4) **da^{c}at**: same meaning, Teshuva 8:2 and 10:6, but note that Maimonides may intend a double entendre there in the sense of "positive knowledge" and "intellect."

The third principal meaning is really a constellation of three sub-meanings: "intellectual capacity"; "intellect" in the technical sense of the intellectualist "link" between God and man (cf. e.g., **Guide,** I:1; II:45; III:51); and a purposeful double entendre intended to convey both of the previous meanings, "intellectual capacity" to the philosophically untrained and "intellect" to the philosophically trained (for Maimonides' use of double entendre, cf. e.g., S. Klein-Braslavy, **Interpretation,** Part One, and the whole literature on Maimonides' esoteric method of writing). I have tried to capture this double entendre with the word "mind."

Note that Maimonides uses the term **dēᶜāh** in seven of the passages listed below (signaled by an asterisk) and the term **daᶜat** in four such passages (signaled by an ampersand). The construct form of both nouns would be **daᶜat** and, in those cases, one cannot tell which noun form is in the back of Maimonides' mind. The passages are:

(1) "intellectual capacity": Yesode ha-Torah 4:8; Gerushin 6:9, etc.

(2) "intellect": Yesode ha-Torah 4:8*; 7:1, end (twice); 7:4; 7:6 (twice); Teshuva 8:2&; 8:3; Melakhim 12:5

(3) the double entendre, "mind": Yesode ha-Torah 1:9; 1:10 (three times); 2:2&; 2:8; 2:10 (four times, once *); 2:12&; 4:11&; 7:1 (three times, two *); Teshuva 3:32; 5:5 (twice); 8:6 ʾIssure Biʾa 20:22*

The following three references are of special significance because they refer to the "mind" and/or "intellect" of God: Yesode ha-Torah 2:10; Teshuva 3:2; and Melakhim 12:5.

The fourth principal meaning of the root **ydᶜ** is "moral disposition" or "character" as in "Hilkhot Deᶜot." Cf. also **MT,** Deᶜot 1:1; 5:11; A.Z. 11:1. The reference in Yesode ha-Torah 7:1 with the parallel in ʾIssure Biʾa 22:20 is interesting because the context lends itself either to understanding "moral disposition" or "intellect," or a double entendre for both meanings.

The fifth principal meaning seems to be "type of knowledge." Cf. Yesode ha-Torah 2:8 (twice); 2:10 (twice); Teshuva 5:5.

For the individual discussion of these terms, cf. the full commentary which I hope to publish, ad loc. Here, Maimonides intends the double entendre and I have chosen, therefore, to render "mind." Baneth's discussion ("On the Philosophical Terminology of Maimonides" [Hebrew], **Tarbiz,** 6 [1935], 16-8, 21) is inadequate.

3. This phrase, drawn from **Talmud**, Berakhot 39b; Yevamot 71a; Bava Meṣiᶜa 31b; etc., is dealt with in **Guide**, I:26, 33, and 46.
4. Heb., **kinnūyīm**. In **PM**, Pereq Ḥeleq, the Third Principle, Maimonides uses **majāz**, as the general term for "image" (Qafih 211). Note Qafih's difficulty in translation, ad loc, though **majāz** clearly means a "figurative expression," a "metaphor," an "image," etc. In **Guide** (e.g., II:29), Maimonides uses **ᵓistiᶜāra** as the general term for "figurative language." He seems to use **kinnūi**, here, synonymously with **māshāl**, the usual term for "metaphor."

The other meaning of **kinnūi** is a quality of God worth imitating. Cf. **MT**, Deᶜot 1:16 for one list and Tefilla 9:7 for another. One may erase these appelatives, an act forbidden for the seven names of God (Yesode ha-Torah 6:2,5) and there is a question whether one incurs the severest punishment if one curses with one of them (A.Z. 2:7). Cf. Assaf, **Concordance,**, for further references and **Guide**, I:54, where Maimonides characterizes these as **derākhīm** and **middōt**, as attributes of action.
5. On God as one who wages war and the rabbinic understanding thereof, cf. **Mekhilta**, Shira 4; **Mekhilta de-Rashbi**, 15:3; **Tanḥuma**, Mishpaṭim 4; etc. Maimonides chose well here.
6. Maimonides uses three terms in **MT** to delineate the different types of figurative language: **kinnūi**, **māshāl**, and **melīṣah** or **ḥīdāh**. I have already dealt with **kinnūi**. Now we must turn to **māshāl u-melīṣāh**. Maimonides discusses these terms in **PM**, Pereq Ḥeleq (Qafih 202-3) and in **Guide**, Introduction (Joel 6:19-9:25; Pines 10-14). The Arabic terms, as used by Maimonides are **mithl / ᵓamthāl** and **lughz / ᵓalghāz**. They occur as a pair as follows: **PM**, Pereq Ḥeleq (Qafih 202:27-8; 203:24) and **Guide**, Introduction (Joel 3:21; 4:19, 26, 28; 5:11); I:31 (Joel 45:15). **Mithl**, in its various forms, occurs alone at ibid. (Joel 6:21, 23) and **Guide**, I:46 (Joel 69:13-17) in the context of the proper understanding of the bodily organs when used of God.

According to these sources the term **mithl / ᵓamthāl** appears to have a general use and two technical usages. In its general sense, it means any figure of speech, i.e., an image with a decipherable religious-intellectual meaning. In this sense, it includes **lughz / ᵓalghāz**. In its specific sense, **mithl / ᵓamthāl** refers to: (1) an image in which each word has a decipherable meaning (e.g., the words in the verses of the story of Jacob's ladder) or, (2) an image in which only the whole has a decipherable meaning (e.g., the verses in Proverbs, ch. 7, on the harlot and the young man).[2*] The term **lughz / ᵓalghāz**, however, appears to have only a technical meaning. It refers to an image that has multiple levels of meaning, each of which has some religious-intellectual value. It has an exoteric meaning (Ar., **ẓāhir**) and an esoteric meaning (Ar., **bāṭin**).[3*]

The difference, in the technical usages, then, between **mithl** and **lughz** is that **mithl** has only one level of decipherment and, without that, it is only an image. Without decipherment, a **mithl** does not even have an exoteric meaning (Ar., **ẓāhir**); it is nothing (Heb., **kelūm**; cf. **Guide**, Introduction [Joel 7:5-15]). A **lughz**, on the other hand, has multiple levels of decipherment and, hence, one can decipher a perfectly comprehensible exoteric meaning (which would be for the masses or the philosophically untrained), as well as an esoteric meaning (which would be for the philosophically initiated). Maimonides shows this contrast nicely in the **Guide** (Introduction [Joel 7:6-8:3]; I:17 [Joel 29:7]; I:33 [Joel 48:4]).[4*] He draws the analogy for the **mithl** to a pearl lost in a dark house. It is valueless until light is brought so that it can be found. And he draws the analogy for the **lughz** to silver filigree set over gold. It has value, from a distance, as silver but greater value when examined closely for its gold underlay. This gold underlay represents "wisdom which profits convictions (Ar., **ᵓiᶜtiqādāt**) concerning the truth in its true reality (Ar., **al-ḥaqq ᶜalā ḥaqīqatihi**)."

If **mithl** and **lughz** are the Arabic terms, what are the Hebrew terms? Maimonides has four choices: **māshāl, melīṣāh, ḥīdāh,** and **kinnūi.** As noted above, **kinnūi** is the parallel of **ᵓistiᶜāra** and is used to denote the broadest meaning of "image," or "figure of speech." **Māshāl**, is the Hebrew parallel of **mithl** and, like its parallel, is used in two senses: generally (and hence synonymous with **kinnūi**), and technically (for an image with only one layer of meaning which is decipherable from each of its words or only from the whole image presented). **Ḥīdāh** is "the [type of] speech the intent of which is on its esoteric level and not on its exoteric level" (**PM**, Pereq Ḥeleq, Qafih 202:31-2). It is, thus, the proper translation of **lughz** and, using Ezekiel 17:2, Maimonides sets it off in direct contrast to **māshāl** (**Guide**,

Introduction; Joel 6:22). **Meliṣāh**, cited from Prov. 1:6 in both **PM** and **Guide**, is more problematic. The verse reads, "To understand **māshāl** and **meliṣāh**, the words of the Sages and their **ḥīdōt**." If the structure of this verse is by stich (aa-bb), then **meliṣāh** is a synonym of **māshāl**; if it is parallel (ab-ab), **meliṣāh** is a synonym of **ḥīdāh**. (The third possibility, chiliastic [ab-ba], would make **māshāl** and **ḥīdāh** synonymous, which is just what Maimonides wishes not to do in these sources.) My suggestion is that, since the conceptual difference between **mithl** and **lughz** is clear and, since this is the proper place to allude to such a distinction, we should adopt the parallel structure and understand **meliṣāh** as a synonym for **ḥīdāh**.

The English equivalents, I propose, then, are as follows: **kinnūi** = image; **māshāl** (general sense) = image, or metaphor; **māshāl** (technical sense #2, the whole has a meaning) = metaphor; **māshāl** (technical sense #1, each word has meaning) = extended or detailed metaphor; **ḥīdāh** and **meliṣāh** = riddle.[5*]

7. Heb., **reʾāyāh**. There is a very interesting Arabic translation of "Hilkhot Yesode ha-Torah" which I hope to publish soon. The Arabic translator renders here, **al-dalīl**. Both these terms seem to refer to a Scriptural proof (as in this case), to an argument (Ar., **ḥujja**), or to a full logical demonstration (Ar., **burhān**; cf. e.g., **MT**, Teshuva 5:5).

8. The point is that God cannot be dressed in red and in white. Therefore, such language is metaphorical. Cf. **Guide**, II:45, the second degree, that Daniel is not quite a prophet. Cf. to the contrary, **Talmud**, Ḥagiga 15a, and correct the reference in Cohen, ad loc. Note too that in **Talmud**, Ḥagiga 14a, the contrast is drawn between God's white hair (Dan. 7:9) and His dark hair (Song 5:11).

9. The history of the text here is fascinating. **Mekhilta**, Shira 4 (ed. Ish Shalom 37b) reads: "He revealed Himself at the Sea as a warrior who makes war as it says, 'God is a man of war' [Ex. 15:3] and He revealed Himself on Sinai as an old man full of mercy (Heb., **zāqēn mālēʾ raḥamīm**) as it says, 'And they saw the God of Israel' [Ex. 24:10] . . . and as it says, 'I saw . . . and his garments were as white as pure snow and his hair was as white as clean wool' [Dan. 7:21]." **Mekhilta de-Rashbi**, 51:3 (ed. Hoffmann 61) reads: "He . . . as a young man who makes war . . . Sinai as an old man wrapped up (Heb., **ke-zāqēn ʿāṭūf**) as it says,

'I saw . . . and his garments were white . . .'" The **Talmud**, however, at Rosh ha-Shana 17b, reads: "This [Ex. 34:6, 'And He passed before him and He said . . . '] teaches that the Holy One, blessed be He, wrapped Himself up as a representative of the community (Heb., **nitᶜaṭṭēf ke-shelīaḥ ṣibbūr**) and showed Moses the proper prayer [for forgiveness] . . ." Maimonides seems, then, to have followed the Talmud in the matter of "representative of the community" and the **Mekhilta de-Rashbi** in the adjectival form of "wrapped up." There seems to be some precedent for that in a fragment from R. Ḥananᵓel to **Talmud**, Berakhot 7a (cited in B. Lewin, **Otzar ha-Gaonim**, vol. 1, part 3, page 4): "in the likeness of a wrapped up representative of the community (Heb., **ke-demūt shelīaḥ ṣibbūr meᶜuṭṭāf**) who passes before the ark as it says, 'And he passed . . . '" Interestingly, in the matter of the substance here, Maimonides does not appeal to R. Ḥananᵓel who, at Rosh ha-Shana 17b, interprets: "God commanded the angel to wrap himself up as a representative of the community . . . " For another kind of wrapping up in a prayer-shawl, cf. **Talmud**, Ḥagiga 14b, where the mystic wraps himself up to study the secrets of the heavenly realms. Interestingly, **Midrash Haggadol**, which usually follows Maimonides, follows the **Mekhilta de-Rashbi** at Ex. 15:3.

NOTES

1* The works most frequently cited in this essay are: (1) Maimonides, **Perush ha-Mishna**, ed. Y. Qafiḥ, 7 vols., Mossad Harav Ḳooḳ, Jerualem: 1963-68, = **PM**; (2) idem., **Mishne Torah** with special reference to **Sefer Madda^c**, ed. J. Cohen, Mossad Harav Ḳooḳ, Jerualem: 1964, = **MT**; (3) idem., **Guide for the Perplexed**, ed. I. Joel, Junovitch, Jerusalem: 1929, = Joel; transl. S. Pines, University of Chicago Press, Chicago: 1963, = Pines; (4) D. Blumenthal, **The Commentary of R. Ḥoṭer ben Shelomo to the Thirteen Principles of Maimonides**, E. J. Brill, Leiden: 1974, = **Comm.**; (5) idem., **The Philosophic Questions and Answers of Ḥoṭer ben Shelomo**, E. J. Brill, Leiden: 1981, = **PQA**; (6) D. Assaf, **Concordance of the Mishne Torah**, 8 vols., Haifa: 1960-, = **Concordance**; and (7) S. Klein-Braslavy, **Maimonides' Interpretation of the Story of Creation** (Hebrew), Jerusalem: 1978, = **Interpretation.**

2* Probably because of this double-meaning of **mithl**, Pines consistently translates **mithl** as "parable" while others render it as "allegory." I prefer "metaphor" for the second sense and "extended" or "detailed metaphor" for the first sense. In **Guide**, Introduction, however, Pines missed the general usage of **mithl** as "image" or "figure of speech" (esp. 12, explaining the double-layered figure of speech and probably in the introductory words to this section on the bottom of 10).

3* Cf. Faur (**Studies in Mishne Torah**, [Mossad Harav Ḳooḳ, Jerusalem: 1978], 130, n.94) with **PM**, Pereq Ḥeleq (Qafih 202), for these exact terms. Pines consistently translates **lughz** as "riddle" and I can find no better word though "riddle" is not quite what is meant.

4* Cf. S. Klein-Braslavy, **Interpretation**, Part One for the theory and Part Two for an application of it to the Biblical Creation narrative.

5* For other uses of these terms, cf. Assaf, **Concordance**, where available. I note the following significant occurrences in **MT**:
(1) **māshāl** and **ḥīdāh** together: on the incorporeality of God and the angels (Yesode ha-Torah 1:12, understanding **melīṣāh** as a synonym for **ḥīdāh**; 2:4); on prophetic language (Yesode ha-Torah 7:3,6); on the world-to-come (**ḥīdāh**: Teshuva 8:2; **māshāl**: Teshuva 8:4,6); on eschatological language (Melakhim 12:1);
(2) **māshāl** alone: on Ma^caseh Merkavah (Yesode ha-Torah 2:12); on Song of Songs (Teshuva 10:3);
(3) I do not find any references to **ḥīdāh** alone.
Note especially Yesode ha-Torah 4:13 that even metaphysics and physics can be known by "young and old, man and woman, well-educated and poorly educated," presumably each on his/her own language and level.

My analysis, then, goes beyond that of Pines and Faur cited above. It also advances beyond S. Klein-Braslavy (**Interpretation**, 39-46) who identifies **māshāl** and **ḥīdāh** as synonymous (39), maintains that the shift to the esoteric level of interpretation is achieved by a transposing of the semantic axis to the philosophic level (40-2), and who offers a four-fold analysis of sub-types of figurative language (44-6). Interestingly, she does not sustain the latter part of this analysis through the rest of the bo͞ok. Twersky (**Introduction,** 366, n.31) also takes **māshāl** and **ḥīdāh** as synonyms and renders them as "allegory." Cf. also, ibid., 355, n.31. The Arabic translator came close here with, **mathālāt wa-ʿibārāt mutarjima,** "metaphors and interpreted images."

I do not know the origin (if any) of this theory of figurative language. Saadia, in his **Translation and Commentary to Proverbs,** ad loc (ed. Qafih 24-5), differentiates four kinds of figurative language, ascribing multiple-level meaning to the **meliṣāh** and the **ḥīdāh.** But the rest of his theory does not seem to parallel that of Maimonides.

ROYAL POWER AND RABBINICAL AUTHORITY
IN 14TH CENTURY FRANCE*

Roger S. Kohn

"The story has been mentioned often yet it is not unnecessary to go back over it again." This is the way in which S. Schwarzfuchs chose to introduce his chapter dealing with the greatest controversy of 14th century French Jewry, the dispute between Johanan ben Mattathias Trêves and Isaiah ben Abba-Mari, in his studies on the origin and development of the medieval rabbinate.[1]

Regarding this controversy, I will attempt to demonstrate that **two** conflicts actually existed where only one has so far been perceived, conflicts involving more parties than Johanan and Isaiah. The latter has previously been considered the leading figure in this affair. But evidence I will cite from non-Jewish sources will prove that Isaiah was not the most prominent rabbi in his community and, hence, not as central a character in this story as previously claimed.

The story, in brief, is as follows: Johanan's father, Mattathias, was the leading religious authority in Northern France after the Jews were allowed to return in about 1380. He was also a close relation of Manessier of Vesoul, the lay leader of the French Jewish community.[2] Mattathias is credited with having strengthened the religious life of French Jewry by establishing the first **yeshivot** in France after the Black Death. Following Mattathias' death, his son Johanan was appointed head of the French Jewish community with the approval of the king. Five years after Mattathias' death,[3] Isaiah ben Abba-Mari, a former pupil who had quarreled with Mattathias and had gone to live in Savoy, challenged Johanan's authority over French Jewry. Isaiah claimed that he had received full rabbinical authority over the Jews in France from Meir ben Baruch ha-Levi of Vienna. According to Isaiah, Meir ha-Levi had decreed that no **yeshiva** could be established without Isaiah's permission, nor could any religious act such as marriage or divorce be carried out without his approval.[4]

Until now, we have known about this dispute only from a few Hebrew sources: two letters from Johanan sent to the Spanish rabbis Hasdai Crescas and Isaac bar Sheshet, requesting that Isaiah be excommunicated; the rabbinical consultation and answer sent back by bar Sheshet; and a letter sent by another Spanish rabbi, Moses Halawa. Although none of the rabbis agreed to issue the excommunication, all affirmed Johanan's basic position. We have no Hebrew sources available stating the arguments in favor of Isaiah ben Abba-Mari, and we know little about him or the rabbis allied with him from these or any Hebrew sources.[5]

For over a century, more than a dozen scholars of various countries have studied the Hebrew sources, in particular the **Responsa** of bar Sheshet. From these texts, together with Johanan's appeals, we can derive some information about the controversy. However, several important points are left open to evaluation.

The Role of Meir ha-Levi of Vienna

There are four different evaluations of the action and attitude of Meir ha-Levi of Vienna, the key figure on Isaiah's side of the dispute. Beside the reference in the bar Sheshet **Responsa**, little is known about him. He was probably born in Fulda, Germany, and later sojourned in the Rhineland, in Frankfort around 1392,[6] in Nuremburg, and in Vienna.[7] He died about 1407. His authority is scarcely attested by direct evidence, but rather through the respect paid to him by later generations of rabbis.

Meir ha-Levi is credited with the revival of the **semikha**, the rabbinic ordination, among Ashkenazi Jewry. In his **Geschichte und Literatur**,[8] Zunz dated the reinstitution of **semikha** around 1360. Writing several years after Zunz, Auerbach gave full credit for the revival to Meir ha-levi: "It seems that Meir ha-Levi who was in Vienna . . . had renewed the ordination around 1360."[9] Güdemann wrote that beside the reinstatement of ordination, little is known about Meir ha-Levi.[10] He speculated that Meir ha-Levi was motivated to renew the institution of ordination because Jewish academies in Germany were in decline, and the community was not enjoying strong religious leadership. Persecutions may have been responsible for this state of Judaism in Germany at this time, Güdemann wrote, and the renewal of the ordination may have been one of several steps taken to strengthen religious behavior.

Meir ha-Levi's ordination affected rabbis ordained through the more informal system where an individual rabbi conferred ordination on those who had studied under him. The new structure established by Meir ha-Levi challenged the authority and prestige of already established rabbis. It may be assumed that the reinstatement of ordination did not at first offend established authorities, including Johanan ben Mattathias.

Meir ha-Levi's direct involvement in the Johanan-Isaiah dispute, however, did not seem obvious to Güdemann. According to him, Meir ha-Levi was a person who generally avoided controversy. In support of this view, Güdemann cited a case in which Meir ha-Levi had defended the right of another rabbi to teach in his neighborhood.[11] From this instance, Güdemann concluded that it made no sense to assume that Meir ha-Levi defended the privilege of exclusivity claimed by Isaiah ben Abba-Mari. No controversy seems to have arisen from the renewal of ordination in Germany, Güdemann noted. The polemic was rather started in France by Isaiah, and no direct responsibility should be attributed to Meir ha-Levi, even though Johanan and the Spanish rabbis had explicitly accused him of interference.

In analyzing the bar Sheshet **Responsa**, bar Sheshet's biographer, Hershman reached the opposite conclusion: that the real question at stake was the right of Meir ha-Levi "to interfere with the internal affairs of the French communities."[12] For one thing, the Spanish rabbis, bar Sheshet as well as Crescas,[13] accused Meir ha-Levi directly of interference. Documents indicate that Meir ha-Levi was aware of the turmoil in the French Jewish community; he had received a written protest from the Jewish communities themselves.[14] Hershman wrote that all the Spanish scholars who gave moral support to Johanan were careful not to step into the controversy themselves. Halawa, for one, wished that the parties would be reconciled and was not ready to decide in favor of one side or the other. Bar Sheshet was even more explicit; he could not intervene, for that would be doing what he had reproached Meir ha-Levi for--interfering in a foreign community's domestic affairs. Hershman, Schwarzfuchs and other scholars, thus, agree that the intervention of Meir ha-Levi was perceived as unjustified by all the Spanish rabbis involved in the dispute.[15]

Accepting and defending the idea of an active intervention on the part of Meir ha-Levi, Mordechai Breuer recently proposed two possible motives for his action.[16] First, Meir ha-Levi may have been disturbed by the prevailing situation in France, where rabbinic knowledge was low according to his standards. Second, Meir ha-Levi may have opposed the idea of a congregation selecting its own rabbi, for fear that an ignorant man could, by political means, have himself installed. To prevent such a situation from occurring, Meir ha-Levi favored an institutionalized form of ordination which would conform with his own standards.

A different analysis of Meir ha-Levi's action supposes that his support was not directed specifically against Johanan, but against earlier opponents of Isaiah, rabbi in Bresse (Savoy). It is possible that Isaiah received a decree from Meir ha-Levi against local rabbinical opponents in Savoy, and then proceeded to apply the document against Johanan, the rabbinical authority of royal France. Such an argument is merely a hypothesis, given the scarcity of documentation, but it may serve to reconcile various conflicting statements concerning the dispute between Johanan and Isaiah. To understand the basis of this hypothesis, one must realize that France in the second half of the 14th century was a pre-modern centralized monarchy. From the time of Philip the Fair, the royal administration had extended its influence over an increasing number of feudal estates and cities. Burghers, though not ruled directly by the king, nevertheless turned to Paris as the final appeal in both civil and criminal cases.[17]

Yet another widely accepted explanation of the controversy between Johanan and Isaiah supposes that Isaiah's objection was based on the claim that Johanan was a rabbi not worthy of his status since he had been confirmed in his office by a non-Jewish ruler. Zunz is the first to allude to the interference of the monarchy in the controversy,[18] but the most elaborate analysis comes from Lauer and Zeitlin.[19] Although their views have been dismissed by later scholars,[20] it is worth confronting the arguments they advanced with what we know today about the governmental structure of 14th century France.

The strengthening of the centralized power had its impact not only on Christian subjects but also on Jews allowed to dwell in the kingdom. Four examples of the assertion of royal power: (1) A special paragraph of the royal ordinances specifically authorized the gathering of Jewish representatives of the various communities in the kingdom in order to collect taxes. (2) The king granted Jewish representatives the right to expel any individual Jew from the kingdom. In doing so, however, the king detailed who those representatives must be: two rabbis and four laypersons. It was the will of the king to organize the community from within.[21] (3) A dispute occurred in 1365 between Manessier of Vesoul, the first lay leader of the French communities, and another Jew, Jacob of Sainte-Maxence. The latter was excommunicated by Manessier's brother, Vivant, who prevented Jacob's son from being circumcised. According to the record,

> n'eust pas esté l'enfant circoncis se le chancelier ne leur eust expressement commandé de par le Roy,"
> The child would not have been circumcised if the Chancellor had not directly ordered it on behalf of the king.[22]

This is an example of direct interference on the part of the royal power in the internal life of the Jewish communities by limiting the power of rabbis to enforce their decisions. (4) A further step was taken about ten years later when the Parliament of Paris completely forbade the use of rabbinical excommunication in royal France:

> Nostra cura inhibet expresse . . . Judeis omnibus . . . utantur sententiis seu pronutiationibus de **nidduy**, **samatha** et de **ḥerem** inter eos.[23]

In the present case, scholars such as Zunz, Lauer and Zeitlin have claimed that the king's interference was the major factor behind Meir ha-Levi's decision to deny the investiture of Johanan and assert that of Isaiah as full rabbinical authority over France. This thesis must be rejected because the selection of a rabbi was not the result of a mere designation by the king. From the expression used in bar Sheshet's **Responsa**--"by the will of the communities and the acceptance of the king"--the function of the king was merely to ratify the choice made by the various communities in France. (Bar Sheshet was careful to refer to the "kingdom" of France in his appraisal of the controversy, although

Johanan in his letters always spoke of France as a territorial entity, without emphasizing the distinction between royal France and French speaking territories.[24]) Furthermore, there is no direct evidence that the king did more than approve the choice of Johanan by the Jewish communities. Finally, from what we know about Meir ha-Levi, such action would not have been sufficient cause for intervention. It seems likely, therefore, that the motivation for Meir ha-Levi's intervention was his desire to limit the control of local Jewish communities over the French rabbinate. The king, for his part, was not likely to have been interested in such a parochial dispute. In general, the king's intervention within the Jewish community was limited to matters of finance, where lay people rather than rabbinical leaders were the main spokesmen.[25]

There are, thus four hypotheses which attempt to explain this conflict: Güdemann (that Meir ha-Levi was not an active participant), Hershman-Breuer (that Meir ha-Levi was active because the French rabbinate did not meet his standards), Zunz-Zeitlin (that Meir ha-Levi was active in order to counter the growth of royal power), and my own (that Isaiah misused an earlier letter from Meir ha-Levi).

A Reconsideration of the Evidence

As noted earlier, most of the existing scholarship on the Johanan-Isaiah dispute has been devoted to the lengthy rabbinical **Responsum** of bar Sheshet (n° 271). Little attention has been paid to the texts of Johanan's two appeals to the Spanish rabbis. A closer examination of these texts, however, reveals that the controversy was a many-faceted one. It was not merely a personal dispute between two rabbis; it was a conflict involving two factions of French rabbinical authorities. Due to the importance of these texts, we shall present both. Text A is the letter sent to the rabbis in Catalonia; text B the personal letter to bar Sheshet:

Text A (**Responsum** n° 268)
And also to cancel the second decree, to excommunicate anyone who would pay attention to it or enforce it, and

> to warn R. Isaiah on such acts as would cross into the bounds of our authority.

> Text B (**Responsum** n° 270)
> Two requests, I have for you: the first to cancel the decree as is seen fit; to take appropriate measures and excommunicate anyone who would pay attention to it.

These texts clearly refer to the decree Isaiah received from Meir ha-Levi which gave him ultimate authority over all religious activities in France. The threat to Johanan, thus, was not only on the personal level, a mere rivalry between two centers of power. What Johanan was more afraid of was the imposition of the German rabbinical privilege on other rabbis. Thus, he not only requested that the decree in favor of Isaiah be cancelled, but also that the Spanish scholars take measures against any rabbi who would dare to acknowledge the decree. From Johanan's request, we understand that a large number of rabbis had become allied with Isaiah. Johanan's second request provides an explanation of the motivations of these rabbis--financial motivations.

> Text A (**Responsum** n° 268)
> I request that you excommunicate publicly all judges, rabbis and positioned rabbis[26] who have been functioning for the last fifteen years; who have forced individuals or communities in any judicial case and who have excluded them so as to force them to pay a fine and have taken the fine for themselves or for their relatives through a judicial fine or a judicial compromise . . . Attention should be given that other rabbis, not from the clan [of these rabbis] be chosen by the remitter, and that the fine not be given to the one who has decreed the fine.

> Text B (**Responsum** n° 270)
> And the second [request] that no rabbi shall fine an individual in any case in such a way that the individual is excluded or forced to compromise, and that the fine money shall not be divided by this rabbi

> but by two other rabbis, chosen by the remitter; and that these rabbis shall not be relatives of the judging rabbi or from his clan.

There are several points worthy of notice in these different versions. Johanan's two requests are not given in the same order in the letters to Catalonia rabbis (n° 268) and to Isaac bar Sheshet (n° 270). In the first letter, he asks first for measures against those rabbis he considers unscrupulous and then for sanctions against Isaiah. The order is reversed in the letter to bar Sheshet. The letter to the Catalonian rabbis also gives details omitted in the letter to bar Sheshet. For one thing, Johanan mentions the fact that these corrupt rabbis have been in office for fifteen years, i.e., five years prior to the death of his father.[27] Isaiah may have been one of the rabbis under questions, but Johanan's request for action against these rabbis is **not** linked with his appeal against Isaiah.

Johanan, in these texts, may be reacting to what he considers to be an alliance of rabbis who have deprived him of part of the fines due to him as rabbinic judge. In the French royal judiciary system, the judge generally received a portion of any fines levied as payment for his role in rendering justice. From Johanan's request, we may understand that such a notion was prevalent among Jews as well.

A final detail is worth noting. In his request to bar Sheshet, Johanan mentions evil done only to individuals, while in the letter to Catalonia, both individuals and communities are said to have suffered. This seems to indicate that the opposing party controlled a fairly large portion of the French Jewish community.

The Non-Jewish Sources

Although the non-Jewish sources[28] cannot give us a full picture of the extent of the opposition to Johanan, they can provide us with some examples that add to what we know from Hebrew sources. In the letter to the Catalonian rabbis, Johanan alluded to a follower of Isaiah, saying that Isaiah

> installed a rabbi on the holy people whom he sanctified through money and without shame; he agreed to ordain

> him and afterwards attracted him with material advantages and allied with him through marriage and elevated him.

In his letter sent to bar Sheshet, Johanan mentions the same person, this time by name:

> He ordained a rabbi whose name is Moses **detushai** who never studied either Bible or oral lore and has never understood a talmudic subject all his life, in order to ally himself with him, and this fellow is still rabbi.

This "ignorant" rabbi lived in the city of Dijon (Burgundy), between 1385 and 1387, the period of the dispute according to most scholars.[29] Johanan's brother, Joseph, was the leading rabbinical authority of the city until the expulsion of 1394. Moses of Toussay is not mentioned in the non-Jewish sources of Dijon with regard to any activity aside from moneylending,[30] except for one last reference in 1387 where he is referred to as "juif, maestre de la loi" (Jew, master of the Law).[31] Apparently he left Dijon shortly afterwards, for a subsequent document from Savoy mentions a "Mossie de Tossey"--without any rabbinic title whatsoever. The last mention of him occurs in 1394 when his name is linked with that of Samson of Louhans,[32] the leading rabbinic authority in Savoy.

Samson is another figure in the Johanan-Isaiah dispute. Following his quarrel with Mattathias, Isaiah had left royal France for the Bresse region of Savoy. A rivalry soon developed between Isaiah and Samson, with the two sides sending letters to various authorities seeking support.[33] The quarrel was a fierce one: Isaiah is said to have tried to dismiss Samson from his office. We know that he wrote bar Sheshet asking him how to react to an excommunication issued by Samson, and was told, in response, to pay no attention to such a move.[34] In some manner the dispute was finally resolved and Isaiah later married Samson's niece. All this we know from Johanan's letter to the Spanish rabbis.

With this in mind, we turn to the sources from Savoy and find that Samson, not Isaiah, is the leading authority of the Jews of Bresse for most of the second half of the 14th century. We assume that the Samson mentioned in bar Sheshet's **Responsa** is the same "maistre Sanson, juif maistre de la loy des Juifs de Breisse" (master Samson, Jew, master of the Law of the Jews of

Bresse),[35] also called "maistre Sansin de Loant, juif demorant à Borg en Breisse"[36] (Samson of Louhans,[37] Jew living in Bourg-en-Bresse). The evidence that he was the leading authority in Bresse is a document showing that he paid for the seal affixed to the charter granted to the Jews of the region.[38] In all known documents, his name is preceded by the title "maistre" in French or "magister" in Latin and in two cases, his name is followed by the specific phrase "maistre de la loy des juifs."

Surprisingly, Isaiah is mentioned only twice in records from Savoy, in both occurrences under the name of "maistre Astruc"--a name rarely mentioned in the Hebrew sources.[39] The identification of Astruc with Isaiah ben Abba-Mari is based mainly on an account of a moneylending transaction carried out by Isaiah and Samson.[40] In a related occurrence, he is described as "magistri Astruti judei qui eidem domine in aliquibus utilibus et gratis servit," a Jew who has usefully served the Count.[41] Isaiah ben Abba-Mari was not the main representative of Bressan Jewry.

From the point of view of Christian sources, Isaiah ben Abba-Mari was not the leading authority among the Jews in Savoy. Samson of Louhans, if he is identical with the R. Samson mentioned by Johanan of Trêves, was the religious and administrative ruler of this Jewish community. Samson did not seem involved in the dispute between Johanan and Isaiah. Johanan gives no evidence in his appeals to the Spanish rabbis that he felt endangered by Samson's position in Savoy. Samson might even have, at first, supported the legitimacy of Johanan's position, since Isaiah was also a direct threat to Samson's authority. He later allied with Isaiah by marrying him off to his niece. According to Johanan, the arranged marriage was an act of reconciliation between enemies. But with Samson's talents in negotiating with the civil authorities of Savoy, undoubtedly his diplomacy also served him in disciplining the rebellious pupil of Mattathias Trêves.

Conclusion

There is no doubt that Isaiah alone threatened Johanan's spiritual leadership over French Jewry. Reconsideration of the Hebrew sources has pointed out that Isaiah was actually involved in two quarrels, one with Johanan, another with Samson. In both cases, Isaiah succeeded in upsetting the Jewish communities of France and Savoy, splitting the rabbinate in the process.

After the Black Death, Jews had come to be more aware of political frontiers. We know that Spanish rabbis refused to take a position in favor of Johanan and were reluctant to overstep territorial boundaries. We can surmise, for the same reason, that Meir ha-Levi of Vienna supported Isaiah in his squabble with Samson rather than in his dispute with Johanan.

From Bresse in Savoy, Isaiah's loud claim of authority over the Jewish communities in royal France conflicted with an equally inaccurate claim of Johanan of Trêves to rule over "all the Jews of Northern France,"[43] i.e., excluding only Provence and Languedoc. Savoy would have been included into the territory as defined by Johanan; but the Spanish rabbis clearly were not willing to grant him this extended authority.

Isaiah's clash with Johanan brought him nothing but grief: he fled the kingdom of France while his supporters had to leave the neighboring duchy of Burgundy,[44] and in Savoy Samson remained as the leader of the Jewish communities.

NOTES

* This paper was presented at the Association for Jewish Studies thirteenth annual conference (Boston, December 1981). I express my thanks to Professor David R. Blumenthal, Laurie Edelman-Fialkoff and her husband Harvey for their assistance in editing, as well as for their substantive comments.

1 Simon Schwarzfuchs, **Etudes sur l'origine et le développement du rabbinat au Moyan Age** (Paris: Mémoires de la Société des Etudes juives, 1957).

2 E. de Laurriere, **Ordonnances des roys de France de la troisiéme race** (Paris: 1723-1747), t. V, p. 497.

3 **She'elot u-teshuvot ha-ribash** (Wilna: Lippmann 5639-1879) = **Responsa . . .**, n° 271, p. 148.

4 The expression used in Hebrew regarding such a rabbi is **litfoś yesiva.**

5 Isaiah ben Abba-Mari is also mentioned in **Responsa . . .** n° 193-194 and 212-213.

6 I. Kracauer, **Urkundenbuch zur Geschichte dur Juden in Frankfurt A.M. 1150-1400**, vol. I, pp. 187-191.

7 Max Grunwald, **History of the Jews in Vienna** (Philadelphia: JPS, 1936), pp. 60-66.

8 **Zur Geschichte und Literatur**, erster Band (Berlin: Veit und Comp., 1845), p. 186.

9 Benjamin Hirsch Auerbach, **Berit Abraham** (Frankfort A.M., 1860), p. 6.

10 Moritz Güdemann, **Geschichte der Erziehungswesens und der Cultur der abendlädishcen Juden** (Wien, 1880), pp. 241-242 and 246-247.

11 Güdemann, **Geschichte . . .**, p. 246.

12 Abraham M. Hershman, **Rabbi Isaac ben Sheshet Perfect and His Time** (New York: JTS, 5704-1943), pp. 206-208.

13 **Responsa** n° 271 in the beginning (p. 148) and at the end (p. 150).

14 **Responsa . . .** n° 271, p. 150.

15 Mordechai Breuer, "The 'Ashkenazi Semikha'," **Zion**, XXXIII (1968), pp. 15-46.

16 Certain expressions used by Johanan are misleading. **Cf. Responsa . . .** n° 268, p. 147: " . . . He received **according to what is spread** from his master, rabbi in Germany . . . "

[17] The Parliament of Paris received cases appealed from Champagne, but also from Burgundy and from Languedoc.

[18] Zunz, **Zur Geschichte . . .** , p. 187.

[19] Ch. Lauer, "R. Meir Halevy aus Wien und der Streit um das Grossrabbinat in Frankreich. Eine Studie über rabbinische Streitfragen im Mittelater," **Jahrbuch der Jüdisch-Literarischen Gesellschaft**, XVI (1924), pp. 1-42. Solomon Zeitlin, "The Opposition to the Spiritual Leaders Appointed by the Government," **J.Q.R.**, new series, XXX:3 (1941), pp. 287-300, reprinted in **Religious and Secular Leadership**, Part I (Philadelphia: Dropsie College, 1943), pp. 58-71.

[20] Hershman, **Rabbi Isaac ben Sheshet . . .** , pp. 205-207 and 208-211; Schwarzfuchs, **Origine et développement du rabbinat . . .** , pp. 55-59.

[21] **Ordonnances des rois de France . . .** , t. III, pp. 473-481, paragraphs 3 & 4.

[22] Text published by Schwarzfuchs, **Origine et développement du rabbinat . . .** , p. 67.

[23] Quoted according to Schwarzfuchs, **Origine et développement du rabbinat . . .** , p. 54. The original text is in Archives Nationales (Paris): X^{1A}1470.167v. (1375).

[24] Cf. Schwarzfuchs, **Origine et développement du rabbinat . . .** , p. 50 who connects the expression **kol leson ha-zarfatim** with "Langue d'Oyl."

[25] An example can demonstrate this point. When Manessier of Vesoul, the first lay leader died between June and October 1375, his sons tried to carry on his activities but were replaced by new lay leaders, Ysaac Christofle and Vivant of Montreal, in the following years. Nonetheless, Mattathias remained the religious figure although he had family links with the Vesoul family, cf. **Ordonnances des rois de France . . .** , t. VII, p. 169; t. VI, p. 118 (June 1375) and for mention of the first son of Manessier of Vesoul, Salomon, to take office, Archives Nationales (Paris): JJ 107.184r. (n° 361).

[26] Same expression mentioned in above n. 4.

[27] **Responsa . . .** n° 271, p. 148.

[28] Conveniently published by Renata Segre, "Testimonianze documentarie sugli Ebrei negli stati Sabaudi (1297-1398)," **Michael**, IV (1976), pp. 274-412.

[29] The question of dating the **Responsa . . .** n° 268-272 has been a puzzling one for several decades. N. Brüll ("Das Geschlecht der Trêves," **Jahrbücher fur jüdische Geschichte**, t. 1, p. 95) gave 1392 as the possible date. Güdemann (**Geschichte der Erziehungswesens . . .** , p. 206) was under the impression that the conflict closely preceded the 1394 expulsion. H. Gross (**Gallia Judaica**, p. 534) provided 1385 as the date of the polemic without any basis offered to the reader. The most elaborate dating is made by Hershman (**Rabbi Isaac ben Sheshet . . .** , p. 28

n. 5, p. 26 n. 46 and p. 231) where he reached the conclusion that the conflict must be dated around 1386.

We arrive at the same conclusions with a different documentation. At the end of the letter sent by bar Sheshet to Johanan (**Responsa** . . . n° 272), follows the mention "of what was written on the letter" with the name "The Rabbi, Our Master, Johanan . . . son of Mattathias . . . Provins."

Provins was read by H. Graetz (**Geschichte der Juden** . . . , Leipzig 4th ed., p. 8) as **provenci** and the same theory is found in Brüll ("Das Geschlecht der Trêves . . . ," p. 91). In fact Johanan is mentioned in **Provins** (Ile-de-France) in the following document:

> "Jehan du Vaul, sergent du roy nostre seigneur demorans à Troies confesse avoir recehu de Eliot de Suerre, juif demorans a Diion, pour et en nom de maistre **Jehanen, juif maistre de la loy demorans à Provins**, la somme de cent francs d'or . . . " Archives départementales de la Côte d'Or: B 11293.36v.B (**1386**, 15 October).

Johanan is also mentioned in Troyes around 1382, cf. J. Simonnet, "Juifs et Lombards," **Mémoires de l'Académie impériale des sciences, arts et belles-lettres de Dijon**, 2e serie, XIII (1866), p. 195.

30 We have record of a dozen of his loans, but most of them concerned only two debitors. The first mention is dated 1385, 6 June (Archives départementales de la Côte d'Or: B 11301.55r.A).

31 Archives départementales de la Côte d'Or: B 11302.52.v.D (1387, 26 April).

32 Segre, "Testimonianze . . . ," p. 392 (n° 378) n. 2 and p. 405 (n° 411) in 1394.

33 **Responsa** . . . n° 268, p. 147.

34 **Responsa** . . . n° 212, p. 111.

35 Segre, "Testimonianze . . . ," p. 395 (n° 388) in 1390.

36 Segre, "Testimonianze . . . ," p. 396 (n° 390) in 1391.

37 Segre, "Testimonianze . . . ," p. 376 identifies **Luenco** or Loant with "Louan, Villiers-Saint Georges, Provins, Seine-et-Marne." Louhans (in the département of Saone-et-Loire) is more likely, cf. also Gross, **Gallia Judaica**, pp. 272-273.

38 Segre, "Testimonianze . . . ," p. 408 (n° 421) in 1391.

39 **Responsa** . . . n° 270, p. 147.

40 Segre, "Testimonianze . . . ," p. 379 (n° 344) in 1387. Samson of Louhans played an important role in redeeming pawned jewels and dresses of the rulers of Savoy to a Jew in Strasbourg and his wife (Segre, "Testimonianze . . . ,' p. 375 [n° 331] in 1386), widowed since 1389 (Segre, "Testimonianze . . . ," p. 390 [n° 374]). She is also called Rael of Strasbourg (p. 397 [n° 393] in 1391 and p. 400 [n° 402] in 1392).

41 Segre, "Testimonianze . . . ," p. 381 (n° 349) in 1387.

42 Cf. Schwarzfuchs, **Origine et développement du rabbinat . . .** , p. 63.

43 **Responsa . . .** n° 270, p. 147, cf. above n. 24.

44 On the close administrative relationship between France and Burgundy, see my article "Le statut forain; marchands étrangers, Lombards et Juifs en France royale et en Bourgogne (seconde moitié du XIVe siècle)," **Revue historique de droit francais et étranger**, vol. 61 (1983), pp. 7-24.

"THE EASTERN DAWN OF WISDOM":
THE PROBLEM OF THE RELATION BETWEEN
ISLAMIC AND JEWISH MYSTICISM

David S. Ariel

Judaism and Islam exerted a profound influence upon each other in the period between the rise of Islam around 630 and the fall of Constantinople in 1453. Almost in spite of themselves, Judaism and Islam absorbed, assimilated and transformed elements of the neighboring cultures with which they came into contact. The depth of this influence was generally minimized, however, by the recipient in order to maintain a sense of cultural homogeneity and to avoid the admission of innovation, the enemy of tradition. This process operated, in different ways, within Judaism and Islam.

The process of religious interaction between Islam and Judaism is governed by the criterion of "vested originality." According to this principle, an innovation or importation is not merely retrojected upon an existing tradition but is placed under the absolute control of an accepted religious symbol. For an innovation in Judaism or Islam to be accepted as part of the tradition, it must be subsumed under an authoritative image and accepted as such. Examples of this type of response to innovation can be seen in the pietistic and mystical trends of medieval Islam and Judaism.

In this essay, the problem of interaction between Islam and Judaism in the area of mysticism will be considered. In particular, discussion will focus on the dialectical nature of Jewish influence upon Islamic mysticism and Islamic influence upon Jewish mysticism. We will see how the origins of mystical systems in Judaism and Islam are related, in part, to external religious influences and how each, in turn, minimizes the extent of absorption through strategies of assimilation and vesting. Finally, we will suggest that an understanding of the origins of Jewish and Islamic mysticism requires further investigation into cross cultural religious interaction.

The Early Period

Considerable research has been devoted to the question of the extent of Jewish influence upon the origins of Islam. Since 1833, when Abraham Geiger published his thesis on the Jewish background of the **Quran**, there have been many attempts to demonstrate an affinity between Muhammad's religious outlook and the religion of Israel.[1] The prophet was undoubtedly well acquainted with Jewish oral lore based on Biblical and rabbinic legends as well as with some of the forms of Jewish practice common to Jewish tribes in the Hijaz in the seventh century. Muhammad may, in fact, have drawn inspiration for his understanding of personal piety and religious justice from tales he heard from Jews concerning the exemplary lives of the Hebrew prophets.

The Hebrew prophetic message concerning the moral recidivism of the ancient Israelites and the call for moral regeneration spoke to the contemporary situation in Arabia in which Muhammad found himself. The call to universal observance of a system of transcendentally ordained moral requirements lay at the very heart of his religious mission. He expected to transform the Arabian tribal social order into a community of faithful adherents through submission to the will of Allah.

Muhammad also wished to bring about the conversion of the local Jewish tribes on the grounds that Islam was the continuation of Biblical religion and the fulfillment of the Hebrew monotheistic mission.[2] His favorable attitude toward Judaism changed, however, when these powerful Jewish tribes rejected his efforts to consolidate them under his leadership. Consequently, Muhammad's disappointment with the Jews is reflected in the many Quranic pronouncements on the moral perversities, treacheries, evasions and idolatries of the Jewish people even as it expresses indebtedness to Hebrew prophecy as the original monotheistic tradition.[3]

Jewish influence upon Islam did not cease with the death of Muhammad and the attempts by his successors to differentiate between Islam and predecessor religions. Many studies in the field have shown that Islam demonstrated a propensity toward absorbing teachings from other religions, including Judaism.[4] The field of greatest Muslim-Jewish religious interaction took place around Baghdad, which was the chief center of Jewish rabbinic learning in the period after 635.

Recent studies in Islamic mysticism have begun to explore the influence of Judaism upon early Islamic pietism and Sufism. Muslim sages of the first three generations (632-750) were familiar with Biblical and rabbinic legends through their acquaintance with literate Jewish converts to Islam who possessed a detailed knowledge of **midrashim** and rabbinic legends. These early converts, especially of the second generation, such as Wahb b. Munabbih (654-732), contributed to the dissemination of legends, known as **Isrāʾīliyāt**, concerning the **Banū Isrāʾīl**, the pious men of ancient Israel.[5] These legends were paradigmatic of true spirituality for early Islamic pietists and mystics. Wahb's contemporary, Ḥassan Baṣri, (d. 728) "the patriarch of Muslim mysticism,"[6] introduced numerous **Isrāʾīliyāt** legends which served as the basis for Islamic devotional and mystical notions of piety. The earliest biographer of Muhammad, Muḥammad b. Isḥaq, collected many of the **Isrāʾīliyāt**, which he attributed to "the people of the Book," (**ʾahl al-kitāb**) and "the people of the Torah" (**ʾahl al-thawrāt**). He was severely criticized by his contemporaries for accentuating the Jewish influences upon the prophet.[7]

An important source for **Isrāʾīliyāt** legends and, therefore, of the nature of Jewish influence upon Islamic mysticism, is the collection of Malik b. Dinar of Baṣra, (d. 748), a Muslim pietist of the third generation and a disciple of Ḥassan Ḅasri. Some of Malik's **Isrāʾīliyāt** were preserved in Abu Nuʿaim of Isfahan's **Ḥilyat al-ʾAwliyāʾ** ("Nature of the Holy Men") of which S. D. Goitein published portions.[8] Goitein has shown that Malik turned to the **Isrāʾīliyāt** and to Jewish sources--**Torah (al-thawrāt)** by which he means Torah and midrashic literature, **Psalms (al-zabar)** and wisdom literature **(kutub al-ḥikmah)**--rather than the well-known **ḥadīth** of the life of the prophet for his model of Muslim devotion and piety. Malik's acquaintance with Jewish sources included familiarity with legends, parables and didactic stories concerning the piety, moral conduct and soteriology of the pietists of the Jewish tradition particularly Abraham, Moses and David. The thirteenth century Jewish pietist, Abraham, the son of Moses Maimonides, who incorporated several Sufi devotions into Jewish practice, was not far off the mark when he observed, in defense of his own practices, that the Sufi virtues of **walīya** ("piety") were native to Judaism from which they were adopted by Muslims.[9]

Perhaps an answer to the question of why Malik preferred **Isrā'īliyāt** to **ḥadīth** will help to explain the conditions under which religious interaction may take place. No doubt, the attempt to convert Jews to Islam contributed to a willingness to proffer models of Jewish piety and to appropriate them as part of Islam. But this does not explain Malik's avoidance of Quranic passages and **ḥadīth** which could have served the same purpose.

The answer to the question lies within the tendencies of the second and third generation of Islam. The opposition of the Khalif ʿUmar to recording **sunnah** ("traditions") reflected a general reluctance to expand the corpus of **ḥadīth** at a time when the **Quran** text was being established. This was based on a concern that **sunnah** might achieve a status equal to that of the **Quran.**[10] This view is reflected in the restrictions against writing down new **ḥadīth** and in the emphasis on **Quran** recitation. The strictures against reliance upon **ḥadīth** led the early pietists, including Ḥassan Baṣri and Malik b. Dinar, to turn to other sources of legitimacy. The sense of veneration for the Hebrew prophets, the presence of Jewish converts around Baghdad and the desire to encourage further conversion led to an unusual openness to Jewish sources. The receptivity to Biblical and rabbinic legends of exemplary spirituality, conceived under the broad heading of **Torah,** as in the case of Malik, made it possible for early Muslims to turn to Jewish models of piety without posing a challenge to the authority of the **Quran.**

The decline of the **Isrā'īliyāt** tradition and the philo-Judaism of the first three generations followed the standardization of the Quranic text and the exclusion of **ḥadīth** from the scriptural canon. By 750, **Isrā'īliyāt** had been effectively assimilated by Islamic pietism and quickly fell into desuetude when the pursuit of Jewish traditions became taboo.

The Later Record

The historical record is replete with subsequent religious interaction and devotional relationships between Muslims and Jews. From the time of the Islamic conquest until the rise of the Mamluk Dynasty, (c. 1250), Jews around Baṣra, Kufa and Baghdad enjoyed a high degree of religious tolerance and self-government.[11] There is ample evidence, for example, of the appearance of "an interconfessional outlook"[12] in which the differences separating the confessional religions were subsumed under the conception of a genuinely universal Islam in which piety is found in equal measure among Jews, Christians and Muslims. Abu Ali ibn Hud, a thirteenth century Damascene Sufi of Andalusian origins, was known to have taught Maimonides' **Guide of the Perplexed** to Jewish students. He is described in al-Kutubi's **Fawāt al-Wafajāt** as wearing an ill-concealed Jewish headcovering under his turban. When asked to give spiritual guidance to a seeker, he asked: "Upon which road: the Mosaic, the Christian, or the Muslim?"[13]

Although the interconfessional outlook is rarely as explicit as in the case of ibn Hud, it is apparent that the area around Baghdad between 635 and 1258 was a center of fertile religious interaction between Muslims and Jews. Still, many historians of Judaism have concluded that the influence of Islam upon the devotional life of the Jews is minimal prior to the thirteenth century. Studies of Baḥya ibn Paquda's **Kitāb Farāʾiḍ al-Qulūb** cite this as the sole example of the adoption of Sufi **ʾaḥwāl** ("states") as religious virtues and the incorporation of **bāṭiniyya**, inner spirituality, into Judaism.[14] Others have argued that Bahya's pietism differs profoundly from Sufism in that it contains no element of ecstatic mysticism and resonates more to the native Jewish traditions of **ḥasīdūt** than to Sufism.[15]

The earliest recorded case of an overt attempt to synthesize Sufism and Jewish pietism is the writing of Abraham Maimonides' **Kifāyat al-ʿĀbidīn**, written around 1220. The composition of this work coincides with the appearance of the Kabbalah in Provence and Castille. There is, however, no direct or indirect relation between the Sufism of Abraham Maimonides and the Kabbalah other than a mutual indebtedness to common literary ancestors including Baḥya and Moses Maimonides. Despite attempts to portray Abraham as a genuine mystic,[16] his writings indicate only a pietistic tendency and an inclination to incorporate minor ritual adjustments into Judaism from Islam.[17]

Subsequent attempts to integrate Judaism and Sufism are more common. Studies by Franz Rosenthal and Shlomo Goitein detail several instances of Jewish Sufism after 1200.[18] They also provide a brief guide to some of the manuscripts in the Geniza collection of Jewish Sufi writings and Hebrew translations of Sufi works.[19]

New Evidence for Islamic Influence on German Pietism

To what extent has Islamic pietism and mysticism had an influence upon Judaism prior to the thirteenth century? Gershom Scholem has argued that Islam contributed nothing to the development of the Kabbalah. In his exhaustive study of the origins of the Kabbalah in Provence and Castille at the beginning of the thirteenth century, he identified several pseudepigraphic works which were attributed to well-known Jewish sages of an earlier period who lived in the Islamic world.[20] However, he denied that these texts represented genuine Islamic influences. Scholem concluded that "the thesis that Kabbalah stands in historical relation with Islamic Sufism and derives from it cannot be taken very seriously."[21] Marshall Hodgson also explains that "we know relatively little about Christian mysticism within Islamdom in this period [i.e., 945-1273] and almost nothing about Jewish (mysticism)."[22] After noting that Jewish mysticism appears to have certain affinities with Sufism including a gnostic orientation and philosophic terminology, he concludes that it is impossible to determine the depth and extent of Islamic influence upon Jewish mysticism. Although Kabbalah does not derive from Sufism, the influence of Islamic mysticism upon Jewish mystical traditions originating in the Muslim world is greater than either Scholem or Hodgson recognized.

The writings of Shem Ṭob ibn Shem Ṭob, the fifteenth century Hispano-Jewish Kabbalist and critic of Jewish philosophy, contain three brief Hebrew texts which were ostensibly written much earlier and which provide valuable material for answering the question of Islamic influences upon Jewish mysticism. The Hebrew style of these passages is that of early thirteenth-century Provencal kabbalistic literature. These texts, themselves, purport to be even older than the thirteenth century. They were, in fact, composed around 1200 in Provence although they reflect even earlier traditions.[23] The first text, not preserved anywhere else, is attributed to a group of unnamed Jewish sages from the area around Baghdad during the tenth century. The second text, also known only through quotations from the writings of Shem Ṭob ibn Shem Ṭob, is attributed to Hai ben Sherira Ga'on, the late tenth century **ra'īs** (Ga'on) of the Jewish community who resided in the area around Baghdad.

The first of these texts, known as "the tradition of wisdom," (**masōret ha-ḥokhmāh**) is of historical importance. It presents a chain of tradition in the manner of early **tafsīr** ("commentary") and Sufi **'isnād** ("chains of tradition") and describes a process of transmission of esoteric Jewish wisdom from the major rabbinic academy in Babylonia during the Abbasid period through Italy, Germany and provence where Kabbalah originated. It traces a line of development from an improbable sage named Rav Qashisha (or "an elder sage") from the academy at Mata Meḥasya, near Baghdad, who relocated to Apulia, Italy. The text states that Rav Qashisha taught his student, Judah the Pious, who came to Italy from Provence. The passage reads as follows: "A great Ga'on, Rav Qashisha from the seed of the **Ge'onim**, the elders of the academy, taught Torah in Apulia where he died. He transmitted this wisdom in a small book, which he gathered in a brief manner, and which he wrote in honor of his pupil, Judah the Pious, who came from Corbeil to learn from him."[24]

Who are the individuals who appear in this tradition? Rav Qashisha is an otherwise unknown sage who is said to be a member of the illustrious academy of Mata Meḥasya. Judah the Pious is known as the leading figure of the German Jewish pietist movement of the late twelfth and early thirteenth century known as **Ḥasidei Ashkenaz.** There is no historical evidence other than this passage to suggest that Judah came from Provence or that he spent time in Italy. Most medieval sources claim that his ancestors came from Italy but that he himself lived all his life in Germany. Finally, this passage states that his supposed teacher, Qashisha, gathered together earlier sources of esoteric wisdom in an unnamed book which he composed for Judah who then assumedly returned to his home, whether Provence or Germany, and passed this book on to his disciples.

What is known about the historical assertions contained in this passage? Mata Meḥasya was often identified with Sura, the seat of the Babylonian Gaonate near Baghdad, until the latter was moved to Baghdad in the tenth century.[25] Baghdad itself was the thriving center of Islamic culture, the seat of the Abbasid Khalifate. The forty thousand Jews of Baghdad enjoyed a high degree of prosperity, religious tolerance, autonomy, self-government and integration within the cultural and intellectual life of the community during this period. Members of the academy at Mata Mehasya were known to have been adept at certain mystical practices and to have enjoyed close ties with certain Muslim pietists.[26]

The Italian region of Apulia, where Rav Qashisha is said to have relocated from Baghdad around the early twelfth century is also known to have been a center of Jewish mystical learning dating from the ninth century. The eleventh century Hebrew **Chronicle of Aḥimaaz** states that another sage from Baghdad, Abu Aharon, settled in Apulia in the ninth century and taught his mysticism to the Kalonymide family who brought these teachings to Germany.[27] Judah the Pious was a descendant of this Kalonymide family. Despite the unlikelihood of Judah ever having studied in Apulia, that city appears in several accounts as a center of mystical activity and as the point of entry into Europe of Jewish mystical teachings which originated around Baghdad. The Provencal town of Corbeil appears in many of the earliest kabbalistic accounts as one of the first centers in which the Kabbalah appeared and the place in which a good deal of contact between early kabbalists and German pietists took place.[28]

Although the details of the line of development from Mata Meḥasya, Apulia, Germany and Provence differ from other accounts, the general historical picture of the ways in which certain mystical traditions came from Baghdad to Italy, Germany and Provence is attested to in other sources and corroborated by this important account. If this account is correct, it should be possible to identify in the writings of the **Ḥasidei Ashkenaz** and the earliest Provencal kabbalists early mystical teachings which originated around Baghdad.

German Ḥasidism stressed the virtues of saintliness, equanimity, indifference to the vicissitudes of life, asceticism and penitence.[29] Scholarly studies have pointed out the affinity between these teachings and those of the contemporary Franciscans.[30] It is, however, possible to identify specific traces of Islamic influences in the writings of the German

Ḥasidim.[31] Popular Sufi anecdotes and legends which exemplify the virtues of a saint appear in Judaized form in **Sefer Ḥasidim** (The Book of the Pious").[32] These materials seem to be based on legends of Muslim pietists and Sufis. Their appearance can be explained only in reference to a line of transmission originating in the Islamic east.

In a similar manner, Jewish mystical traditions originating in the Muslim world, particularly around Baghdad, can be discerned in the earliest records of the Kabbalah of Provence. Gershom Scholem has shown that **Sefer ha-Bahir**, ("The Book of Clear Light"), the first kabbalistic text, was composed around the turn of the thirteenth century in Provence partially on the basis of earlier mystical and esoteric fragments of a work of angelology and demonology called **Raza Rabba** ("The Great Secret"). **Raza Rabba**, an Aramaic text, in fact, was known among circles of Jewish sages around Baghdad, including Hai ben Sherira Gaʾon, in the tenth century. It was also read by German Ḥasidim of the late twelfth century who were likely responsible for its reception in Provence.[33] Now, the "tradition of wisdom" states that Rav Qashisha, in the twelfth century, gathered together a book based on earlier sources and transmitted it to Judah the Pious who passed it on to his own disciples. In this book the very same **Raza Rabba** which Hai Gaʾon knew in the tenth century and which reappears in the late twelfth century among German Ḥasidim and the first Provencal kabbalists? At the very least, the existence of the chain of tradition from Baghdad, Italy, Germany and Provence coincides with the facts surrounding the transmission of the **Raza Rabba**, the proto-text of the **Sefer ha-Bahir**, from an Islamic milieu to the Jews of Christian Europe.

A Text on Mystical Calligraphy

So far, we have suggested the likelihood that certain elements of German Hasidism and the Provencal Kabbalah had their origins in the area around Baghdad. Is it possible to discern a specifically Islamic mystical content in these sources? The second Hebrew passage, which also dates from early thirteenth century Provence, is attributed to Hai ben Sherira Gaʾon, the Jewish sage who resided outside of Baghdad in the tenth century. Hai was an adept of an early form of Jewish mystical practice involving visionary and ecstatic experiences which involved a replication of the supposed ascent to the heavenly throne attributed to the Biblical prophet Ezekiel.[34] Such practices utilized magical divine names as passwords and immunization devices which would allow the mystic to ascend from one stage to the next without danger. Hai was acquainted with this tradition even though he rejected the theurgic manipulation of divine names for the purpose of influencing future events or for violation of the laws of nature.[35] The passage exhibits a direct link between the Provencal Kabbalah and Islamic traditions current around Baghdad in the tenth century.

This text describes a technique for the calligraphic inscription of the Tetragrammaton, the divine name. It begins with the following superscription:

> We find this language in the Responsum of the **Geʾonim**, in the name of the great **Gaʾon**, who lights the eyes of this Exile from east to west, our well-known Rabbi Hai, son of the **Gaʾon**, our Rabbi Sherira, the seed of the kings of the House of David, peace be upon him.[36]

The introduction to the calligraphic technique reads as follows:

> In earlier times in Jerusalem there was an elder--wise, learned in tradition (**mequbbāl**), and knowledgeable in the secrets of Torah--Rabbi Ḥanina by name, from the seed of the house of kings, from among the great men of Jerusalem, pious and perfect in his character. He was learned in the tradition of the forms of the holy letters and in their inscription. One of his pious students, who studied under him year after year, sent to our elders some of these forms. We found them engraved in their form and likeness on a thin parchment. The form of the four letters and their inscription is according to the tradition and instruction of the wise **Gaʾon** to his students.

After the description of the pointillistic technique,[37] the following colophon appears:

> This is what we heard from what was sent by our master, the **Gaʾon** (Hai), the light of the Exile, once or twice, to the great rabbi, the wise Rabbi Paltoi and to his esteemed academy, in secrecy, by promise, vow, and concealment. (It was brought) by the pious Talmud

scholar, modest in his character, the liturgist, and man of great authority . . . Rabbi Elijah ha-Babhli.

The introduction to this technique thus explains that it was sent from Jerusalem by a sage named Ḥaninah to Jewish sages around Baghdad, including Hai, who sent it on to his compatriots in Europe, probably Provence where this was written down. Ḥanina, often referred to as Ḥanuniah in early Kabbalistic texts,[38] is an otherwise unidentifiable figure portrayed as a Jerusalemite of noble descent. The identity of Elijah ha-Babhli is likewise unclear although it may refer to Elijah ben Solomon ha-Kohen, an eleventh century **Gaʾon** from Jerusalem. This passage suggests a line of tradition from Hanina to Paltoi to Elijah to Hai Gaʾon. The existence of such a chain of transmission finds no corroboration in any other text.

The use of magical names is common is talmudic literature, Syrian-Aramaic magical papyri, Jewish "throne mysticism" of the high middle ages, German Ḥasidism and the early Kabbalah. The specific form attributed to Hai, however, can be traced to Arabic calligraphic techniques known in Damascus and Baghdad during the ninth and tenth centuries.

Ibn Waḥshiyya, a ninth century Damascene, composed "The Book of Longing for Participation in Knowledge of the Symbols of Languages" (**Kitāb al-Shauq al-mustahām fī maʿrifat rumūz al-ʾaklām**) in which he presented a catalogue of ancient semitic, hellenistic, hermetic and astrological symbols. His writings were widely disseminated throughout the Middle East and were even known among Jews, such as Maimonides, who quoted him in the late twelfth century.[39] In the **Kitāb al-Shauq** we find a pointillistic technique of calligraphy ascribed to the ancient Nabateans. This technique is reproduced identically in the second Hebrew passage under consideration as a method for the writing of the Tetragrammaton.[40] The technique of magical and mystical calligraphy current among Muslims around Damascus and Baghdad beginning in the ninth century found its way into Jewish mystical traditions of the twelfth and thirteenth centuries.

The technique of mystical calligraphy in Islam is based on Sufi teachings on divine names. Is there a connection between this doctrine and the kabbalistic theory of divine names? The kabbalistic theory of divine language maintains that emanation is a linguistic process in which the means of divine expression is the medium of language. Kabbalists explain this process whereby the **Sefīrōt** are the linguistic expression of God since speech is a process of auto-representation. Each individual **Sefīrāh** constitutes a stage in the process of the unfolding of divine thought and speech. As the intellectual process of emanation continues, God's wisdom culminates in the linguistic expression of wisdom in the Torah. Divine language finally becomes the language of Scripture so that the Torah is ultimately the repository of divine wisdom and the final stage in the process of auto-representation.[41]

The initial moment in the process of divine speech is the act whereby God gives himself His own Name, the Tetragrammaton. All other names are elaborations of this original name and come about through the unfolding of divine language, that is, through the emanation of the **Sefīrōt**. The **Sefīrōt** are, therefore, the divine names and these names are essential names, inseparable from the essence of God. This conception parallels Islamic teachings of divine names and represents a Jewish variation of the Sufi doctrine of mystical names.

Light Mysticism and the "East"

The passage on mystical calligraphy specifically asserts that Jewish wisdom, that is, Kabbalah, originated in the "east," a theory introduced in regard to the origin of Islamic esoteric doctrines by ibn Waḥshiyya and ibn Sina but elaborated by Suhrawardi as the doctrine of "eastern wisdom" or "illuminationism" in his **Ḥikmat al-ʾIshrāq** in the twelfth century.[42] The superscription to this Hebrew passage describes Hai ben Sherira, the alleged author of the passage, as "the great Gaon who lights the eyes of the Diaspora from east to west." This is a Jewish variation of Suhrawardi's own notion of the primacy of "eastern wisdom" in regard to the "western exile," which became known to the Jews in Provence through Hebrew translations of Suhrawardi's writings.

Suhrawardi elaborated a system of "light mysticism" according to which the deity is "pure light" beyond all positive determination and is causative of all existent things which are themselves constituted as lights. This very same Hebrew passage which begins with an **ʾishrāq** or oriental superscription goes on to describe the divine realm as a pleroma of "spiritual lights" which are interposed between the absolute deity and the world. These lights--"the internal, primordial light" (**ʾōr penīmī qadmōn**), "the clear light" (**ʾōr ṣāḥ**), and "the polished light" (**ʾōr meṣuḥṣāḥ**)--generate subsequent "spiritual, pure and internal lights."[43] This elaborate scheme of divine light mysticism entered the Kabbalah through illuminationist or Suhrawardian sources rather than by way of neo-Platonism. Neo-Platonism adopts the symbol of light as a metaphor for the description of the process of emanation not as an actual theory of being, as we find here and in the case of Suhrawardi. Nevertheless, this **ʾishrāq** notion was incorporated into the neo-Platonic hierarchy of the early Kabbalah and, thus, its origin has been somewhat obscured.

The way in which Suhrawardi's notion of illumination and "eastern wisdom" has been incorporated within the kabbalistic scheme of neo-Platonic emanation and gnostic divine powers is evident in the **Sefer ha-Bahir** which, as we have already seen, contains earlier strata which originate in an Islamic milieu. Suhrawardi, in the **Ḥikmat al-ʾIshrāq**, also developed the opposition of "east" and "west" in a non-geographical sense. Since the "east" is equated with the world of divine lights beyond the sphere of the fixed stars and the "west" with the terrestrial realm, "orient" and "occident" are located on a vertical, rather than a horizontal, plane. We find the same orientation in one of the passages in **Sefer ha-Bahir.** "East" and "west" are described as two distinct stages of being within God, a gnostic conception, which stand in a vertical relation to each other. "East," which is higher on the vertical plane, is the archetypal seed of the Jewish people and the lower "west" is the field in which this seed is planted.[44] In this passage we have the elements of "orient" and "occident" on a vertical axis coupled with a Judaized form of the notion that the seeds of wisdom originate in the "east" and bear fruit in the "west." In many other passages of **Sefer ha-Bahir,** which undoubtedly reflect the eclectic nature of the world and the diversity of the sources upon which it drew, an elaborate system of light mysticism is presented alongside gnostic descriptions of the divine powers. The same vertical scheme of lights is presented in which the first light, "the light of perfect life" (**ʾōr ha-ḥayyīm shelēmīm**),[45] is called "the clear light" (ʾōr bāhīr),[46] as is the third light which is also "the primal light" out of which the world is formed.[47]

Conclusions

These earliest kabbalistic texts appeared in Provence around the beginning of the thirteenth century even though they were preserved in works, such as the writings of Shem Ṭob ibn Shem Ṭob, which were composed much later. The first text, "the tradition of wisdom," and the second text, ascribed to Hai Gaʾon of the tenth century, are apparently thirteenth-century writings which purport to be much older. Nevertheless, the fact that these texts were composed in the earliest period of the Kabbalah does not lead us to the conclusion that they are wholly pseudepigraphic. In both of these passages, and in the selections from **Sefer ha-Bahir** which were analyzed, the existence of a probable line of transmission of Jewish esoteric mystical teachings, which originated in Jewish circles around Baghdad in the tenth century and reached the Ḥasidim of Germany and the first Kabbalists of Provence, has been proposed. We have seen in several cases, as well, that these teachings which appeared among Jewish groups derived from Islamic Sufi, magical and illuminationist sources of the tenth through twelfth centuries. These teachings, which were transformed into Judaized form around Baghdad or in the course of their transmission to Europe, reflect a high degree of interaction among Muslim and Jewish pietists and mystics.

The degree of influence of Jewish pietism upon Islamic mysticism and the extent of Islamic influence upon the origins of Jewish mysticism are greater than has generally been recognized by historians of Islam and Judaism. In the case of Sufi pietism and mysticism, the Islamicization of Jewish concepts of **ḥasīdūt** was made possible because of the respected position of predecessor monotheistic traditions within early Islam. The overt philo-Judaism of the first three generations of Islam came to an end with the establishment of the canon of the **Quran**. The virtues of **ḥasīdūt** were no longer accepted as the legacy of the **Banū Israʾīl** but were not subsumed under the absolute authority of the Sufi virtues of **walīya**.

The origins of Jewish mysticism are likewise illustrative. The genesis of Kabbalah is rooted, in part, in a pre-history of Islamic mystical teachings which were conveyed to Jewish pietists living around Baghdad in the ninth through twelfth centuries and passed on to Europe by way of German Hasidism and Provencal Kabbalah in the twelfth and thirteenth centuries. The Islamic techniques of mystical calligraphy and the conceptions of holy names and illuminationism thus entered Jewish mysticism and were subsumed under the authority of the tradition of Hebrew letter symbolism. Perhaps the reason for the smooth incorporation into Judaism lies in the fact that they also represented native Jewish traditions which were preserved by pre-Islamic Jewish pietists.

The full account of interaction between Jewish and Islamic mysticism remains to be written. This paper is intended to suggest possible lines of further investigation into the traditions of the **Banū Isrāʾīl**, the appearance of Sufi virtues of **walīya** in German Ḥasidism, the questions of Islamic traditions assimilated into Judaism around Baghdad and the resurgence of Jewish Sufism in the thirteenth century. The solutions to these problems will ultimately tell us a good deal about the process of religious interaction between Islam and Judaism.

NOTES

1 A. Geiger, **Judaism and Islam** (New York, 1970), intro. See also S. D. Goitein, **Jews and Arabs** (New York, 1954), pp. 52-58.

2 See Sura 2:40, 57, 64, 122; 3:64; 4:23; 5:3, 26, 32; 29:41.

3 See Sura 2:86; 5:70, 82; 9:29; 59:2.

4 S. D. Goitein, **op. cit.**, pp. 125ff.

5 G. D. Newby, "Tafsīr Isrā'īliyāt," **Journal of the American Academy of Religion** 47 (1979), pp. 685-697, discusses the role of **mawālī** in early Islam in connection with the incorporation of **Isrā'īliyāt** legends in **Quran** commentaries. Newby credits the introduction of Isra iliyat also to Ubayy b. Kaʿb, Kaʿb al-Aḥbar, Abu Hurayra, Abdullah b. ʿAmr al-ʿAs, and the ibn Abbas.

6 A. M. Schimmel, **Mystical Dimensions of Islam** (Chapel Hill, 1975), p. 30.

7 S. D. Goitein, "Isrā'īliyāt," **Tarbiz** 6 (1935), p. 89, n.2.

8 S. D. Goitein, **ibid.**, pp. 89-101, 510-522.

9 Abraham Maimonides, **The High Ways to Perfection**, ed. S. Rosenblatt (New York - Baltimore, 1927-1938), vol. 2, p. 253.

10 N. Abbot, **Studies in Arabic Literary Papyri** (Chicago, 1967), V. 2, p. 10.

11 E. Strauss (Ashtor), **Toledot Ha-Yehudim be-Miṣrayim ve-Suriah Taḥat Shilṭon ha-Mamelukim** (Jerusalem, 1944), v. 1, p. 47.

12 S. D. Goitein, "A Jewish Addict to Sufism," **Jewish Quarterly Review** 44 (1953), p. 39.

13 E. Strauss, **op. cit.**, V. 1, P. 352-353; see also I. Goldziher, "Ibn Hud, The Mohammedan Mystic, and the Jews of Damascus," **Jewish Quarterly Review** (O.S.) 6 (1894), pp. 218-220.

14 F. Rosenthal, "A Judaeo-Arabic Work Under Sufic Influence," **Hebrew Union College Annual** 15 (1940), p. 439.

15 D. Kaufman, "Torat ha-'Elohut shel R. Baḥya ibn Paquda," **Meḥqarim be-Sifrut ha-ʿIbhrit shel Yemei ha-Beinayyim** (Jerusalem, 1965), pp. 11-77.

16 Such is the view of Rosenblatt in Abraham Maimonides, **op. cit.**, v. 1, pp. 48 ff.; v. 2, p. 418. Rosenblatt's translation of **wuṣūl** as "mystical union" leads to the erroneous impression that Abraham Maimonides was an ecstatic mystic. The section on the meaning of **wuṣūl** is missing from the printed edition of Rosenblatt but is found in Bodleian Ms. Heb. d23 (Neubauer-Cowley

Cat. 2572). These eleven folios, however, are badly damaged and cannot be readily deciphered. The only major study, so far, of Abraham Maimonides is G. D. Cohen, "The Soteriology of R. Abraham Maimuni," **Proceedings of the American Academy of Jewish Research** 35 (1967), pp. 75-98: 36 (1968), pp. 33-56.

17 N. Wieder, **Islamic Influence on the Jewish Worship** (London, 1948) pp. 31 ff. For possible Sufi influences on A. Maimonides, see also Al-Qushayri, **Ar-Risāla fi ᶜIlm at-Taṣawwuf** (Cairo, 1911-1912); and F. Meier, "Qushayri's Tartīb as-Sulūk," **Oriens** 16 (1963).

18 F. Rosenthal, **op. cit.**, pp. 433-484, and S. D. Goiten, **op. cit.**

19 F. Rosenthal, **ibid.**, p. 438, n. 16. See also S. D. Goitein, **op. cit.**, p. 38. See also the extensive bibliography in P. Fenton, **The Treatise of the Pool** (London, 1981), pp. 140-146.

20 G. Scholem, **Ursprung und Anfänge der Kabbala** (Berlin, 1962), pp. 308 ff.

21 G. Scholem, **ibid.**, p. 4 referring to F. A. Tholuck, **Commentatio de vi, quam graeca philosophia in theologia tum muhammedanorum tum Judaeorum exercuerit.** II. Particula: De ortu Cabbalae (Hamburg, 1837).

22 M.G.S. Hodgson, **The Venture of Islam** (Chicago, 1974), v. 2, p. 202.

23 These texts are generally identifed as belonging to the **ᶜIyyun** school. For a study of these texts see Scholem, **op. cit.**, pp. 273-292. For **ᶜIyyun** passages which appear in the writings of Shem Ṭob, see D. Ariel, **Shem Ṭob ibn Shem Ṭob's Kabbalistic Critique of Jewish Philosophy** (Waltham, 1981), unpublished diss., p. 28-35.

24 The text appears in Shem Ṭob's **Sefer ha-ʾEmunot** (Ferrara, 1556), IV:14. I have corrected the text on the basis of a superior manuscript, JTS Micr. 1969, fol. 47v-48r. This text may be preserved in only one other source. Scholem, in "Peraqim me-Toledot Sifrut ha-Qabbalah," **Kiryat Sefer** 7 (1930-1931), p. 262, n. 1, states that this work also appears in Shem Ṭob Ibn Gaʾon's **Sefer Baddei ha-ʾAron** (Oxford Ms. 1630', fol. 1-89b). It does not, however, appear in the printed edition of this work published as **Sefer Tagin** (Paris, 1866) by Senior Sachs and by M. Steinschneider in **Catalogue Bodleiana**, column 2520 and **Catalogue Paris**, 840.

25 B. Lewin, **Rav Sherira Gaʾon** (Jaffa, 1917), p. 21, n. 3.

26 E. Strauss, **op. cit.**, v. 1, p. 47.

27 Y. Dan, **Torat ha-Sod Shel Ḥasidei Ashkenaz** (Jerusalem, 1968), p. 14, n. 1. M. Saltzman, **The Chronicle of Aḥimaaz** (New York, 1966), pp. 63, 76 (English section). Another version suggests that Hai ben Sherira, the tenth century Gaʾon of Pumbedita, was the source of this esoteric wisdom. See H. Gross, "Zwei Kabbalistische Traditionsketten des R. Eleasar aus Worms," **Monatsschrift für Geschichte und Wissenschaft des Judentums** 49 (1905), pp. 692-700.

28 G. Scholem, **Reshit ha-Qabbalah** (Jerusalem, 1948), p. 163, n. 3.

29 See G. Scholem, **Major Trends of Jewish Mysticism** (New York, 1941), pp. 80-118.

30 Y. Baer, "Ha-Megammah ha-Datit veha-Ḥebhratit shel **Sefer Ḥasidim**," **Zion** 3 (1938), pp. 1-50.

31 G. Scholem, **op. cit.**, pp. 96, 102.

32 Jehuda Wistinetzki, ed., **Sefer Ḥasidim** (Frankfurt a. M., 1924), p. 6 and passim on "ᶜAbhadim."

33 G. Scholem, **Ursprung und Anfänge**, p. 96.

34 Y. Dan, **op. cit.**, pp. 124 ff.

35 B. Lewin, **Osar ha-Geʾonim**, v. 4 (Hagiga), (Haifa, 1928) pp. 16-27.

36 Quoted in D. Ariel, **op. cit.**, pp. 18-19 (Hebrew section). According to Scholem in **Ursprung und Anfänge**, p. 285, n. 228, this entire passage was published by Kabak in **Jeschurun** 3 (1859), pp. 55-57. It does not, however, appear there.

37 See also Scholem, **op. cit.**, p. 291.

38 Ḥanina is also referred to as Ḥanuniah in other **ᶜIyyun** texts. See Scholem, **op. cit.**, p. 290, n. 240.

39 See Pines, S. and Strauss, L., **The Guide of the Perplexed** (Chicago, 1963), p. 518.

40 See J. Hammer, **Ancient Alphabets and Hieroglyphic Characters** (London, 1806), p. 101.

41 See G. Scholem, "The Name of God and the Linguistic Theory of the Kabbala," **Diogenes** 79 (1972), pp. 59-80; 80 (1972), pp. 164-194, and D. Ariel, **op. cit.**, pp. 140 ff.

42 This notion was actually introduced by ibn Waḥshiyya and ibn Sina and elaborated by Suhrawardi. See A. M. Schimmel, **op. cit.**, p. 262. S. H. Nasr, **Three Muslim Sages** (New York, 1964), pp. 65 ff., 82.

43 Quoted in D. Ariel, **op. cit.**, p. 78 (Hebrew section). Another version of the text is quoted in A. Jellinek, **Beiträge zur Geschichte der Kabbala** II (Leipsig, 1852), pp. 11-14.

44 G. Scholem, **Das Buch Bahir** (Leipsig, 1923), n. 104.

45 G. Scholem, **ibid.**, n. 88.

46 G. Scholem, **ibid.**, n. 1.

47 G. Scholem, **ibid.**, n. 97.

THE **HAQDAMAH** OF IMMANUEL OF ROME TO THE BOOK OF RUTH

Murray Rosenthal

The Jews of Franco-Germany and Spain contributed greatly to the development of Biblical studies during the Middle Ages. Personalities, such as Rashi, Rashbam and Nachmanides, are well-known. However, Jews of other lands also gave of themselves to the study of the Bible. Limited attention, for instance, has been accorded to the Jews of Italy, despite the fact that Italian soil has nurtured some of the most ancient Jewish communities in all of Europe.

Immanuel ben Solomon of Rome (ca. 1261 - ca. 1336) represents but one in a host of individuals who contributed to the Jewish interpretation of the Bible among Italian Jews prior to the Renaissance. His literary output was great and, as such, an exhaustive study lies beyond the scope of this present monograph. Instead, we shall endeavour to understand some of the forces at work in Immanuel's commentaries by investigating a sampling of his exegesis of the Book of Ruth. However, before proceeding directly to the commentary itself, let us first examine the historical context in which Immanuel lived.

Historical Background

The thirteenth century represents one of the most decisive turning-points in history due, in great measure, to important political,[1] economic[2] and cultural[3] shifts. It ushered in a period of internal, geopolitical consolidation. Energies expended for the sake of religious beliefs during the Crusades were not being channeled into the art of state-building. Feudalism had begun its decline, thus yielding to the new realities of nationhood.[4]

Yet, for all its attempts at consolidation, the thirteenth century remained an age of flux and instability. While religious and pietistic norms of the past were faithfully guarded, a newly-developing social order was making itself felt. The once arbitrary designations of lord and serf no longer applied, as society came to terms with concepts such as growth, freedom and hope.

Notwithstanding, society still meant a Christian society and growth, freedom and hope were comforting promises only to those who aligned themselves with the Church. The Jews of Europe, in the midst of this upheaval, found themselves in as precarious and uncertain a position as before. They remained subject to government strictures and had the dubious distinction of having to faithfully yield to the many decrees, doctrines and laws promulgated especially for them. Forming a religious and cultural minority within the general framework of Christian society, the Jewish presence posed unique theological, as well as practical, problems. These grew more acute and required greater attention as Europe experienced the birthpangs of a new reality; the reality of Church and State.

The greatest demonstration of this reality manifested itself in Italy. During the first half of the thirteenth century, the Church waged an on-going battle with the most infamous of its detractors, Frederick II. Strategically, Frederick's control of Italy south of the Papal States, as well as his control of Germany, made the Papal borders vulnerable and subject to attack. In matters of religion, his orthodoxy was challenged as the Church sought to prove him a heretic. Eventually, he was excommunicated by Innocent III.

In an attempt to vindicate himself in light of these accusations, Frederick found a scapegoat in the Jews. By drawing attention away from himself, he was able to maintain a certain degree of credibility with the Church. Ironically, Frederick himself favoured the Jews inviting, for example, Jacob Anatoli of Marseilles to settle in Naples where, in 1224, a university was established and lectures on the Hebrew language were reportedly given. Nonetheless, it was the same Frederick who, in 1222 at Messina, acting upon the recommendations issued at The Fourth Lateran Council, decreed that the Jews of Sicily, Naples and Pisa distinguish themselves not only by wearing a badge, but by also allowing their beards to grow.[5] This kind of compliance with the authority of the Church placed the Jewish population in an uncertain situation, one that would continue throughout the thirteenth century.[6]

Given the ambiguous relationship that existed between Church and State, it is not surprising to encounter a similar phenomenon within the Church itself regarding the Jews. The promulgation of official Church policy was one matter, its acceptance by the masses quite another due, in large measure, to the fact that the vast majority of the Christian population could not accept the Church's more moderate approach towards the Jews. Consequently, doctrinal issues were either misunderstood or not understood at all by the uneducated faithful.

The first glimpses of this ambivalence already surface in the Papal decrees of the twelfth century. A temperate attitude towards the Jews is expressed in the bull first issued by Calixtus II (1119-1124), beginning **Sicut Judaeis**,[7] which afforded the Jews protection from assaults against their persons, property, religious observances and conversionist pressures. On the other hand, a more hostile approach was advocated by The Third Lateran Council of 1179, presided over by Alexander III. Among other things, Jews could not own Christian slaves, and many of the privileges previously extended to them were nullified.[8]

With the dawning of the thirteenth century, this latter, less tolerant approach continued. In the 1230s, the Inquisition, under the supervision of the Dominican friars, began its investigations of the Jews. The repercussions of the Paris Disputation of 1240 soon reached Italy, where copies of the Talmud were seized and burned. The fanatical, religious fervour, occasioned by the Flagellants as they moved through Italy in 1260, placed the Jews in a dangerous situation.[9] In 1278, Jews in Lombardy were forced to attend conversionist sermons. Between 1265 and 1294, anywhere between 12,000 and 15,000 Jews were converted in southern Italy after sovereignty of the area passed from the Hohenstaufens to the Angevins. The new dynasty of Charles II, resigned to the reality of the Church's direct control and influence, developed the charge of a blood libel against the Jews of Trani which took nearly three decades to quell.[10]

Yet, in spite of these and other dark moments, the intellectual creativity of the Jews continued.[11] In Rome and other Italian cities and towns, Jewish notables, such as Menahem ben Solomon ben Isaac, Zeraḥyah ben Isaac ben Shealtiel Ḥen, Hillel ben Samuel of Verona and Isaiah ben Mali of Trani the Elder, wrote and researched in the areas of Biblical exegesis, philosophy, halakhah and liturgy. It was in this milieu that Immanuel of Rome wrote his commentary to the Book of Ruth.

Although influenced by and aware of the historical and cultural currents of his day, Immanuel does not deal with these in his commentary to the Book of Ruth. One can only speculate as to why this is, although the phenomenon itself is not new. Many commentators, both before and after Immanuel, made exegesis the focal point of their commentaries. The commentator's sole purpose was to explain the text without becoming involved in tangents. Of course, not all commentators subscribed to this approach. The fluidity and freshness in Jewish exegetical activity is directly related to the variable of priorities that each commentator assigns to his work. For Immanuel, at least, the historical, social, economic and political realities of his day could not be artifically dovetailed with the Biblical text so that it might appear natural. This, in fact, is true of the balance of Immanuel's exegetical output that has thus far been studied and published. It seems clear that any critiques that Immanuel formed and activities that he engaged in as a social observer were deliberately left for the **Maḥbarot.**[12]

The Manuscript

There is but one extant text of Immanuel's commentary to the Book of Ruth which forms part of the de Rossi collection, housed in the Biblioteca Palatina di Parma. The best description of the MS is given by G. B. de Rossi himself:[13]

> Psalms, Ruth, Lamentations and Esther with the Commentary of R. Immanuel son of Solomon and with an anonymous Dissertation upon the words, "The Tables, moreover, are the work of God, and the writing is the writing of God" [Exodus 32:16]. Parchment, quarto, 2 volumes and 2 columns, 15th century.
>
> The commentary is written in rabbinic letters, the sacred text partly in rabbinic, partly in square letters with points. The manuscript is most precious and of the greatest price because of the comments, which it exhibits, of the celebrated Immanuel on those four books, comments which are unedited and most rare, unknown even to all bibliographers. For, so far as I can see, both we and the literary writers of the Jews

> maintain profound silence about them. So far as the commentary on the Book of Ruth is concerned, I suspect and am almost certain that a certain R. Immanuel, who wrote a commentary on Ruth - a commentary which the Plantavitius manuscript [i.e., Jean Plantavit de la Pause (1576-1651), **Florilegium Rabbinicum** (Lodeve, 1645)] number 359, claims it has - and who is mentioned by Wolf [i.e., J. C. Wolf, **Bibliotheca Hebraea** (Hamburg, 1715)] under number 1785, vol. I, p. 947, is our Immanuel, and that the Plantavitius manuscript must be referred to him [i.e., to our Immanuel]. 149 Psalms are enumerated, and at their conclusion the word Chaiim [sic] is mentioned with points, without doubt for designating the name of the scribe. The dissertation of the anonymous author, which is added at the end of the second volume of the manuscript, has been written by another hand, nevertheless of the same antiquity as that [of Immanuel] and sometimes has supplied some supplements to the text of Immanuel.

Insofar as the designation **memb.** is concerned--translated here as "parchment," it should be noted that this term may simply be a generic reference, including vellum as well.

The MS has been paginated by a hand later than that of the original scribe. Page numbers appear in the lower right-hand corner of the recto pages and the lower left-hand corner of the verso pages. There are forty-one pages.

Verse and chapter numbers are not indicated, although each verse and its commentary are distinguishable by a few empty lines. Explanations of individual words and phrases are noted by the relevant catch-words from the Biblical verses themselves.

De Rossi informs us that the MS was written in the fifteenth century by one "Chaiim." We may speculate that our scribe is to be identifed with Chaim ben Isaac ha-Levi Ashkenazi who, while in the employ of Joseph ben Jacob Gunzenhauser and his son Azriel, assisted in the publication of Immanuel's commentary to Proverbs in Naples, 1487.[14] Judging from the hand in which the MS is written, southern Italy is a possible location.[15]

Along with Immanuel's commentary, there are notes that appear in the margins and, as far as can be adduced, are of a hand different than that of our scribe. In all, there are close to thirty.

The marginal notes do not deal with exegetical matters. Instead, they offer stylistic revisions of words and phrases in the commentary itself. Their function is to clarify and enhance the reader's understanding and appreciation of the ideas expressed in the commentary. They do not appear to reflect variations in other texts.

The **Haqdamah:** Mystical vs. **Peshaṭ**-Exegesis

Before beginning the commentary proper, Immanuel offers an introduction in which he discusses various interpretations given to the Book of Ruth. Although he is clearly writing an introduction, the word **haqdamah** is wanting in the MS as the title-word for this opening section.

The absence of the designation **haqdamah** is significant for, insofar as the literary genre of **haqdamah** is concerned, an introduction is either physically distinguishable and distinct from the commentary itself or else it is preceded, in MS editions, by the catch-word **haqdamah.** Here, however, neither of these situations obtains.

In mediaeval Hebrew literature--especially works written by Sefardic authors[16]--the **haqdamah** took the form of a preface appended to the halakhic, philosophical or exegetical tract being written. The author would state his motives in composing the word and would usually mention something about its contents. In time, the art of writing introductions developed to such a degree that it became a literary genre unto itself.

Immanuel wrote introductions to his commentaries on the Pentateuch, Proverbs and Song of Songs. These deal with the various ways--literal and philosophical/mystical--in which the Biblical text can be understood.

Immanuel's introduction to the Book of Ruth addresses itself to the tensions then surfacing between a literal, **peshaṭ**-exegesis of the text, on the one hand, and a kabbalistic approach, on the other.

The Kabbalah did not lie beyond the influence of philosophy. In the fourteenth century, the Kabbalah underwent something of a systemization with the application of the terms **kabbalah ᶜiyyunit**

--"speculative Kabbalah"--and **kabbalah ma^{c}asit**--"practical Kabbalah"--terms that had already been used by Maimonides in his division of philosophy into speculative and practical categories.[17]

Immanuel's intention of offering a literal approach, as outlined in the **haqdamah,** is realized quite faithfully in the commentary itself. Let us now present the **haqdamah** in its own right.[18]

The Translation

The Book of Ruth records the genealogy of David, peace be unto him. The text mentions his ancestry because he is the source of the Jewish monarchy. It would have sufficed had we only been informed of this at the end of the book where it is written, " And these are the generations of Peres: Peres begat Hesron" (4:18)--from that point on until the end of the book. However, the author mentioned the entire story because it brings to mind the good characteristics, the generosity and benevolence of Boaz, and the righteousness of Ruth the Moabitess and the pleasantness of her manner in clinging to her mother-in-law--as a consequence of which she foresook her people and her god--so that she might eventually cleave to the holy nation [of Israel]. The author likewise recounts the attributes of Naomi and the compassion that she demonstrated with her daughters-in-law when she said, "Go, return, each woman to her mother's house" (1:8), as well as her endeavours in trying to marry Ruth to Boaz. The author also reminds us of the great kindness that God rendered to Ruth because of her cleaving to the true God, namely, that she was privileged in having worthy offspring from which issued the king of Israel.

When you consider the entire Bible, there is not one story in any of the books that does not store great value concerning true opinions that affect belief, as well as the teaching of good opinions--to say nothing of those that have been lost because of the length of the Exile and the books that are no longer in our possession but which existed among the Jewish people since ancient times. Would that these books were in our possession today, not one single detail concerning anything written in any of the books of the Bible would have been lost to us. That is why this particular story was written according to the plain meaning among the other books of the Bible.

However, the Rabbis, of blessed memory, have reminded us, in the collection **Midrash Ruth,** of the mysteries of the world that exit in this book. They believed that, aside from the literal meaning that can be ascribed to the Book of Ruth, there exist, without any doubt, marvelous matters concerning the secrets of the soul that the imagination cannot grasp. In this regard, there exists no interpretation that is empty or meaningless--save those that are unknown to us because of our own limitations. It is very much analogous to the situation that obtains with the verses in the Account of Creation where the names of the four rivers are recorded (Genesis 2:10-14). No one in the world would argue that these verses should not be understood literally, since these rivers are known, as are their locations. Nonetheless, these same verses allude to marvelous matters. The same thing is true of the Book of Ruth, for even though the incidents recorded in it can be interpreted literally, there is no doubt that they also allude to hidden, divine secrets.

It seems to me that the Rabbis, peace be unto them, were moved to infuse the stories in the Book of Ruth with secrets and enigmas. The verse tells us, "And the name of the man was Elimelech and his wife's name was Naomi" (1:2). We are told that they had two sons and two daughters-in-law and that their son's names were Maḥlon and Chilyon and that those of the daughters-in-law were Orpah and Ruth. Concerning these individuals, we are told nothing save that they died, that is, that Elimelech and his two sons died, leaving Naomi alone with her two daughters-in-law. We are told that Orpah left her mother-in-law immediately and departed from her, while Ruth clung to her mother-in-law and that Oved issued from Ruth. The Rabbis, peace be unto them, thought that since the Book of Ruth mentions the passing of certain individuals and the incidents that befell those still alive, the story, albeit literal in its entirety, also alludes to what will happen to the soul after death. In this light, the figure of Elimelech represents something else, as does that of Naomi. So, too, is the situation with their two sons, Maḥlon and Chilyon: both represent other things. Orpah represents that thing which turns away after death, in the same way that she turned her back to her mother-in-law. Ruth represents the existent thing that is part of the soul of man, which gives the individual continuity after death.

These matters are the deepest of the deep. Not every person can understand them, only those privileged few whom God has designated "the ones who shine forth like the light of the heavens" (Daniel 12:3), those who are proficient in the science of Nature and what will follow after Nature and to whom the emotional and intellectual properties of the soul are most certainly known--to them alone has this wisdom been given as an inheritance. We, however, shall leave these matters to the proper authorities who can readily expound upon things of this nature. We shall, instead, satisfy ourselves with interpreting the verses according to their simple meaning while, at the same time, allowing room for those who will come after us to interpret.

NOTES

1 See Brian Pullan, **A History of Early Renaissance Italy: From the Mid-Thirteenth to the Mid-Fifteenth Century** (London, 1973), pp. 17-80, especially pp. 26-49.

2 For a good introductory source, see G. Luzzatto, **An Economic History of Italy from the Fall of the Roman Empire to the Beginning of the 16th Century**, trans. P. Jones (London, 1961), pp. 121-36.

3 F. A. Gregorovius, **Rome in the Middle Ages**, trans. Annie Hamilton (London, 1894-1902), VI, pp. 1-25.

4 With regard to Italy and national consciousness, see John Larner, **Italy in the Age of Dante and Petrarch, 1216-1380** (London/New York, 1980), pp. 1-15.

5 " . . . ut in differentia vestium et gestorum a Christianis discernantur." For the complete text, see Bartolomeo and Guiseppe Lagumina (eds.), **Codices diplomatico dei Giudei di Sicilia** (Palermo, 1885), I, p. 17, no. 19; J.L.A. Huillard-Breholles (ed.), **Historia Deiplomatica Frederici Secundi, sive constitutiones, privilegia, mandata, instrumenta quae supersunt istius imperatoris et filiorum ejus** (Paris, 1852), II, p. 178.

For the text of the Fourth Lateran Council, see Solomon Grayzel, **The Church and the Jews in the XIIIth Century: A Study of Their Relations During the years 1198-1254, Based on the Papal Letters and the Conciliar Decrees of the Period** (New York, 1966[2]), pp. 308-9.

6 A number of studies discuss the life and personality of Frederick II, including those by E. H. Kantorowicz, **Frederick the Second**, trans. E. O. Lorimer (London, 1957[2]) and T. C. Van Cleve, **The Emperor Frederick II of Hohenstaufen: Immutator Mundi** (Oxford, 1972).

7 Julius Aronius (ed.), **Regesten zur Geschichte der Juden im fraenkischen und deutschen Reiche bis zum Jahre 1273** (Berlin, 1902), no. 313a. Cf. Solomon Katz, "Gregory the Great and the Jews," **Jewish Quarterly Review** XXIV (1933/4), pp. 113-36; Solomon Grayzel, "The Papal Bull **Sicut Judeis,**" **Studies and Essays in Honor of Abraham Neuman** (Philadelphia, 1962), pp. 243-80.

8 Grayzel, **The Church**, pp. 296-7.

9 See Ariel Toaff, "Hints to a Messianic Movement in 1261," (Hebrew) **Bar-Ilan** XIV/XV (1977), pp. 114-22.

10 Joshua Starr, "The Mass Conversion of the Jews in Southern Italy (1290-1293)," **Speculum** XXI (1946), pp. 203-11.

11 Some scholars have suggested that the extent to which the Jews were involved in this creativity ought to be modified somewhat. Cf. Attilio Milano, "Italy," **Encyclopaedia Judaica,** IX, p. 1211, who asserts that Jewish scholars of the period

"interested themselves in various fields without predominating in any."

A similar sentiment is echoed by Gershom Scholem, "Kabbalah," **Encyclopaedia Judaica,** X, p. 537, with regard to the Italian Kabbalists:

> . . . there was little independence in Italian Kabbalah, and for a long time it consisted of no more than compilations and interpretations, following the **Zohar** and the **Ma'arekhet ha-Elohut,** and, to an even greater extent than in Spain itself, the writings of Abraham Abulafia.

The themes of persecution and suffering in Jewish history, on the one hand, and the continuation of Jewish learning and scholarship under these conditions, on the other, have formed the basis of an important debate among Jewish historiographers, the most noted being S. W. Baron and Yitzhak Baer. For a more complete treatment of the subject, see the references in B. S. Bachrach, **Early Medieval Jewish Policy in Western Europe** (Minneapolis, 1977), p. 144, note 2.

12 This may help to explain the rather weighted evidence against Immanuel that has been formulated by rabbinic authorities over the centuries. For a cursory survey, see Moshe Carmilly-Weinberger, **Censorship and Freedom of Expression in Jewish History** (New York, 1977), pp. 214-17. For the longest time, none of Immanuel's Biblical commentaries were published, thus resulting in a misrepresentation of Immanuel's personality and outlook. While it is true that the **Maḥbarot** couches certain ideas in language and phrase disturbing to certain rabbinic personalities, it ought to be remembered that these individuals did not have access to the Biblical commentaries also written by Immanuel. It has only been within the last century that Jewish scholars have attempted to correct the misconception surrounding the personality of Immanuel of Rome, based on the entirety of his extant literary output. However, because of the relative infancy of this enterprise, we are still today in a position where conjecture and speculation are the rule. As time goes on and as more students of Jewish Studies devote themselves to Immanuel and his writings, a true and accurate evaluation will be reached.

13 G. B. de Rossi, **Mss. codices hebraici bibliotheca G. B. de Rossi** (Parma, 1803-4), pp. 105-6, no. 615:

> Psalterium, Ruth, Threni, et Esther cum Commentario R. Immanuelis fil. Salomonis et anon. Dissertatione in ea verba Tabulae autem opus Dei sunt, et scriptura scriptura Dei, memb. in 4° 2 voll. ac 2 col. sec. XV.
>
> Commentarius rabbinicis descriptus est litteris, sacer textus modo rabbinicis, modo quadratis hisp. cum punctis. Pretiosissimus maximque pretii codex ab ineditos, ac rarissimos, immo et bibliographis omnibus hucusque ignotos, quos exhibet, celebris Immanuelis in quattor eos libros commentarios. Quotquot enim ob oculos habeo sive nostros, sive judaeorum scriptores rei litterariae, profundum de iis servant silentium. Quod spectat tamen ad comm. in librum Ruth suspicor ac

> fere pro certo habeo, eum R. Immanuelem nescio quem, cujus comm. in Ruth ms. se habere testatur Plantavitius n. 359, a Wolfio relatum sub no. 1785 T. 1 p. 947, Immanuelem nostrum esse, ac Plantavitianum codicem ad eum referendum. Psalmi numerantur 149, et ad eorum calcem punctis notatur vocabulum Chaiim, procul dubio ad designandum nomen scribae. Quae sub fin. II vol. ac codicis additur anonymi auctoris dissertatio, alia manu est exerata, antiqua tamen eademque cum ea, quae in Immanuelis textu interdum nonnulla supplevit.

With reference to de la Pause, see G. E. Silverman, "Plantavit de la Pause, Jean," **Encyclopaedia Judaica**, XIII, p. 613; F. Secret, **Les kabbalistes chrétiens de la Renaissance** (Paris, 1964), pp. 336-7.

Reverend Simeon Daly, Librarian at St. Meinrad Abbey, St. Meinrad, Indiana, has drawn my attention, in his corespondence of August 17, 1982, to some biographical information on de la Pause in **Nomenclatur literarius theologiae catholicae theologos exhibens aetate, natione, disciplinis distinctos**, ed. Hugo Hurter (Innsbruck, 1906-26), III, col. 1053. I thank him for this reference.

Although de Rossi has no. 359 as the citation from **Florilegium Rabbinicum**, it is, in truth, no. 559. See, however, Leopold Zunz, "Rom J. 1270 bis 1330," **Wissenschaftliche Zeitschrift fuer juedische Theologie**, IV (1839), pp. 188-99, especially pp. 195-6 and note 54.

14 His precise responsibilities regarding the publication of Immanuel's commentary to Proverbs are unclear. J. Jacobs, "Incunabula," **Jewish Encyclopedia**, VI, pp. 578-9, is of the opinion that he was the printer; however, M. Marx, "A Catalogue of the Hebrew Books Printed in the Fifteenth Century Now in the Library of the Hebrew Union College," **Studies in Bibliography and Booklore** I (1953/4), p. 29, delegates him a position as either the typesetter or proofreader.

The date 1487, as representing the correct year of publication, is not subscribed to by all scholars. Moritz Steinschneider, **Catalogus Librorum Bibliotheca Bodleiana** (Hildesheim, 1964[2]), p. 162, no. 1066 and p. 1058, no. 5269(8), decides for 1486, as does L. F. T. Hain, **Repertorium Bibliographicum, in quo libri omnes ab arte typographica inventa usque ad annum MD., typis expressi ordine alphabetico vel simpliciter enumerantur vel adcuratius recensentur** (Stuttgart, 1831), II, no. 8346. Joseph Zedner, **Catalogue of the Hebrew Books in the Library of the British Museum** (London, 1867), p. 125, argues for 1486-7. M. Sander, **Le livre à figures italiens depuis 1467 jusqu'à 1530** (Milan, 1942), II, no. 5931, remarks that the commentary was publishec ca. 1487. Cf. Aaron Freimann, "Ueber hebräische Inkunabeln," **Centralblatt fuer Bibliothekswessen** XIX (1902), p. 115; J.C.T. Oates, **A Catalogue of the Fifteenth-Century Printed Books in the University Library Cambridge** (Cambridge, 1954), no. 2525. Cf. F. R. Goff, **Incunabula in American Libraries: A Third Census of Fifteenth-Century Books Recorded in North American Collections** (New York, 1964), pp. 318-9.

[15] Concerning the commentaries of Immanuel that have been published, we have some information as to who the scribes are. David Goldstein, "Longevity, The Rainbow, and Immanuel of Rome," **Hebrew Union College Annual** XLII (1971), p. 244, reports that text A of Immanuel's Commentary to the Pentateuch was written by a certain Solomon, while text B was written by one Abraham. Both texts appear to antedate 1500. As far as Immanuel's Commentary to Song of Songs is concerned, S. B. Eschwege, **Der Kommentar des Immanuel bar Salomon zum Hohenleide** (Frankfort a/M, 1908), p. 2, has noted that in the case of Munich MS 25, the scribe is one Isaac ben Elias Manus of Leitmeritz (Bohemia), ca. 1550. Cf. Moritz Steinschneider, "Die hebräischen Handschriften der k. Hof - und Staatsbibliothek in Munchen," **Akademie der Wissenschaften, Munich: Sitzungberichte der philosophisch-philologischen und historischen Classe** II (1875), pp. 169-206, especially p. 178.

[16] Notwithstanding, for example, Rashi's introductory remarks to Zechariah and Song of Songs or Rashbam's opening words to Genesis 37:2.

[17] Moses ben Maimon, **Millot ha-Higgayon**, ed. M. Ventura (Jerusalem, 1969), pp. 71-7.

[18] Parenthetical references and notations in brackets, as well as paragraph divisions, in the Hebrew text, are my interpolations. The English translation aims at a figurative, not a purely literal, rendition of the original.

בזה הספר נכתב יחש דוד ע״ה והזכיר הכתוב יחושו בעבור היותו שורש למלכות ישראל. והיה מספיק להודיע יחש דוד מה שהזכיר בפרשה אחרונה מזה והוא אמרו אלה תולדות פרץ פרץ הוליד את חצרון (רות ד:יח) עד סוף הספר. אמנם הזכיר מחבר הספר כל זה המאורע בעבור מה שיש בו מזכרון המדות הטובות והנדיבות והחסידות של בועז ומזכרון צדקת רות המואביה ונועם מדותיה שדבקה בחמותה כדי להדבק בעם הקודש ולא שבה אל עמה ואל אלהיה ומזכרון מדות נעמי וחמלתה על כלותיה באמרה לכנה שבנה אשה לבית אמה יעש יי עמכם חסד וגומר (רות א:ח) והשתדלות הגדול להשיא רות לבועז וזכרון החסד הגדול שהפליא השם יתברך לעשות עם רות בעבור שדבקה באלהי אמת שזכתה להקים זרע כשר ויצא מזרעה מלך ישראל.

וכשתתבונן בכל כתבי הקודש לא תמצא באחד מהם ספור שלא יקבץ תועלות גדולות מנתינת דיעות אמיתיות באמונה ולמוד דיעות מדות טובות מלבד קצת שנעלמו ממנו לאורך ימי הגלות ושאינן נמצאים בידינו ספרים שהיו בישראל מימי קדם. ולו היו נמצאים אצלנו אותם הספרים לא היה נעלם ממנו דבר אחד פרטי מספרי כתבי הקודש שלא היתה ידועה אלינו הסבה שנכתב בכתבי הקודש. זאת היא הסבה שנכתב זה הספור בין כתבי הקודש לפי פשוטי המקראות.

אמנם רז״ל זכרו במדרש רות דברים שהם בכבשונו של עולם והוא שהאמינו כי עם היותו כפשוטו מאין שום ספק נרמזו בו ענינים נפלאים מסודות הנפש לא יכילם רעיון ואין בו [2] דבר ריק כי אם ממנו שנעלמו סודותיו וחידותיו ממנו. והוא על הדרך שנכתב במעשה בראשית: ונהר יוצא מעדן להשקות את הגן ומשם יפרד והיה לארבעה ראשים שם האחד פישון וגומר, ושם הנהר השני וגומר, ושם הנהר השלישי וגומר, והנהר הרביעי הוא פרת (בראשית ב:י-יד), שאין ספק אל שום אדם בעולם שאלה

הפסוקים הם כפשוטם והנהרות הם ידועות ונמצאות במקומותם ועם כל זה ירמזו אילו הפסוקים אל ענינים נפלאים. כן הענין בזה הספר שעם היות כל הסיפורים אשר בו כפשוטם מאין ספק ירמזו אל סודות אלהיות נעלמות.

ויראה לי שהדבר אשר בעבורו התעוררו רבותינו ע"ה להשיב באילו הסיפורים סודות וחידות הוא דאותם שהזכיר הכתוב - ושם האיש אלימלך ושם אשתו נעמי (רות א:ב) והזכיר שהיה לו שני בנים ושתי כלות ושם הבנים מחלון וכליון ושם כלותיו ערפה ורות - ולא הזכיר מאודותיהם דבר רק המיתה בלבד ר"ל שמת אלימלך ושני בניו ונשארו נעמי בלבד ושתי כלותיה. והזכיר כי ערפה הניחה חמותה מיד ונפרדה ממנה ורות דבקה בה וממנה יצא עובד. ובעבור ראותם ע"ה כי מיד בהתחלת הספר הזכיר מיתת המתים והזכיר במקרה הנשארים חשבו שעם היות הספור הזה כולו כפשוטו יהיה הספר בכללו רמז לכל מה שיקרה אל הנפש אחר המות. ויהיה אלימלך עם היותו כפשוטו רמז לדבר אחר ונעמי רמז לדבר אחרים [sic] ושני בניו מחלון וכליון רמז [sic] לשני דברים אחרים וערפה רמז לדבר אחר הפונה עורף מיד אחר המות. ורות רמז לדבר נמצא ודבק בנפש האדם ויהיה לו השארות וקיום.

ואלה הענינים עמוקים בתכלית העומק לא יבינם כל אדם רק השרידים אשר יי קורא המזהיר כזוהר הרקיעים (ע"פ דניאל יב:ג) הבקיאים בחכמת הטבע ובמה שאחר הטבע והתבררו אליהם כחות הנפש המרגשת והמשכלת על אמתתם, אליהם לבדם ניתנה חכמת זה הספר למורשה. ונניח זה הענין אל החכמים הראויים לבאר דבר כזה ואנחנו נסתפק בפשוטי [3] המקראות ונניח מקום לבאים אחרינו.

INDEX

BROWN JUDAIC STUDIES SERIES

Continued from back cover

140040	*Israeli Childhood Stories of the Sixties: Yizhar, Aloni, Shahar, Kahana-Carmon*	Gideon Telpaz
140041	*Formative Judaism II: Religious, Historical, and Literary Studies*	Jacob Neusner
140042	*Judaism in the American Humanities II: Jewish Learning and the New Humanities*	Jacob Neusner
140043	*Support for the Poor in the Mishnaic Law of Agriculture: Tractate Peah*	Roger Brooks
140044	*The Sanctity of the Seventh Year: A Study of Mishnah Tractate Shebiit*	Louis E. Newman
140045	*Character and Context: Studies in the Fiction of Abramovitsh, Brenner, and Agnon*	Jeffrey Fleck
140046	*Formative Judaism III: Religious, Historical, and Literary Studies*	Jacob Neusner
140047	*Pharaoh's Counsellors: Job, Jethro, and Balaam in Rabbinic and Patristic Tradition*	Judith Baskin
140048	*The Scrolls and Christian Origins: Studies in the Jewish Background of the New Testament*	Matthew Black
140049	*Approaches to Modern Judaism*	Marc Lee Raphael
140050	*Mysterious Encounters at Mamre and Jabbok*	William T. Miller
140051	*The Empire and the Subject Nations: The Middle Eastern Policy of Imperial Rome*	Eliezer Paltiel
140052	*Sparda by the Bitter Sea: Imperial Interaction in Western Anatolia*	Jack Martin Balcer
140053	*Hermann Cohen: The Challenge of a Religion of Reason*	William Kluback
140054	*Approaches to Judaism in Medieval Times I*	David R. Blumenthal
140055	*In the Margins of the Yerushalmi: Glosses on the English Translation*	Jacob Neusner
140056	*Approaches to Modern Judaism II*	Marc Lee Raphael
140057	*Approaches to Judaism in Medieval Times II*	David R. Blumenthal
140058	*Approaches to Ancient Judaism VI*	William Scott Green
140059	*The Commerce of the Sacred: Mediation of the Divine Among Jews in the Graeco-Roman Diaspora*	Jack N. Lightstone
140060	*Major Trends in Formative Judaism I: Society and Symbol in Political Crisis*	Jacob Neusner
140061	*Major Trends in Formative Judaism II: Texts, Contents, and Contexts*	Jacob Neusner
140062	*A History of the Jews in Babylonia. I: The Parthian Period*	Jacob Neusner
140063	*The Talmud of Babylonia: An American Translation. XXXII: Tractate Arakhin*	Jacob Neusner
140064	*Ancient Judaism: Debates and Disputes*	Jacob Neusner
140065	*Prayers Alleged to Be Jewish: An Examination of the* Constitutiones Apostolorum	David Fiensy
140066	*The Legal Methodology of Hai Gaon*	Tsvi Groner
140067	*From Mishnah to Scripture: The Problem of the Unattributed Saying*	Jacob Neusner
140068	*Halakhah in a Theological Dimension*	David Novak
140069	*From Philo to Origen: Middle Platonism in Transition*	Robert M. Berchman